Bodacious and Beautiful

Gini Noble

Copyright © 2023 Gini Noble
All rights reserved.
ISBN: 979-8-8513-4890-7

Unless otherwise indicated, all Scripture quotations are from The ESV® Bible (The Holy Bible, English Standard Version®), © 2001 by Crossway, a publishing ministry of Good News Publishers. Used by permission. All rights reserved.

Scripture quotations marked TPT are from The Passion Translation®. Copyright © 2017, 2018, 2020 by Passion & Fire Ministries, Inc. Used by permission. All rights reserved. ThePassionTranslation.com.

Scripture taken from the New King James Version®. Copyright © 1982 by Thomas Nelson. Used by permission. All rights reserved.

Scripture quotations marked (NIV) are taken from the Holy Bible, New International Version®, NIV®. Copyright © 1973, 1978, 1984, 2011 by Biblica, Inc.™ Used by permission of Zondervan. All rights reserved worldwide. www.zondervan.comThe "NIV" and "New International Version" are trademarks registered in the United States Patent and Trademark Office by Biblica, Inc.™

E.E. Cummings poem from, Tulips and Chimneys, E.E. Cummings, (pp. 78, 79) VI, Liveright publication.

DEDICATION

This book is dedicated to all the people who blessed me during this time. There are too many to count, but you are woven throughout my story. Thank you for blessing me in so many ways.

CONTENTS

	Introduction	3
	Prologue	15
1	Season of Waiting (Winter and Spring 2019)	29
2	Season of Wondering (Spring and Summer 2019)	45
3	Season of Strife (Fall 2019)	113
4	Season of Surrender (Fall and Winter 2019)	157
5	Season of Acceleration (Winter 2020)	221
6	Season of Solitude (Spring 2020)	255
7	Season of Lingering (Spring 2020)	313
	Epilogue	367

*"Your words were found, and I ate them,
and your words became to me a joy
and the delight of my heart"*
Jeremiah 15:16, ESV

Bold, Bodacious and Beautiful

INTRODUCTION

I have never been one to talk much about my spiritual life. It felt so personal, strange and difficult to explain, even to close friends, much less total strangers. When I encountered street preachers shouting and handing out tracts in New York City, I tended to cross to the other side of the street. I felt embarrassed to be associated with them, yet on the other hand, I also felt vaguely guilty that I was not out there proclaiming my faith as they were. For me, it was challenging to find the words to describe my beliefs, so I generally didn't talk about them.

I lived on the Upper West Side of Manhattan, and for the better part of three decades an elderly black man I nicknamed "Jesus Man" lived about a block away from me. He typically dressed in a dark suit and a hat, and walked down the street shouting, "Jesus! Jesus! Jesus! Hallelujah! Hallelujah! Hallelujah!" On Sundays, I knew it was 7:00 AM, because he exalted, "Praise him! Praise him! Praise him!" at the bus stop beneath my bedroom window until his bus arrived. By 2020, Jesus Man's walk had become more of a shuffle and his booming voice was raspy. Yet he still proclaimed his faith for all to hear, and he gave out tracts to anyone who cared to take one. In all those years, I never spoke to him even though we shared the same neighborhood and faith.

Given my reticence to talk about faith, writing a book about my faith and the very personal words I believe I received from God has been a challenge. As much as I wanted to share what I felt I heard from God, I had no desire to share *my* personal story. I've always been a behind the scenes type of person. I stayed quiet in large groups; I was timid. I also didn't consider myself much of a writer, and I had no idea how to write a book. Yet in spite of my doubts, I couldn't shake off the feeling that I was supposed to write about my experiences.

I knew that the Bible spoke about the "gift of prophecy" and even went so far as to say we should desire that gift above the other spiritual gifts [1 Corinthians 14:1-4]. But I didn't think of my encounters with God as prophecy and didn't realize people still received the gift of prophecy today. So, when a friend sent me a post by Lana Vawser, an Australian woman who described herself as "a wife, a mother, an author, a prophetic voice and an itinerant speaker," I was intrigued and more than a little skeptical. The words *prophetic voice* caught my attention.

Did prophets or people with the gift of prophecy still exist? Lana seemed perfectly down to earth and normal except that she heard from God, and she shared what she heard with others. After reading many of her posts, I realized her "downloads" from God aligned with the words in the Bible. She also heard from God quite frequently. After following her for the better part of a year, I decided I wanted what she had, and I wondered if it was possible? It didn't happen immediately, but after praying, reading the Bible and journaling, I began hearing what I felt were words from God.

Why should I care that you hear from God, and why should I read this book? you might ask. I believe God exists, and he wants to communicate with you and me. That is why I decided to write this book. I wanted to share the words that blessed me because I believe they could be a blessing to you, even though you and I are complete strangers.

During the winter of 2019 to the spring of 2020, I discovered and internalized the fact that God loves me. Deeply. I had been taught from a very young age that God loved me, and God's love for all mankind is clearly revealed in the Bible. The problem was, I didn't necessarily *feel* deeply loved by him. Then he began to tell me over and over again, "I love you." and after hearing it for months, it began to sink in. He really did love me. I hope that as you read my story, you will discover that God feels the same way about you. But maybe I am getting ahead of myself. Just what do I mean by the term "God"?

I am not a theologian, but I believe there is one God who exists in three forms: God the Father, God the Son and God the Holy Spirit. God the Father could possibly be likened to God's soul. God the Son is Jesus, or God in human form, who came to earth. He was fully God and yet also fully man. When Jesus lived on the earth he proclaimed the Kingdom of God by calling himself "the Word that became flesh" [John 1:14]. At that time, the Jewish people living in Israel expected the Messiah to free them

Bold, Bodacious and Beautiful

from Roman oppression, but instead, he freed them from the worst part of themselves. Jesus freed them from sin. After three years of public ministry, he was executed by being nailed to a cross and was buried in a tomb [Luke 23]. After three days, Jesus came back to life [Luke 24]. After that, he appeared to his followers (and others), and later, right before their eyes, he was taken up into heaven and sat down at the right hand of God the Father [Mark 16:19, Colossians 3:1]. Jesus promised we wouldn't be left alone: His Spirit would be our immediate connection to him. Soon after, he sent his spirit into the world, the Holy Spirit [Acts 2:1-41, John 14:16-17].

The Father, Son and Holy Spirit make up the Trinity or "the fullness of God." When I was a child in Sunday School, the Trinity was compared to the three forms water could take. Boil water and it becomes steam; freeze it and it becomes ice. No matter what form it takes, it is still water. It is not a perfect analogy, but it is still the best way I know to explain someone who is, in many ways, inexplicable.

The Holy Spirit is active on the earth and within the lives of his followers. These are people who have invited Jesus, or his spirit—the Holy Spirit—to reside in them. In ancient times, God spoke to many people including Moses, Elijah, Daniel and David. Later, Jesus spoke to people he encountered on earth as well as to his disciples. And today, the Holy Spirit speaks to us, and through us, to others.

How does he speak? you might be wondering. He can speak through the Word, which is also called

Bold, Bodacious and Beautiful

the Bible or the scriptures, or through a song, a sermon, an encouraging word from a friend, or a whisper in our minds. He can speak through a prayer, and he has been known to speak through the lips of children.

I knew this in theory, but I hadn't experienced it very often in my day-to-day life. I knew God spoke to me sometimes as I read the Bible. Once in a while, a verse would leap out at me at exactly the right time. At other times, he would speak to me through a sunset or as I walked in the woods or even around the reservoir in Central Park—-I felt his presence more keenly when I was out in nature. Or sometimes I felt he spoke to me when I sang or listened to music. I also knew I could pray to God (talk to him) or be silent with him. But did he speak directly to people now, and was this a common occurrence? I have often heard pastors say, "God put this sermon on my heart" or "God gave me a word for you," but I never considered what they meant. I had rarely, if ever, encountered anyone who openly admitted that God spoke directly to them, and I wondered why.

Before I began to hear from God regularly, I had heard in my mind what I thought was his voice at least twice in my life. The first time was when I was working at a youth hostel in Amsterdam in 1986. I was sitting by myself on a bench by a canal, exhausted and angry. One of my coworkers, who also happened to be my friend and roommate, had abruptly left Amsterdam in the middle of the night without telling anyone when she realized *my* boyfriend was not

Bold, Bodacious and Beautiful

interested in her. This was high drama for everyone on the staff of the hostel. How could she have attempted to steal my boyfriend, disappear without so much as a goodbye and leave the staff shorthanded all at the same time? I felt a deep sense of betrayal and debated returning home even though I had not finished my six month work commitment.

What should I do, God? I prayed. I didn't actually expect to hear an answer, but I hoped an idea would pop into my mind.

Then I heard these words in my head: "*I am your God, and I have brought you here for a reason.*"

I had never experienced anything like it before. It was a clear, almost loud voice inside my head; it wasn't my inner voice. Had God just spoken to me? The words were deeply comforting, and all of the sudden my situation didn't seem as dire as it had before. I decided to stay in Amsterdam, and my last few months turned out to be quite exhilarating. Not only did I fall in love for the first time, meet wonderful lifelong friends from all over the world, but I also grew in my faith. As staff members, we led Bible studies and shared our faith with any of the guests who were interested.

I experienced living in a different culture which was fun as well as challenging. As an American living in the Netherlands, I often felt like a bumbling idiot. I didn't speak Dutch; I didn't know much about the history of the Netherlands; and there were social mores in Holland that didn't exist in America. I grew

Bold, Bodacious and Beautiful

in many ways during my final months in Amsterdam that I never would have had I left.

Several years later, when I was living in New York City I felt God spoke to me a second time. I was having dinner with friends, and a new man had joined our group. He was funny and flirting with me. I was having a good time when all of the sudden, I heard a clear voice in my head say, "*No.*" Just one word. I was taken aback and wondered what it meant. I knew the voice. It was the same voice I had heard in Amsterdam, so I thought I should take it seriously. Within the year, the man had married someone in our circle, but the marriage was short-lived and did not end well.

In later years, I sometimes found myself thinking about that word, "No", and I wondered when, or if, I would ever "hear" God's voice again. Almost three silent decades passed before I directly heard from God again, and after that, he began to speak to me as often as I took the time to listen. I was moving from a season of spiritual famine into a divine feast where there was plenty of delicious food continually available whenever I chose to eat it. It was strange and wonderful and, at times, felt like almost too much to fully digest.

After almost two years of hearing from God almost daily, I had filled several journals. Some of it was personal, but much of it could be for anyone or possibly everyone. The words I received from God were too good to keep to myself, so I decided to write this book.

Bold, Bodacious and Beautiful

You might be wondering if I am crazy. After all, who hears from God anymore? And how do you know if God is speaking or the voice is just your vivid imagination? Or even Satan? When I asked God this same question, I felt him answer, *"My words line up with my Word [the Bible], and that's how you know it's me."*

Believe it or not, hearing from God isn't as rare as I once thought. In fact, various people I've encountered throughout the years hear from him often, if not daily. I just didn't pick up on it at the time, and they didn't come right out and tell me.

The truth is, God wants to speak to all of us, probably for the same reasons our friends want to speak to us or we want to speak to them. We like our friends and want to get to know them better. Being with our friends is fun. They provide companionship, someone to lean on during the difficult, heartbreaking seasons and someone to laugh with in the joyful ones. God doesn't just love you, he likes you. He delights in you. You are the focus of his love, and he wishes to spend time with you. He also wants *you* to fall in love with *him*. Deeply and passionately in love. He wants you to *want* to spend time with him. He desires to be part of your life, your day, your thoughts, your moments. The God of the Universe desires you. All of you.

I realized that if God already knows us deeply and wants *us* to know *him* deeply, then I had the opportunity, and perhaps even the obligation, to share the words he had given with the hope of sparking that same intimacy in other people's relationships with him.

This is the story of how I began to hear from God as well as the words I believe I heard.

Bold, Bodacious and Beautiful

SUGGESTIONS FOR READING THIS BOOK

Hearing from God revolutionized my life—not all at once, but over time. I often didn't remember his words (even after I reread them a second time), much less respond to what I felt God was saying. Many of the words were repetitive, and after hearing them for months and later, years, I finally began to internalize them. For instance, I didn't know how to truly trust God or how to live a joy-filled life. I didn't understand how to resist the negative thought patterns that had become habitual for me. I had no idea how to discern my internal voice from God's voice or the evil one's voice. I thought it was all me. But slowly, over time, I began to grow in discernment and developed a deeper awareness of all of these areas.

The words I felt were from God are italicized in the story, and when I added my own words for clarification or if I removed the name of a person who was mentioned, I put those words in brackets. As you read these words, I encourage you to read them aloud as if they were written to you, because I believe they were.

I encourage you to mark up this book. Highlight or underline parts that stand out to you or speak deeply to you or challenge you. Make notes. Write questions that come up for you. You may want to write your thoughts in a journal, and you may want to address them to God.

I have included scripture verses throughout my story as well as references in brackets. The

Bold, Bodacious and Beautiful

passages can be found at the end of this book, and as you read, you might want to take the time to flip back to compare how the words I felt I heard compare to scripture. Unless otherwise specified, the Bible verses are taken from the English Standard Version (ESV).

There are different ways to read this book. You could use it as a devotional by reading a small section each day and meditating on the scripture references. You could memorize the scriptures that speak to you or write them on cards and put them up where you can see them. You could also read my story to follow the progression of my relationship with God or simply as an autobiographical journey. No matter how you choose to read my book, I pray it will bless you.

Bold, Bodacious and Beautiful

Bold, Bodacious and Beautiful

PROLOGUE

Have you ever noticed someone enjoying something you didn't possess? You may never have thought about that particular thing, much less wanted it, but once you discovered someone else enjoying it, a seed of desire was planted. That is what happened to me. I had never considered that God could or would speak to people today. Wasn't that messaging reserved for his prophets in ancient times? But when I discovered modern people who heard from him, I wanted him to speak to me as well. I didn't realize the *desire* to hear from God, then *hearing* from him and actually *internalizing* his words would bring me so much joy—joy that my job, friends, accomplishments or possessions were incapable of providing. Joy that had been that hitherto elusive ingredient in my life.

When I was twenty-three, I moved from Arizona to New York with two suitcases, and began my career as an assistant childrenswear designer. I had attended the Fashion Institute of Technology (FIT) a few years earlier, so New York City was familiar to me. Originally, I had gone to college in California with the plan of becoming an elementary school teacher, but when I discovered I had to go to school for five years to become certified, I began to consider other career options. I loved art, but I didn't think I could make a living as an artist. I realized I could combine my desire to create art with the more practical need for people to wear clothes and become a fashion designer. After attending FIT for two years,

15

Bold, Bodacious and Beautiful

I decided I would take my associate degree and begin working rather than finish college. Why pay money to learn in school what I could learn on the job? I would gain valuable work experience too.

Sometime during my four year career as a children's wear designer, I read a book called *God's Smuggler* about a man named Brother Andrew who smuggled Bibles to Christians behind the Iron Curtain into Eastern Europe and Russia in the 1960's. That book led me to Russian literature and a general interest in Russian history. A few years later, in the early 1990's when Russia had opened its doors to Western tourists again, I heard about a mission's trip to Ukraine and Russia sponsored by Christian Solidarity International (CSI), and I jumped at the opportunity.

CSI advocates for people who have faced religious persecution and human trafficking around the world. At the time of my trip, CSI had been instrumental in working for the release of Christians who had been imprisoned for their faith under the communist regime. We were invited by several Baptist and Pentecostal Christian churches in Kiev to speak to their congregations and encourage believers who had not been free to openly practice their faith since Stalin had come to power in the early 20th century. I was excited to bring Russian Bibles with me to give to the people I met along the way.

Most of our time was spent in or around Kiev. I learned about how deeply and passionately Ukrainians desired their independence from Russia. I

Bold, Bodacious and Beautiful

was also profoundly blessed by the generosity of the church members who had so little themselves, yet chose to give the best of what they had to a small group of Americans in their twenties. One family gave up their two room apartment they shared with another family (housing eight or nine people) so four of us girls could stay there. Each morning, one of the wives came and prepared meals for us. We were fed fresh pressed cherry juice, brown bread brought to us in briefcases, borscht, and on our last day, pancakes with sour cream and caviar. I assumed they brought the bread in briefcases because shopping bags were nonexistent. We had also brought gifts for them, but our gifts were given out of abundance; they gave us the best of what they had. Many differences exist between our culture and theirs. They drank hot tea from samovars and their vending machines had only one cup, which would be refilled with juice for each new customer. During one meal, I observed a mother chew her food, put it on a spoon and feed her infant.

We spent our time visiting cancer hospitals filled with victims of the Chernobyl nuclear accident, as well as churches that had suffered under the communist regime. During those visits we sang, someone gave a message of greeting and an encouraging word from the Bible and then we chatted with the patients and church members. After the service at one small country church, people brought out saw horses and planks of wood creating a very long table in just minutes. Tablecloths and food appeared seemingly out of nowhere, and we had a

Bold, Bodacious and Beautiful

delicious feast with all the members of the church. Most of the women were elderly and wore babushkas, or head scarves, and dresses. We also visited a school and a dacha (country home). We explored beautiful churches and a crypt that contained coffins with clear glass covers where embalmed remains of saints or priests or other important church members were laid to rest. One afternoon, we witnessed Christians getting baptized in the Dnieper River, and on another day we helped one of our hosts care for the grave of her family member. It was a rich, life-changing experience that ended with a quick visit to Moscow before we returned home.

After the trip, I decided to become a missionary to Russia or Ukraine, so I began taking Russian language classes at the Russian embassy in New York City. I also took a job as a receptionist at my Episcopalian church on the Upper West Side just to earn enough money to live.

Soon after, a job opened up for the director of Children and Youth Ministries. I decided to apply and was surprised when I got it. I quickly realized this role was much more than a job, it was a ministry and more time consuming than I had anticipated. I discovered a passion for teaching children about Jesus.

My Russian language studies fell by the wayside. I was terrible at learning languages and no longer had the time. During those years I often felt out of my depth, and I learned about the power of praying to God by myself and also with friends.

Bold, Bodacious and Beautiful

Several years later, when my position was unexpectedly cut to part time, I had no idea of what I would do next. I loved teaching children, so I decided to go back to school and get my degree in Elementary Education.

Three careers, and several lifetimes later, I was in my mid-fifties and a veteran teacher at an elite private school in Manhattan. My colleagues were brilliant, passionate and driven, and several of them had become dear friends. I taught a delightful class of articulate, bright and funny fourth graders who kept me laughing (and on my toes). My work days flew by, and I felt grateful that I didn't have a boring job.

A rent-stabilized, one bedroom apartment on the Upper West Side had practically fallen into my lap, and it was my haven. Twenty years earlier, some dear friends had lived in the building, and they informed me that an apartment had just become vacant. Did I mention it was rent-stabilized? They suggested I offer the super some cash if I wanted it, which ended up being the better part of a month's rent, but it was worth it. It was large (by New York standards), and bright with a Northern exposure, which was a big plus during the steamy summers. I loved the original wood floors from the 1920's and the old fashioned 1940's sink in the kitchen, and the location was perfect. It was situated right between Riverside Park and Central Park.

I soon discovered I could walk across Central Park to the school in about the same time it took me to catch the subway uptown and then transfer to a

Bold, Bodacious and Beautiful

bus which took me to the East Side. This revolutionized my mornings and evenings because I was able to get lots of fresh air, avoid the cramped and airless subways, and enjoy the beauty of the park. Those walks were times of physical exercise, mental rest and contemplation all wrapped up into one glorious green (or sometimes gray or white) package. Central Park was my place of peace and contentment in every season.

My gym was only a block (or two) away as were my favorite Italian, Thai, Ethiopian and Vietnamese restaurants, not to mention a fabulous French bakery and Dunkin Donuts. I also loved the art and theater that Manhattan offered. The Metropolitan Museum of Art and the Frick Collection (and mansion) were old friends. And the theater! I was able to enjoy at least a few musicals or plays each year, which added up to quite a bit of theater over the span of three and a half decades.

New York is the therapy Mecca of the country and maybe the world, and I had found an excellent therapist. I originally sought out therapy when I began having memories of sexual abuse from my childhood, but years later, I continued it because I felt there was always room for growth. I was part of a therapy group which was both cheaper than individual therapy, and in many ways, more challenging for me. I tended to stay quiet in many group settings, so I thought this would give me practice in speaking up. The group was comprised of highly successful New Yorkers who were smart,

Bold, Bodacious and Beautiful

articulate and honest, and they were not afraid to call me on my s***. It was a far cry from the hilarious and quirky therapy groups I had seen in the movies and on TV.

I had gone on many, many dates over the years and known some wonderful men, several of whom I had loved. Yet for one reason or another, being with them didn't feel like "home" to me, or perhaps I wasn't "home" for them, so we eventually parted ways. The breakups were sometimes heartbreaking and took me years to get over, but at other times I felt pure relief to be free. Yet, I often felt vaguely disappointed by my inability to feel connected—-especially on a spiritual level—-with some of the men I had dated. Part of the problem was that I dated a fair number of men who either didn't believe in God or if they did, they were not part of any active faith community such as a church or synagogue.

When I turned forty, I realized I didn't have *any* of the things a successful American was supposed to have: a husband, children, a car, a dog and a house. I sank into a period of mourning for several weeks. Then I realized that I actually had *many* of the things successful New Yorkers had: good friends, an awesome job, the fabulous therapist, a rent stabilized apartment and close proximity to two parks as well as numerous restaurants that weren't too expensive. And unlike many New Yorkers, I went to a lovely Catholic church in my neighborhood, and I had a relationship with God.

Bold, Bodacious and Beautiful

However, as I look back on that period of my life, knowing God and spending time talking to him and reading his word weren't priorities even though I faithfully went to church every week. I was slipping farther and farther away from him and I didn't even realize it.

I had grown up in a Protestant Bible-believing church as a child, and I loved the small Episcopal church where I had attended and worked on staff for over a decade. Yet in the 1990s, I felt drawn to the Catholic Church. After meeting with a wonderful priest for several months, I converted to Catholicism. This was a shock to my Protestant family, and it was somewhat shocking to me too, but overall, I loved it. Yet, after being a Catholic for about a dozen years, I felt that I wanted more. I wasn't sure exactly what had happened or what I was lacking, but I craved a deeper relationship with God.

A friend had told me about a non-denominational Protestant mega church that was known for its worship music, and I also knew about a Presbyterian church that was known for its Bible teaching. I decided to try the worship-oriented church first, and I never attended the second. I loved this new church. As I trudged up the seven-flights of stairs to the theater where the church met on that first Sunday, volunteers were on each landing greeting visitors with smiles and signs that said "Welcome Home" and offering us small cups of water on trays. The theater was dark, the music was loud, and the sermon was simple yet profound. I had never experienced anything like it. I loved it.

Two years later, though, I hadn't met any new friends and felt disconnected. The church had a variety of small Connect Groups that met each week, so I decided to visit a women's Bible study that was led by two vibrant and deep-thinking women who welcomed me with open hearts. Who would have thought I would find a small community of friends within a mega church in New York City?

***

My parents became Christians when I was a baby, and as I grew up, my dad loved to tell me the story about how he met Jesus. One Sunday evening in the 1960s, he turned on the television intending to watch Bonanza but a Billy Graham Crusade was on instead. It was the last thing he wanted to watch, so he got up to change the channel. He made it about halfway to the TV, but something captured his attention, and he backed up and watched the whole program. "So that's how it all fits together," he thought to himself. That evening, my dad prayed Billy Graham's prayer:

"Dear Lord Jesus,

I know that I am a sinner, and I ask for Your forgiveness. I believe You died for my sins and rose from the dead. I turn from my sins and invite You to

Bold, Bodacious and Beautiful

come into my heart and life. I want to trust and follow You as my Lord and Savior. Amen."

The following week, a Billy Graham Crusade happened to be in town at the Sun Devil Stadium, and my mom and dad were there. At the end of the evening, they both went forward to accept Christ into their lives even though my dad had already done so during the previous week. The "altar call" was the culminating moment of Billy Graham's program; it was the invitation to become a Christ follower. Accepting Jesus into their lives involved praying the same prayer my father prayed in front of the TV and speaking with a counselor about their next steps as Christians. They were encouraged to read the Bible every day and pray to God as well as attend a Bible-believing church so they could be a part of a Christian community.

I was raised in a Protestant Bible-believing church. We were not part of a denomination, and church services were quiet and well-ordered. I have fond memories of attending Vacation Bible School as a child. A week-long day camp in the summer, VBS was a place where we would sing, listen to Bible stories, play games, eat snacks and make crafts. I especially loved the crafts and winning prizes for memorizing the daily Bible verse. In middle school, I liked church a lot less, mostly because my main friend became best friends with someone else. In high school, my parents began attending a new church that had charismatic worship services. People danced in

Bold, Bodacious and Beautiful

the aisles with tambourines while loudly singing to the Lord. After a childhood of well-ordered and somewhat sedate church services, this new church was a shock. My sister and I would pretend to go to Sunday School and then sneak back to the car and play cards until the service was over. Thankfully, my family eventually found our way back to my quiet childhood church.

Outside of church, my parents took my sister and me to see modern day heroes of the faith, including Corrie ten Boom, who had hidden many Jewish people in her home in Amsterdam during World War II and was betrayed by an informant. She and her family were sent to a concentration camp where she was the sole survivor. After the war, Corrie traveled around the word speaking about the love of God.

My parents also took us to a few Billy Graham crusades where, like them, I went forward to accept Christ as my savior. I was ten or eleven. They also introduced us to Christian music, and took us to see Evie Tournquist, Andre Crouch and Amy Grant. We always had a good time. Those seeds of faith took root, and I was still following the Lord, sometimes more and sometimes less, over forty years later.

***

I lived a simple but busy life in New York. I was content to take a walk in the park, or curl up on my couch with a book or have coffee with a friend. To me, New York City was the greatest city in the world (along with Amsterdam and Rome), and although I missed my family, Manhattan felt like home. After over thirty years of relative contentment, in 2019 shifts began to occur in my otherwise predictable life.

I stepped into a leadership role at my church, and my teaching responsibilities changed. These changes weren't monumental, but my equilibrium was thrown off enough that I no longer felt "on my game." In hindsight, I wish I had been more adventurous about leading our Connect Group at church or open to trying new ways of teaching at school. If I had cut myself more slack, I most likely would have done the same for others and avoided unnecessary conflicts in both situations. I didn't have confidence in myself, or for that matter, God. Not knowing exactly how to tackle these changes and, as a result, do my jobs well made me uncomfortable. Nonetheless, God used this season of discomfort to grow my confidence and strengthen my trust in him.

Then the world shifted, and the Covid virus appeared, shutting down New York City for a season. Around this time, a friend sent me a post from Lana Vawser. When I first read that she thought God spoke to her directly, I assumed she was a religious fanatic. After reading more of her posts, though, I realized her messages from God reflected the words in the Bible. I didn't know then that God wanted to speak to me, too.

***

Bold, Bodacious and Beautiful

The story of *Bold, Bodacious and Beautiful* highlights seasons of struggle in my life, but mostly I wanted to write about the words I felt I heard from God so that I could share them. The words encouraged, challenged and inspired me. Sometimes they even made me laugh. I had no idea that God had a sense of humor. I also began to believe that God actually liked me. I'd always heard that he loved me, but loving others was something that we were commanded to do, even if we didn't like them we could show love to them. God didn't just love me, he liked me. I began to trust God and his purposes for me. It didn't happen all at once, but my ideas about God slowly began to shift during this time. God's words allowed me to walk through difficult and unexpected seasons.

Why share my story about hearing from God when people might think I'm crazy? Because I knew it was too good to keep to myself. I believe that reading about my experiences could bless you, too. I don't know why God chose to speak to me, except that I asked and he said yes. I hope you might also be inspired to ask him to speak to you, too.

Bold, Bodacious and Beautiful

1
SEASON OF WAITING
(WINTER AND SPRING 2019)

1

Waiting has never been my strong suit, and I don't like surprises either. I prefer to have what I want when I want it and know what to expect when it arrives. However life doesn't usually work that way, does it? When I was a child, waiting until Christmas to open all of the beautifully wrapped gifts just sitting there under the tree was painful. They called out to me every time I walked past the Christmas tree, *Come take a closer look. Pick me up. Shake me. Can you figure out what's inside?* I learned early on that the gift did not always match the shiny silver paper in which it was wrapped.

When I was ten or eleven, I sneaked under the tree a week before Christmas and carefully unwrapped one of my gifts because I had to know what was inside the box. It was a flannel nightgown. Needless to say, I was disappointed and annoyed that I had to rewrap such an unexciting gift and then pretend to be surprised (and not disappointed) when I unwrapped it for real on Christmas Day. I'm pretty sure that was the last time I opened a gift early.

Even as I write this book, I find myself wishing that God would let me know a bit about my future. But if finding out what is going to happen next month is anything like the experience of unwrapping that nightgown, maybe it's best to wait.

Bold, Bodacious and Beautiful

At fifty, my spiritual life exploded–an unexpected surprise, but this time, a welcome one. I had broken up with a wonderful man who was an ideal match in many ways, but he didn't share my faith and that was a deal-breaker for me. After we broke up and got back together several times, I realized I needed to relinquish him to God and stop getting back in touch whenever I felt lonely and missed him.

On the morning before we broke up for good, I visited the church that became my home church and fell in love with it. It was unlike anything I had ever experienced. I especially loved the music, and it took me deeper into worship than I had ever gone before. The theater where we met was dark, and people sang with abandon—eyes closed and hands raised. I had asked my boyfriend to join me, but he declined and said he would meet me afterwards for lunch. As I sat alone in church for the zillionth time, I decided I would wait for a man with whom I could share my faith journey. Someone who wanted to be a part of a church community with me. Lunch that day was the last time we saw each other, and I mourned the loss of this man for a long time.

However, I had found my new church. Even though I had always liked quiet and contemplative church services, I loved the thunderous passion of this one. What was happening to me? These people acted like they were in love with God, and quite simply, I wanted to fall in love with him, too.

After immersing myself in worship at this church for about a year, I suspected that as much as I

Bold, Bodacious and Beautiful

loved to *worship* God, I did not feel much love for God *himself*. I loved the experience of singing to God more than I loved God. I loved the music, but more than going to a concert, I took great pleasure in worshiping God. I just wasn't sure how much I actually *loved* God. How did one quantify one's love for God? And was it okay to love worship more than the object of one's worship?

I began to pray that God would fill my heart with love for him and for all the people I encountered, too. (If I was being honest, I didn't like some people any more than I liked God.) I prayed this prayer for about two years even though I didn't feel much change in my heart or my circumstances. I wasn't capable of filling myself up with love. God had to do that, so I knew I was on the right track. But would he do it? And did I trust him to fill me up with love? I wasn't sure, but I kept asking anyway. For two years.

In hindsight, he did increase the love in my heart, especially for him. He did for people, too, but he put increasingly challenging people and situations in my path which required more love and forgiveness. Years later, as I write this book, I've begun to pray this prayer again: Lord, please fill me with love for you and love for people. All people. Amen. [Matthew 22:37-39]

***

Bold, Bodacious and Beautiful

2

It was during this season of waiting for God to answer my prayer that a friend sent me the post by Lana Vawser. A self-described "prophetic voice," she claimed to hear from God directly. This sounded a bit suspicious to me yet sparked my imagination, too. Did people with the gift of prophecy still exist? Lana would receive "downloads" from God that she shared on her website. He spoke to her in all sorts of ways, in words, dreams, visions, and even numbers. When she asked him, "Lord what are you dreaming about?" and "What is on your heart?" God would answer her.

Lana was sixteen when God first spoke to her. He said three simple words, "I love you." After that, each morning she would get a cup of coffee, sit down and talk with the Lord. And he would answer her. Lana believes that God desires to speak to everyone. He desires our company, and all we have to do is ask. Before reading Lana's posts, I never imagined I could ask God to speak to me. Honestly, it never occurred to me that I should. The idea of God communicating directly with people today seemed strange yet also intriguing. So, I began to follow Lana, and the more prophetic words I read from her, the more I wanted to hear from God for myself.

Several months later, I finally asked. I fixed myself a hot beverage and sat in my big gray comfy chair with my Bible and journal. Using Lana's questions, I asked the Lord what was on his heart and what he was dreaming about. I sat in silence for a few minutes. Nothing. What if the questions didn't work?

Bold, Bodacious and Beautiful

Or was it just me? Restlessness, anxiety and boredom quickly set in, so I decided to write in my journal about the two times in my life, in Amsterdam and New York, when I had heard from God.

Kris Vallotton, a pastor at Bethel Church, defines prophecy as "calling things that aren't as though they are. Prophecy is foretelling the future but also forth telling, [as in] I'm causing the future." Two prophetic people had given me messages in the past. These were people who walked closely with God—they lived with a sense of his presence—and their words were strongly influenced by their relationship with him. I decided to write down those messages while I waited for God to speak to me.

In 1986, these prophetic words were given to me by Adith, a manager at the youth hostel in Amsterdam where I worked.

"You will know that [God] is truly to be trusted at all times and will carry you through the rough times if you let him…. Bear witness of Light he has given you, so that the people around you will find our Lord as well…. Don't be afraid to use the knowledge He has given you—and your laughter. You've been a blessing."

A dear friend from college gave me my second prophetic word. She told me very simply but powerfully that my prayers were like "fire wiping out the evil one."

Recalling these prophetic words from my past heartened me, but I still hadn't heard anything directly from God. I decided to copy a few verses from the

Bold, Bodacious and Beautiful

Bible into my journal. I felt God's peace in the room, and it seemed that I was on the right track. I felt God's presence in several powerful Bible verses I found as I was flipping through the Psalms. Here are two:

> He will be standing firm like a flourishing tree planted by God's design, deeply rooted by the brooks of bliss, bearing fruit in every season of life. He is never dry, never fainting, ever blessed, ever prosperous.
> Psalm 1:3 (The Passion Translation)

> It is much better to have little combined with much of God...
> Psalm 37:16 (The Passion Translation)

God spoke to me through his word that day. It wasn't quite what I had asked for, but it was enough.

Meanwhile, Lana Vawser had started a weekly YouTube series called, "Coffee with Jesus." The calm, down-to-earth manner in which she shared spiritually monumental, earth-shattering and inspiring revelations resonated on a deep level with me. The name of her program cracked me up, but the content brought me deeper into God's presence while reminding me that God still spoke to people, even if he hadn't spoken to me. I didn't realize it at the time, but my curiosity was evolving into a desire to pursue

34

this type of relationship with him. I wanted to hear from him myself.

> ...he will display at the proper time—he who is the blessed and only Sovereign, the King of kings and Lord of lords, who alone has immortality, who dwells in unapproachable light, whom no one has ever seen or can see. To him be honor and eternal dominion. Amen.
> I Timothy 6:15-16

***

3

A few weeks later, during my second attempt to hear from the Lord, I wrote this verse in my journal:

> Call to me and I will answer you, and I will tell you great and hidden things which you have not known. Jeremiah 33:3

I also wrote a prayer that began, "Lord, I pray for my city. I pray that you will lead me to be near my family." One of the benefits of writing down prayers is the ability to go back later to see which ones have been answered. I had no idea that my prayer to be closer to my family would be answered a few years later.

I don't remember if Lana provided any tips about hearing from God. She simply encouraged her

Bold, Bodacious and Beautiful

followers to ask God to speak, so I continued to ask, read the Bible, write down Bible verses that resonated with me, wait, pray, write in my journal and wait some more. These practices are excellent ways to spend time with God, but at the time my goal was to hear God's voice. After about an hour or so, I usually gave up.

In another episode of "Coffee with Jesus," Lana spoke about a vision she had of dancing with Jesus like a child standing on her father's feet, letting him teach her the steps. The vision reminded me of the ballroom scene in *Beauty and the Beast,* and it brought tears to my eyes. Would I ever have visions and dreams like that?

***

4

Several weeks later, author and actor Priscilla Shirer came to speak at our church. Priscilla wrote a Bible study called *Armor of God* that my Connect Group had loved. In her Instagram account she describes herself as "Just a girl …with a Sword." She told a story about a woman who asked for an oak tree so God gave her an acorn.

How many times had I prayed for certain outcomes only to have those prayers answered in vastly different ways than how I'd imagined they would be? God's answers sometimes required more work and more waiting on my end. I would definitely need to learn patience. Later that same day, as I was

Bold, Bodacious and Beautiful

making tea, I happened to read the quote on the teabag.

"The creation of a thousand forests is in one acorn." --Ralph Waldo Emerson

A *tea bag* had expounded upon Priscilla Shirer's sermon. Had God just used a tea bag to speak to me? Or was this an extraordinary coincidence? I don't think so. I don't believe there are coincidences in God's world. That night I wrote in my journal, "Lord I love how you speak to me—even through a tea bag. Haha!"

> ...grant to those who mourn in Zion— to give them a beautiful headdress instead of ashes, the oil of gladness instead of mourning, the garment of praise instead of a faint spirit; that they may be called oaks of righteousness, the planting of the LORD, that he may be glorified.
> Isaiah 61:3

***

5

As I waited on God, I had to decide whether or not to lead my Connect Group made up of a small group of ladies from church. Our leaders had both stepped down and asked me if I wanted to lead. I was conflicted. I really didn't know how to lead a small Bible study. Being a fourth grade teacher didn't

Bold, Bodacious and Beautiful

automatically qualify me to lead a women's Bible study effectively.

Though I didn't realize it at the time, I wanted God to speak to me about this decision. Perhaps it was one of the driving forces that propelled me to follow Lana's lead and seek his voice.

One of the hurdles to leading the Bible study was my perfectionism. Being a perfectionist deterred me from taking risks since it was impossible to do something new "perfectly." I already felt too busy with school and liked my down time on weeknights. My church was huge, and I had no idea how to navigate a new role in such a large place. Mostly, though, I was afraid of failing. Everyone in my group was a friend, but my insecurities overwhelmed me. What if they didn't want me to lead them? What if they didn't like my leadership style? What if they were too afraid to tell me and just left the group? What if new members didn't like me? The "what ifs" list was long.

God, what would you have me do? I wrote in my journal. *What would you have me be? Are these the right questions, or do I simply need to go deeper into you?*

My journal during that time of waiting was a concoction of my prayers, questions and observations, Bible verses that spoke to me, and memories. With all of my effort, I felt that God was not answering my prayer. Now I can see that he was showing me how to go deeper with him by using the tools I already had at my disposal: prayer, reading scripture, sitting in silence with him and journaling.

Bold, Bodacious and Beautiful

He was showing me how to slow down and "be" with him. I could never have imagined, a year later, I would be in quarantine, forced to spend weeks on end by myself with God as my only companion. These times of quiet contemplation were preparation and training for what was to come.

Since I started hearing words from God, I've discovered that we are rarely, if ever, "qualified" to do the things God asks us to do. Many times, God asks us to step out and take a risk, and *then* he empowers and enables us to do what we have been called to do. Not perfectly, but we grow and learn along the way.

> And your ears shall hear a word behind you, saying, "This is the way, walk in it," when you turn to the right or when you turn to the left. Isaiah 30:21

***

6

On April 14th, I was writing in my journal about the arrival of my great niece. She was the first child to be born into our family in over thirty years, and my family was over the moon with excitement. I remembered holding my nephew, her father, when he had been born, and not for the first time, I wished I lived closer to them. I would have to wait until the summer to fly to Arizona and meet her. In the meantime, I gobbled up photos of her like a starving person. I was thinking about all of this when a rush

Bold, Bodacious and Beautiful

of words entered my mind, one word or phrase at a time. These are the words that I feel came to me.

> *Be still and know that I am God. Know I am your God. The King of Heaven. The one who is first and the last and who is to come. I am here. I am now. I am always and forever. I am here. I am now. I am always and forever.*

What was happening? Was this what I had been waiting for? I had no idea, but I was scrambling to write quickly, and I didn't have time to think.

> *I go before you and behind you and place my hand of blessing on your head. I Am. I was. I will be. I am forever. I am now. I Am that I Am. All you need, I Am. All you need to know, I Am. All you need to live, I Am. All you need to love, I Am. I am all. I am all in all and never ending. You don't know time. I am time. I am future. I am past. I am all. I Am that I Am.*

Was I making this up?

> *Who are you that you ask what is on my heart? My heart is unknowable, unsearchable, so far beyond you. Can you touch the stars? No. But you can see them. Can you see me? No, but I will, and have, revealed myself to you. Don't spend time rehashing how the Word came to be or who chose it. It is and it was, and it is to come. Take what you have. Learn it. Love it. Make time for me. Make time for what matters. I make time—all time—and give it to you to use.*

Bold, Bodacious and Beautiful

As I was writing I kept thinking, "Oh my gosh! Oh my gosh!" This was it. This was what I was praying for and waiting for and wanting.

> *I am the Refresher of spirits, the Alpha and the Omega. I am the first and the last, the beginning and the end. I am what was and what is to come. I wait, and I don't wait. Don't wait too long. Use the time wisely. It won't always be like this, like now. Use the time I give to you. Love my world. Your time and days are in my hands. Don't worry about home. My home is yours. I am your home. Your home is here. I have brought you here for now, and for always. I brought you here, and you had no idea why. Not for fashion. For now. I am your strength. I stand by you and fight with you and for you.*

What did "It won't always be like this" mean? It sounded slightly ominous.

> *I am the beginning and the end. I am now. I am forever. I am now. Come to me now. I will direct your steps. I will step with you. Step in my steps—in my tracks. I go before you and I place my hand of blessing on your head. Know me. Let me be your guide. I am your focus. Look to me. Look at me. Look at me, and I will reveal my heart, but wait. Wait for me. Wait on me. Wait for the Lord. Be still. Be solid. I am your rock.*

The sheer vastness of God overwhelmed me. The beginning and the end. My guide. My rock.

Bold, Bodacious and Beautiful

> *I am yours now and forever. No man, no friends, no family—just me. Always me. Only me. I am a jealous God. I want all of you. Not moments of your choosing. I want your time, your body, your mind, all of you—not the scraps you give to me. You have lived on scraps of me, now feast on me. Let me make a feast for you. Feast on me and dine with me, my love. My only.*

I immediately regretted the "scraps" of myself I had given to God as well as the scraps of him that I had lived on. I wanted to feast on him and with him. I wanted him to make a feast for me.

> *My table is large, large enough for only you and only many others. I desire you. Stay with me. Be with me. Be me. Be mine. Be with me. Be before me. Be.*

In my mind I saw a huge wooden table. We were at one end, but the table was so long, I couldn't see the other end. I asked, "Lord, is there more?"

> *There is so much more, but how much do you wish? How much do you want? How much do you desire? How much can you fathom? Be careful what you ask. The burden is heavy and light. The burden is cumbersome and small. It is loaded with bricks and feathers. It is.*

When the words stopped, there was a heavy silence in the room that was palpable. I sat for a while just savoring it. Something remarkable had just occurred unlike anything I had ever experienced, and

Bold, Bodacious and Beautiful

I wasn't sure what to make of it. The words had come powerfully into my mind, and I had to write quickly to get them all down. I knew the words I had written weren't my thoughts, but at the same time I couldn't quite believe I hadn't made it all up. They weren't me, but it was such a strange feeling that they had come into me, or flowed into my mind. It wasn't like hearing God's voice in Amsterdam or years earlier in New York. It was different, a softer impression rather than the loud voice I had heard years ago, but unmistakable.

That first "download" was powerful. I didn't fully recognize the Biblical references that were woven throughout until later. I didn't know how to measure the significance of the reminders and warnings. I wasn't sure what to make of his message, but I did realize one thing: God loved me and he wanted my love. In fact, he wanted my whole being.

A sense of urgency grew about using my time more wisely. I had never really considered how I used my time, wisely or not, but I now realized I spent much of my time outside of school working, reading novels and on social media. This realization made me vaguely uneasy. I *had* to work in my free time, didn't I? And I had *always* read lots of novels. I loved them. And *everyone* spent time on social media. Right?

I pushed these thoughts out of my mind to focus on other questions. Was this a one-time event? Was there any significance to the timing, coinciding so closely with the birth of my great niece? I didn't know the answers to these questions. How could I be sure

Bold, Bodacious and Beautiful

the words *were* from God? I couldn't help but wonder if he would speak to me again. I wasn't really expecting it, but I secretly hoped he would.

> Behold, these are but the outskirts of his ways, and how small a whisper do we hear of him!
> Job 26:14a

Bold, Bodacious and Beautiful

2
SEASON OF WONDERING
(SPRING AND SUMMER 2019)

1

A week later, it was Easter Sunday, and I was still hoping I would hear from God again. I had reread the words several times, and their meaning wasn't any clearer than they had been a week earlier. I continued to feel a deep sense of God's love for me, his sheer awesomeness, and the nagging feeling that I should reevaluate how I spent my free time. I also shared the words with my sister and one of my dear friends because they both knew me so well. My friend lived in California and went to Bethel Church where hearing from God was a common occurrence. Even though the idea of hearing from God sounded strange, I thought they would believe me, and they did. But I didn't feel comfortable sharing the words with my New York friends just yet.

Because it was Easter, my church had seven back-to-back services with lines snaking around the block from 9am until 9pm. I loved the service, and I sat with a friend from my Connect Group. However, she had plans with her family afterwards, so I decided to come home and spend some quiet time with God. It didn't feel like a festive way to celebrate Easter.

I wrote in my journal, "I don't feel like I deserve any more words from God. The last ones

45

Bold, Bodacious and Beautiful

could last a lifetime. But God, is there anything more you would say to me? I feel your presence so strongly. Easter [has been] so full and empty at the same time —perfect though…. I miss my family as they gather in sunny Phoenix. It looks so fun. I'm glad I booked my flight in July!"

As I was thinking about my family and missing them, the words came for the second time.

> *I am your God who goes before you. I died for you and rose again for you and only you and only the rest of the world. Know me. Embrace my peace. Embrace my joy. I will fill your heart with love—for me and mankind. Be open. Be my vessel. Be. Be prepared. Don't hesitate. Don't squander—don't squander time, money, resources. Do all in memory of me and for love of me. I go before you. Step in my tracks. Don't be afraid. Fear isn't of me. Fear is from the pit of hell. How do you know that what you fear will even happen? Don't squander time. Don't squander thoughts or love or joy or dedication to that which is not of me.*

There it was again—wasting or "squandering" time. And fear. Fear was an old companion of mine. I could barely remember a time in my life when I had not felt its slimy presence.

> *…Walk with me—by my side. I am with you. You are never alone and never have been…. Feast on me. Feast with me. Feast with others. I prepare a feast for you in the presence of your enemies. I am not your*

enemy. I don't seek your destruction or to undermine you.

That was a reference to Psalm 23:5. "You prepare a table before me in the presence of my enemies..." It brought to mind a memorable sermon by Louie Giglio called, "Don't Give the Enemy a Seat at Your Table" where Louie actually sat at a food-laden table at church when he preached his sermon.

I go before you. You are my child. I love you more, more, more, so much more than you love [your great niece] or a mother loves her precious child. You are my beloved… and I shelter you under my wings and in the palm of my hands. You are safe. Even in the midst of danger and uncertainty you are safe— enclosed, protected, divine. You are divine only because I am divine. You are mine, Child. My baby, the one I shelter with all my love. You are gorgeous and beloved and precious. Don't hesitate to love the gorgeous, beloved and precious world I made. Everyone is beloved by me and so must be loved by you. You are only one, but with me you are a battalion—a mighty army. You go before me. I am behind you and beside you and before you. Stay in me. Stay with me. Stay for me. Stay by my side. I am yours. Your lover, your friend, your family, your all. Only me. Only me. Only me. Amen. So be it. Amen.

"Was that me?" I thought to myself.
"No," was the reply.

Bold, Bodacious and Beautiful

...there is a God in heaven who reveals mysteries...
Daniel 2:28a

***

2

God had now spoken to me twice, and I couldn't quite wrap my mind around how to take in his words. I had been feeling lonely on Easter, and he told me I was never alone. I felt honored and loved as I reread his words.

Later, I typically had little recollection of what I wrote down when God gave me his words early in the morning. I was so distracted and busy, I also tended to forget what God had said to me almost the moment I closed my journal after rereading the entries. Consequently, God often repeated himself. It took months of hearing from him before I slowly began to internalize what he was saying.

***

3

The New York City spring had been rainy and cold but beautiful, as usual. There was nothing like watching the bare, brown winter trees begin to blossom and grow leaves each year. I absolutely loved walking home from school through Central Park. It was the perfect time to unwind and enjoy the beauty of my rather limited access to nature. It didn't matter how tired I was, when I caught sight of the park I almost always felt energized, and the cares of the day dissipated. I spent most of my life inside or in the shadow of tall buildings outside. To walk on a dirt path in the wide open space of the reservoir on my way home was life affirming. I loved hearing the sounds of the water lapping, the cries of seagulls and the rattle of wind in the leaves. I made a goal for myself to stay off my phone (except to take photos) for at least half of the walk, and this was almost always a challenge. I tried to "be" in the moment and spend at least some of the time talking to God or simply being silent with him.

Summer was just around the corner, and I was making plans to travel and researching fun outings around the city. My first trip would be a girls weekend in Savannah with two of my Connect Group friends. I had been a part of this small group of women for a couple of years. During the previous year, I had declined to lead the group, so we had decided to meet together informally, without a leader, and slowly complete Priscilla Shirer's *Armor of God* Bible study. We also got together socially, and enjoyed concerts, movies and Broadway shows as well as dinners and picnics. I was excited to travel to Savannah with some of these friends.

A four-week series of classes called "growth track" had begun at my church, which I was required to attend in preparation for leading my Connect Group. I was still afraid to lead the group, but I felt God leading me in that direction. The more I prayed,

Bold, Bodacious and Beautiful

the more I felt my mind change. I prayed someone from the group would volunteer to co-lead it with me.

I also planned to spend two weeks with my family in Arizona and two weeks in Scotland to visit an old friend whom I hadn't seen in decades. I was thrilled to have so many travel plans as well as friends to visit and friends with whom to travel.

Throughout the Spring, I continued to set aside time to hear from God, usually about once each week. One weekend in late April, I was writing some verses from the Bible in my journal when I felt I heard from God for the third time.

> "So then, as we have the opportunity, let us do good to all men, and especially to those who are of the household of faith."
> Galatians 6:10

> "If we live by the Spirit, let us also walk by the Spirit."
> Galatians 5:25

> Then the words came into my mind.
> *Stop taking ownership of your students. I own them. I own them. They are mine. You cannot save them, [and] you cannot speak of me.... I am bringing you... to a place where you can freely speak of me. Do not be afraid. I will provide. You are all I need. You are all I need. You are all I need. Not anything else. Only you.*

50

Bold, Bodacious and Beautiful

"But I always thought you don't *need* me or anyone. Why me? Why do you need me?" I asked. He didn't answer my question.

...Move free. Come away. Come away with me.

"But to where, God?" I asked.
I will show you in time. Be ready. Be ready to move, to come, to go. Stay for now and stay with your whole heart, but not with your whole self.... I am key.... Be bold, be brave, be mighty in me and for me.... Be bold, be brave, be the beauty I created you to be. Be my beauty...

I rarely, if ever, felt beautiful. What did it mean to be the beauty God created me to be?
Rise above your petty and complaining spirit. Walk in my spirit with joy and thankfulness and forgiveness. Do not be bowed down. Rise up. Rise up. Rise up. My chorus sings louder than Hamilton [the musical]. Louder than an orchestra. Louder than [your church].

Unfortunately, or perhaps fortunately, I knew exactly what God was talking about when he mentioned my "petty and complaining spirit." I had slipped into a habit of complaining about many things in my life, and I knew then and there it was a habit I needed to break. I wasn't sure I could change, but I could at least try.

Sing with me and for me and about me.... Be strong and brave and bold and beautiful. Amen.

Bold, Bodacious and Beautiful

Looking back, I realize I had begun to ask God questions as he spoke to me. I'm surprised that I felt comfortable so soon. After all, it was only the third time. On the other hand, I had been praying, or speaking, to God for decades, so communicating with him felt familiar. He was also calling me to BE "strong and brave and bold and beautiful." I didn't feel that I possessed any of those qualities, and if I didn't possess them how could I "be" them? I didn't know, but I had a sense that he would help me if I asked.

***

4

As April melted into May, Central Park was in full bloom. I loved this time of year: the soft pink, white and almost purple-colored blossoms on the trees, the lime-green color of new leaves and all of this abundance beginning at the end of winter with a few green crocus sprouts. But then again, I enjoyed every new season.

As Spring bloomed, I began to take time to listen to God's words a few times a week rather than just on the weekends. "Lord, do you have anything to say to me?" I would ask. I might start out copying a verse from the Bible into my journal, and the words that I felt were from him would soon follow. I only seemed to hear from him when I was holding a pen and my journal. I did not hear from him when I was walking in the park, although I felt his presence and I felt close to him.

Once, when I wasn't sure about what I had been writing, this came to me.

> *When you are sure then you should be wary. Never be sure in yourself, only me. Only me. Only me. I am your surety. I am your escape, your strength in and out of season.*

How perfectly the Lord knew me and my love of the seasons.

> *Walk in my steps. Walk beside me, walk in me. Walk through the desert, and I will be your umbrella. Walk through the rainforest, and I will shelter you under my wings. [Psalm 91:4] Fly and I will fly beside you. When you are drowning I will be your aqualung. Breathe my life and my breath. When you walk through fire you will not be burned. [Isaiah 43:2] Take the first step. Step in me. Step with me. Hold my hands. Know I am near you, not just close by but in you and on you and around you. I fortify you. I am your fortress. [Psalm 91:2] I am your song. [Psalm 118:14] You are my song. I sing of you. Now sing of me every day. Speak of me and speak for me.*

During these early days, many of the words I received were about walking with my hand in his and stepping in his steps. Over and over the words came, until I began to think of him, talk to him and sing of him as I walked through my days.

Bold, Bodacious and Beautiful

I also heard these words that I felt were for a friend of mine. I knew they were about her because her name was mentioned.

> *...I will minister to you in the night watch. You will be in darkness and only see light. The light of my love and the reflection of my kindness [are] like the light of the moon at midnight. Call to me in the night. Hang on to me, but lightly, because I already carry you on my shoulders as the shepherd carries his lamb.*

I was thrilled to hear what I felt were words from God on behalf of my friend, and I was quick to send them to her. I have since learned to be more circumspect when sharing. After several missteps, I now know that it is always a good idea to ask God if his words should be shared and when, and to ask the person if they want to hear them.

For my own growth, in hindsight I can see now that God wanted a much closer relationship with me and was preparing me for the coming year. At the time, however, I simply accepted they were beautiful words from a God who was actually there and speaking to me. That was special enough, and I would soon learn that he was enough.

> The Rock, his work is perfect, for all his ways are justice. A God of faithfulness and without iniquity, just and upright is he.
> Deuteronomy 32:4

***

Bold, Bodacious and Beautiful

5

The school year was winding down, but my work as a teacher was ramping up, and I found it more difficult to set aside time for God. The cost of hearing from God was time, time I wasn't in the habit of giving up.

Do you think this is a waste of time? Are you so focused on children's papers or reports? I am what matters. I am the Alpha and the Omega. The beginning and the end. I Am that I Am. Go before me. I will be right behind you and beside you and in front of you. I am your armor. The armor isn't something of your making. I even put it on you. Use it. Use it well. Use it now. It's on. Now use it. Don't let petty feelings or misunderstandings trip you up or stop you. I will not be stopped unless I choose to stop.

"I hear you, Lord. Is there anything else you wish to say to me?" I responded.

Only this—don't stop. Don't let the opinions of others stop you. Don't let your own doubts stop you. Don't let fear stop you. Fear is an entity—a being. But I am more powerful than fear, and with me, so are you....

Have I not commanded you? Be strong and courageous. Do not be frightened, and do not be dismayed, for the LORD your God is with you wherever you go.
Joshua 1:9

Bold, Bodacious and Beautiful

6

With the end of the school year in sight, I needed both stamina and rest. I didn't know what it meant to "rest in God" or "let God be my rest," much less do it. Now I know I need boundaries and can say no. I can also ask God to expand the hours of my sleep, so I feel more rested. Or I can ask that I accomplish three hours of work in one hour. I don't always get exactly what I want, but I've found I get what I need.

I was drowning in Pilgrim stories to read and student reports to write. In mid-May I wrote in my journal, "Thank you for this day off [for report writing]. I have so much on my mind. I'm tired and busy, but not too stressed. God do you want to speak to me? I'm a bit worried about where our Connect Group leadership will land. I'm worried to share what I've been receiving from you with our group…. You are so good and faithful, God. Thank you."

I also wrote several Bible verses in my journal including this one: "…and he will be the stability of your times, abundance of salvation, wisdom, and knowledge; the fear of the Lord is Zion's treasure." Isaiah 33:6

These were some of the words I felt I heard that day.

Take me into your life and your days and your hours…. Don't forget me in the busyness of the day,

Bold, Bodacious and Beautiful

and take time to be with me. Think of me and about me and all I am doing and have done for you.

God was giving me the first step of "resting" in him.

I am your all in all—your beginning. Even in the womb I was with you. I am with you in the womb you've created for yourself. Break forth. Be born. Be birthed. Step out of the womb. Be bold and be beautiful and teach others to be…. Rest with me— even in the midst of chaos- rest."

For thus said the Lord GOD, the Holy One of Israel, 'In returning and rest you shall be saved; in quietness and in trust shall be your strength.' But you were unwilling…
Isaiah 30:15

7

The following week, some of the words that came to me included these.

Sing my praises daily…. Stay in my word, and I will heal the deep sorrow in you. I will fill those places with the substance of my joy and praise. You will mount up with wings like eagles, and you will walk and not faint. [Isaiah 40:31] …I am your joy. Your joy is in me and in me alone, deep everlasting joy that bubbles up like a spring that will never run dry. Deep and cleansing joy; joy that will water your spirit and soul. Deep joy. Come drink of my joy. Let it fall down onto you… and cleanse you. Drink of it now. Drink

57

Bold, Bodacious and Beautiful

> *deeply. It will not run dry. It will always be there just for you. You. You alone. Only you. It is for you—but you must drink of it. It is there. Take it. Drink deeply. Now. Take it now. Drink now. Take my joy. Take it now. Take it now.*

"How?" I asked. But no more words came that day.

I wasn't sure how to "take" the joy that God described, but I wanted to. I thought back on my perception of joy, and to be honest, the whole idea of joy irritated and confounded me because it had always felt elusive. When I was a young child I remember seeing a banner at VBS that read:

Jesus
Others
Yourself

We students were taught that we should think about Jesus first, others second and yourself last. Only then would we have true joy. There is wisdom in this aphorism, but I grew up believing I shouldn't think about myself, and I should ignore feelings that were not positive. To be honest, I didn't feel a lot of joy as a child or a young adult, and I often felt like I was surrounded by Christians who were chronically happy. Was it all for show? Were they faking it? If they weren't, then where did all that joy come from? And why did they have it and I didn't? I didn't feel like I belonged in youth groups or other church settings because I wasn't a joyful person even though I knew

Bold, Bodacious and Beautiful

and loved Jesus. In fact, I often felt burdened by a heavy sadness that I tried to push away.

Later, when I had just turned thirty and was living in New York City, I began to have disturbing flashbacks of sexual abuse that I had experienced as a very young child at a neighbor's house. After working hard in therapy, it began to make sense why I felt such a lack of joy during my childhood and early adulthood. However, even with years of therapy, at times, joy still felt elusive.

What did it mean to have joy? Was it something I could take hold of? Should I pray for it? Could I be joyful in the midst of sorrow? What *was* joy, and how did it differ from happiness?

Now I know that joy is like fine wine while happiness is more like powdered grape juice. I've heard it explained that happiness depends on circumstances, but joy is possible *in spite* of circumstances.

So what *was* the secret of feeling deep and abiding joy? I didn't know, but I felt that I was on the right track. I was feeling more joy than I ever had in my life, especially when I was singing and worshiping in church. I would often come to church feeling the weight of the world on my shoulders, but after singing and praising God, even for just a few minutes, I felt the worry, fear and anxiety dissipate and be replaced by a feeling of joy, peace and even exhilaration. What was the connection between praising God and feeling joy?

Bold, Bodacious and Beautiful

> I will bless the LORD at all times; his praise shall continually be in my mouth. My soul makes its boast in the LORD; let the humble hear and be glad. Oh, magnify the LORD with me, and let us exalt his name together! I sought the LORD, and he answered me and delivered me from all my fears. Those who look to him are radiant, and their faces shall never be ashamed.
> Psalm 34:1-5

***

8

On the thirtieth of May I wrote, *God, I'm so tired and so joyful and so ready for this year to be over. I'm heartbroken about [a few of my students]. Help me to let go in a healthy way and stay loving until the last day. Amen.*

Letting go of my expectations and failures was often a challenge at the end of school. My students had grown in many ways, but as the year drew to a close, feelings of frustration and failure nagged at me. I wouldn't be able to help a few of them as much as I had hoped.

A few days later, I was still thinking about those students and my own shortcomings when I wrote my favorite Bible verse in my journal.

"Be still and know that I am God. I am exalted among the nations. I am exalted in the earth! The Lord of hosts is with us; the God of Jacob is our refuge." Psalm 46:10-11

Then these were the words I heard in my spirit.

Do you not know? Have you not heard? The Lord is the Everlasting God [Isaiah 40:28], the one high above all others. I am your God, the one to turn to....

The image of God on his throne came to my mind, and my perspective shifted. My problems were dwarfed by the enormity of the universe and God high above it all.

Keep me in your heart, close to your heart. Memorize my words [Bible verses] as you memorize songs and poems and phone numbers. Memorize my Word [the Bible]; keep it in your heart. Fill your hours with my Word, not on things of this earth. You have wasted time, hours, days, months, years. Waste it no more. The time is short. Use it well. Use it now. Fill your mind with me. What is in your mind is who you will be....

I hadn't memorized Bible verses much during the last few decades, but thanks to our Connect Group Bible studies, I had begun writing Bible verses on index cards and would put them up in my bathroom and kitchen so I was reminded of them throughout the day. One of my favorites was from Song of Solomon 4:7:

"You are altogether beautiful, my love; there is no flaw in you."

Bold, Bodacious and Beautiful

I had rarely even felt cute, much less beautiful, but after seeing this verse right below my bathroom mirror for two years, I began to believe that God saw me as beautiful. If he created me to look this way, then who was I to say his workmanship was flawed?

> *I want to speak to you. I will speak to you, but you need to clear your time and spend it with me. Don't fill the empty space with things that don't last. Only I last. I am everlasting. I am jealous of the time you spend with your phone, books, movies, [and] friends. The noise is deafening. Let it go. Be still before me.*

In addition to God's encouragement to memorize scripture, he delivered two warnings about wasting time again. I didn't want to hear it. How could I live without my beloved novels or spend less time on social media? I felt I could not, so I chose to set aside this request—at least for the moment.

> *Don't be afraid of the empty space. Let me fill it. Let me make you a feast in the emptiness and silence. I am your friend, your lover, your music. The one who whispers to you of my deep and abiding love for you. You are mine. Be fully mine. I will ignite your spirit; I will set you on fire, but you will not burn. Glorify me. I am your glory. You need me more than you need anything else. Everything else is secondary.... Seek me first and build my kingdom here on earth.*

But seek first the kingdom of God and his righteousness, and all these things will be added to you.

Matthew 6:33

9

The words continued to poke and prod my mind as well as my conscience.

> *Don't fear the fearful ones in your life. Fear only me. I am the one you will answer to, and I love you far more deeply than they do. Their love is nothing. I am all. Be in me. Be of Me....I am the most holy God, and I have spoken.*

I was fearful, though, afraid of what people would think if they knew that I felt I heard from God. In hindsight, the people I shared this phenomenon with were interested and curious. Perhaps they secretly thought I was delusional, but if they did, they didn't let on. I should have been more bold. I had many other fears, though. At the top of my list was my fear of failing as a teacher and a Bible study leader. I hadn't defined what I meant by failure, but almost any negative response to me or my ideas qualified as a failure in my mind.

As for the gift of these words, I did wonder sometimes if I was making it all up. Deep down I knew I was writing what *came* into my mind rather than what was *in* my mind, but it was difficult to explain the difference. The experience was like taking dictation; I wrote what came to me.

The more I wrote, though, the more I wanted to spend time with God. I needed his presence like a thirsty person drinking cold water, and I didn't let my

Bold, Bodacious and Beautiful

own doubts or the perceived doubts of others deter me.

> As a deer pants for flowing streams, so pants my soul for you, O God. My soul thirsts for God, for the living God.
> Psalm 42:1-2

***

10

Before I knew it, the school year had ended, and I was on my way to Savannah. Summer had arrived! Sitting on the plane, allowing the exhaustion and busyness of the school year to melt away, was exhilarating. I had always loved summers in New York, but this one held the promise of travel and time spent with friends and family.

The next afternoon, I sat on the second story porch of our charming Airbnb surrounded by southern live oaks draped in Spanish moss reflecting on the previous day. We had meandered around the quaint and charming squares of Savannah and stopped for lunch (and air conditioning!) at an elegant wood-paneled apothecary. Later that evening, we enjoyed a leisurely and delicious dinner of fried chicken, greens, mac and cheese, cheesy cornbread and sweet iced tea. It was the perfect celebration of summer: talking, laughing and enjoying fabulous food. This was our first time traveling together, and we were having the time of our lives—or at least I was!

That morning, we all had toured the Owens-Thomas House and Slave Quarters. The tour began in the slave quarters as the docent told the story of the place from the point of view of the enslaved people who had lived and worked there. Only then did we move to the garden and finally the mansion.

I had been captivated by the tour, everything from the "haint blue" paint used in the slave quarters to the first indoor plumbing used in the main house to Major-General Lafayette's visit in 1825. Afterward, I returned to our Airbnb while my friends continued to explore the city. I did not want to miss out on more adventures, but I needed a nap and time to reflect.

I ventured out onto the porch with my journal and Bible. It was late afternoon, and the warm air was dense; charcoal gray clouds warned of an approaching thunderstorm. I would have liked to have been out with my friends, but time to sit down in such a delightful, albeit steamy, setting was wonderful. I wrote these Bible verses in my journal.

"...give us life, and we will call upon your name!" Psalm 80:18b

"In distress you called, and I delivered you; I answered you in the secret place of thunder; I tested you at the waters of Meribah." Psalm 81:7

Then I wrote a letter to God.

"Lord, this trip has been so full. Full of new friends and adventure, full of my own [physical]

shortcomings and health, and full of history and the failings of our country and this city (and New York City, too). I've only been in Savannah for twenty-four hours, and I'm changed for having been here. The history of slavery is grizzly and disturbing—deeply disturbing. Teach me what you would have me learn, O Lord."

> Teach me good judgment and knowledge, for I believe in your commandments.
> Psalm 119:66

11

While enjoying the mini vacation with my friends, I was also researching urban slavery in Savannah. Every year in fourth grade as part of our year-long focus on Immigration, we taught a unit on the Transatlantic Slave Trade. Since much of the material we covered focused on plantation slavery, I thought it would be beneficial for my students to learn about urban slavery, especially since we were urban dwellers. I was surprised by how few museums, statues, or historical plaques made mention of it.

I had done some research before the trip, so I knew where to go, but the sites of barracoons (slave holding cells), slave markets and other places of interest were largely unmarked. I was feeling judgmental about the South, but God reminded me that New York City was the second largest slave-holding city in the country, second only to Charleston, South Carolina. (thenation.com, The Hidden History

Bold, Bodacious and Beautiful

of Slavery in New York, Adele Oltman, Nov. 7, 2005). Except for the African Burial Ground National Monument, very few historical markers, statues or museums commemorating slavery existed in New York City much like Savannah.

As I was mulling over all of this, I received a text from my friends who were at a museum. It was a painting of a warrior wearing armor and the perfect illustration for Priscilla Shirer's *Armor of God* study we had recently completed.

While reflecting on the painting and the day, the following words came to me.

> *I am the God that thunders in the heavens. I am great and mighty to behold. I roar in the waters—yet the water and the heavens were made by me. I am so much greater than them. I hold them in the palm of my hand as I hold you.*

These words gave me chills, even though the air outside was muggy and warm.

> *…I will use you in spite of your frailties and shortcomings; I will be glorified in your frailties and shortcomings. Do not fear. I desire not perfection but a willing and contrite heart. I desire your heart….*
> *Don't trust in your own heart and your own ability to love. Trust in my love and let me fill you with it….*

I couldn't imagine God being glorified in my exhaustion, which I believed was a shortcoming. On the other hand, because of my exhaustion, I had

Bold, Bodacious and Beautiful

come back early from sightseeing and received this intensely deep time with the Lord.

> *Stay with me…. Look only at me. I am yours and you are mine…. In me you have a vast expanse of riches: peace, love and divine forbearance. You will have streams in the desert, food during famine and songs during desolation. I will be a garden in the midst of chaos and pain….*

A garden in the midst of chaos and pain? The garden sounded nice, but not the chaos and pain. I thought this was the end, but it wasn't.

> *I am not finished…*
> *I desire you. All of you. I thunder in the heavens; I roar in the oceans. Be mine; be fully mine. I will show you the way, one step at a time.*

The sound of far-off thunder reverberated in the distance.

> *…Do not fear drought. I am your water—your living water [John 4:13, 14]. You will not die in the dry places. Instead, you will find cool pools of refreshment along the way. I am all you need, more than enough. More than you imagine. More than you could possibly need. Enough. I am enough. Money won't help you. Money won't save you. Only I can carry you through what is to come. Do not fear it. You have been fearful; now be brave like the photo your friend sent [of the warrior]. Be brave and strong. Surround yourself with brave and strong people. People who are brave and strong in me and only me. Let all others go….*

Bold, Bodacious and Beautiful

The painting of the warrior standing on a stormy beach with both hands wrapped around the hilt of a long sword was fresh in my mind.

> *...I will use you in spite of, and because of, your frailties and shortcomings. No one is perfect. Stop trying to be perfect. Stop it. Stop it now.... Be who I made you to be. Step into it with me by your side, surrounding you and protecting you, uplifting you and empowering you. Take my words and use them well. Do not forget them....*

The words about being perfect spoke to so many aspects of my life: my teaching, leading the study and even needing a nap.

"Is there anything else?" I asked.

Yes, much more, but this is all for now.

When my friends returned from the museum, I wanted to share all about the afternoon, the painting and thunder and how it all blended together with the words I felt I heard from God, but they seemed tired, so I told them that I had had a wonderful and restful time with God and left it at that.

On our final evening in Savannah, we walked along the waterfront at sunset and enjoyed a leisurely and delicious Greek dinner. In all, it was a fun, informative, delicious and even spiritual adventure, and I felt deeply grateful for these women from our Connect Group. I hoped it would be the first of many such trips, but due to the onset of Covid, we

Bold, Bodacious and Beautiful

have not been able to travel together again. However, I am still hoping for many reunions in the years to come.

> A man of many companions may come to ruin, but there is a friend who sticks closer than a brother.
> Proverbs 18:24

***

12

As summer settled in, I looked forward to relaxing for a few weeks in the city. I loved watching cheap Tuesday night movies with my Connect Group, and a few of us were taking a summer intensive Bible class together. A dear friend who taught in the classroom next to mine lived in Kensington Gardens, so I rode the B train and met her at Brighton Beach. Afterward, we spent the evening at her house: sitting on her porch and walking to a nearby restaurant called Hamilton's for dinner. Even working out at spin class at the grungy gym a block from my apartment was fun, as was relaxing afterward with a novel.

I wouldn't lead our Bible study until the fall, but in the meantime, figuring out my responsibilities and expectations was a challenge. I could tell that a member of the group wasn't thrilled about the change in leadership, which wreaked havoc on my insecurities. There were over 200 Connect Groups at my church, and from where I stood, the other leaders

Bold, Bodacious and Beautiful

seemed more charismatic, confident and successful—successful enough to attract large numbers.

My Connect Group was small, about six members. I did not feel charismatic, confident and successful, but shy, insecure and fearful. I was afraid of failure, whatever "failure" means in a Bible study.

After our leaders stepped down, our group had transitioned from being an official Connect Group to a group of friends that met on our own. We met whenever and wherever we wished, and it worked well. Moving back into being an official church group meant more structure: agreeing on a set day, time and place; taking attendance and welcoming and communicating with new members; going to leaders' meetings and having a "coach" who would occasionally check in with the group and maintain close contact with the leaders.

I felt strongly that God was calling us back to official status, especially so we could welcome more women into the group. Most of the group agreed to go back, but not everyone, and I was uncomfortable with the lack of agreement. I hadn't expected that leading a church group would push my emotional buttons, but the responsibility seemed to shine a spotlight on my insecurities. Over the coming months, I learned to make peace with people disagreeing, questioning me and coming and going. Thankfully, another member of the group stepped up to co-lead, and her wisdom and pragmatic perspective proved to be a support and blessing to me in the next

Bold, Bodacious and Beautiful

months. I was deeply relieved when she came alongside me.

> Whoever walks with the wise becomes wise, but the companion of fools will suffer harm.
> Proverbs 13:20

13

I was continually amazed by how precisely God's words spoke directly to my inner angst. He knew how susceptible I was to becoming deflated in the face of criticism or disagreements.

> *...Don't let the words of man knock you down. They are words, and they come from a place you know nothing (or little) about.... Don't stop; keep going. I will be your strength. You are not perfect and you never will be, but you can and will be perfected. Allow me to do this for you. Don't resist me and my love and my correction. I am not your enemy. I will not harm you or let you come to harm. You will pass through waters and not drown, fire and not be burned.... I am your boat and the sail on your boat. You need only step on, and I will do the rest. Be still. Let your mind be still. Let your heart be still. I am in the midst of the clamor and the stillness.*

Did I truly think God was my enemy? I didn't want to admit it, but I didn't fully trust that he wanted the best for me. Instead, a deep part of me believed God would set me on a treacherous path with few creature comforts and people who disliked me in

Bold, Bodacious and Beautiful

order to strengthen me. And maybe, at times, he would.

> Jesus answered him, "What I am doing you do not understand now, but afterward you will understand."
> John 13:7

***

14

A few days later, I read this verse in the book of John, "And I have other sheep that are not of this fold. I must bring them also, and they will listen to my voice. So there will be one flock, one shepherd." John 10:16

This verse had always intrigued me; I have wondered if it spoke of life on other planets in different galaxies as well as to people on Earth who did not know Jesus. I wasn't a fan of science fiction, but I was intrigued by the possibility. As I was mulling it over, these words came to me.

> *I have other sheep in other pastures. They also hear my voice. You are not the only one. You will be surprised when you get to heaven.*

> "Am I making this up, Lord?" I asked.
> *No. The world and universe are so much bigger than you can imagine. Allow me to show you and guide you. In time, I will. You need not see or know it all. I know it, and that is enough.*

Bold, Bodacious and Beautiful

These words were high and lofty, and they gave me a lot to think about. I wondered who (or what) I would see in heaven.

> Lead me in your truth and teach me, for you are the God of my salvation; for you I wait all the day long.
> Psalm 25:5

***

15

When I was in college, a song called "Friends are Friends Forever" by Michael W. Smith was popular. I grew up believing friendships were forever, but over the years as friends came and went, I realized a long-time friend was a rare and treasured gift. I was saddened that my friend and I had disagreed over the leadership of our Connect Group, but I was also having conflict with another friend that summer, and I wondered if both friendships would survive.

I needed to learn how to voice and receive criticism with grace and love. Too often I remained silent through multiple disappointments and misunderstandings rather than calmly and kindly speaking up as they occurred. Then something would happen that would be the final straw, and I would react with more vehemence than the situation warranted. Thankfully, over the summer, one friend and I were able to work through miscommunication and hurt feelings, and we are close friends now. The

Bold, Bodacious and Beautiful

other one drifted off, and after one failed attempt to reconnect, completely disappeared.

Both of these women were in my thoughts as I read the story of Esau and Jacob in Genesis. In Genesis 33:4 the brothers finally reunite after having spent many years apart. The verse reads, "But Esau ran to meet him and embraced him and fell on his neck and kissed him and they wept." Not for the first time, I wished there could be reconciliation and forgiveness between all people, especially Christian friends.

The words that came to me that day spoke to both friendship situations and helped guide me forward.

> *...Know that I love you, my precious daughter. You are beautiful in my sight. Be bold and bodacious and beautiful. Not everyone will like you or seek you out. Be who I've called you to be, and I will do the rest....*

It had never occurred to me that people might not like me or seek me out. For most of my life, I had believed that I could be friends with everyone who crossed my path if I tried hard enough. It was one reason I stayed silent in groups; I didn't want anyone to dislike me. Yet, no matter what I said or didn't say, there were still people who weren't my fans. God seemed to be calling me to be more than just myself, he seemed to be challenging me to be *more* than who I was. He was challenging me to be bold, bodacious and beautiful.

A few days later, the words continued.

Bold, Bodacious and Beautiful

> *Forgive her and love her. I will help you. I can give you more than enough love to forgive....Don't let bitterness spring up. I forgive you and I love you, so you should do the same for her. Love her. Forgive her. Don't talk about her or think unnecessarily about her. It is in my hands. This isn't such a big step, and you aren't as important—right or wrong—as you feel or think.... People will hurt you. Expect it. But they will also love you and bring you tremendous joy and laughter. You will cultivate a community, and I will show you how....*

It was a relief to learn I wasn't as important as I had imagined. Most people were inside their own heads as much as I was inside mine. Most of the time, they weren't thinking about me at all. I realized that I would benefit from getting out of my own head to focus on bigger things, such as God and world events and how other people were doing. This grown-up idea was surprisingly similar to the acrostic on the old VBS banner from my childhood that had pointed the way to JOY. Think about Jesus first, Others second and Yourself third.

Jesus
Others
Yourself

Was I beginning to understand the path to joy?

> Whoever says he is in the light and hates his brother is still in darkness.
> 1 John 2:9

Bold, Bodacious and Beautiful

***

16

A shift in my sleep began in June, and I started to wake up in the early morning hours, around 3:00 AM. I was accustomed to waking up multiple times during the night. My apartment was several blocks away from both the fire and police stations. In the summer, the windows were wide open and sirens, street fights and the bus stop below often jolted me out of sleep. During the school year, anxiety and other worries sometimes kept me awake.

This waking felt different. Was God actually waking me up? One night I woke up at 2:00 AM and lay there for a while before I asked God if he had any words for me. He did.

> *Is sleep so important to you? Is it a god or an idol? I am your rest. I am the one who gives you health and rest. Rest in me; allow me to calm your mind…..Stop your mind from running away with you; stop listening to the evil one….*

I wondered how I could stop listening to the evil one? I didn't even know I was.

> *You are learning to hear me and follow me. Put on the full armor [of God] and stand. [Ephesians 6:10-18] Stand with me. Learn to discern the voices that aren't yours…. Keep seeking me and cutting away what isn't of me. You hear my voice, now seek my face.*

Bold, Bodacious and Beautiful

"How?" I asked.

Keep on this path. I am waking you up. Stay awake…. Awakened to me. Praise me daily and often. Praise is the key to surrendering your mind to me and silencing the evil one and your own worries. Praise me daily and often—especially now….

I had been thinking about praise being a bridge to joy, but not necessarily in connection with silencing my own worries or connecting my mind to God's mind. I had always loved music, and now I was beginning to see the multiple benefits and blessings of singing and praising God.

I will give you the rest you need, but not necessarily the rest you want. Trust me to keep you rested and whole and healthy. Keep trusting. Sleep and stay awake…. Always with me and for me and in me.

Typically, I would go right back to sleep after writing the words that came to me, and later I would have little to no recollection of what I had written. I was grateful and glad to receive the words, but I was also relieved to go back to sleep. When my alarm went off in the morning, and it was actually time to get up, I would open my journal to see what God had said to me.

Later that day, these words also came to me.

I long to be your God. Your only God. Not one of many. Set aside the other gods. Set them aside. They are not me….

"You keep saying that, Lord," I said.

Because you need to hear it. Have no idols before me. Not your computer, phone, retirement, money, food, comfort. Put it aside. Dwell in me. Be mine....

What did it mean—did I have idols? Did I put anything or *many* things before God? Why did I constantly compare myself to others and want what they had? How could I truly enjoy the people and possessions in my life without making them more important than the God who gave them to me?

How strange. What would people think of me if I told them I felt like I was actually hearing from God? I wasn't sure what I thought about receiving these "downloads" early in the morning only to have no recollection of them until later when my alarm went off and I reread the words. I couldn't wait to talk about all of this with my sister when I went to visit my family in Arizona.

You shall have no other gods before me.
Exodus 20:3

***

17

My second trip of the summer was only a few days away, and I was eager to see my family, and meet my baby great niece. Living in New York City so far away from my family in Arizona, California and Hawaii was difficult. I was the only member of our clan who

Bold, Bodacious and Beautiful

ended up on the East Coast. When I had arrived in New York to attend the Fashion Institute of Technology thirty-five years earlier, it never occurred to me I might spend the major part of my adult life there. As one year ran into the next, more than three decades had quickly passed. I wanted to retire in Arizona in five or six years, but retirement seemed a long way off. Would it be possible to move closer to my family any sooner? I had thought about moving back to Arizona for at least a dozen years, but the timing had never felt right.

On July 1st, I wrote this verse from 2 Chronicles 15 in my journal. "...for they had sworn with all their heart, and had sought him with their whole desire, and he was found by them, and the Lord gave them rest round about. 2 Chronicles 15:15b"

I asked God if he had a word for me.

I do. I am round about you; I surround you as I surrounded the Israelites in the desert.... I'm quick to love and slow to anger. [Psalm 86:15] I'm not as angry as you think I am. I am an infinitely patient God, rich in mercy, rich in peace, rich in joy, [and] rich in love. These riches I will and do share with you. Open your hands and take it. I long to give you more than you can hold.... Enough to share with others. Be generous with what I give to you. Be free with your time and love and money. Be free and full and abounding in love for me and those who walk across your path.... You are all connected. You are brothers and sisters. See humanity as your family, as your

Bold, Bodacious and Beautiful

sisters and brothers. See yourself as my beloved child....

If only I could see humanity as my family, as my sisters and brothers. I wanted to.

My load is easy and my burden is light. I am light. Light and light. I am your light. I will light your path and guide your way....

I loved the way God played with language. I would like to say that I read these words and took hold of the riches of peace, joy and love, and then I generously showered them all onto everyone I encountered. To be honest, more often than not, I forgot the words as soon as I read them. They made an impression in the moment, but the worries and busyness of life crowded them out. Not until I wrote this book and read through my old journals was I reminded of the treasure trove of wisdom and guidance I grasped for a moment and then let pass me by.

Wisdom cries aloud in the street, in the markets she raises her voice; at the head of the noisy streets she cries out; at the entrance of the city gates she speaks: "How long, O simple ones, will you love being simple? How long will scoffers delight in their scoffing and fools hate knowledge? If you turn at my reproof, behold, I will pour out my spirit to you; I will make my words known to you."

81

Bold, Bodacious and Beautiful

Proverbs 1:20-23

***

18

Arizona was sweltering, but I relished every moment with my family. I spent time with my dad, my sister and her husband, two nephews and their partners and the new baby. The joy from holding my great niece was indescribable. She was so alert, and I could see signs of her sense of humor when she smiled. I was in love. My mother had passed away a few years earlier, and in many ways, we were still mourning her absence. She would have loved getting to know her first great granddaughter.

I especially loved swimming, hiking and biking at sundown with my sister. The lavenders, pinks, oranges and yellows of the desert sunset brought to mind a poem by e. e. cummings, "The / sky / was / can dy lu / minous / edible / spry / pinks shy / lemons …"

My dad, sister, brother-in-law, nephew, his family, and I took a trip to the mountains of Prescott to escape the heat. The house where we stayed had multi-levels and a deck where deer and javelina passed by in the early morning and at sunset. It was rustically magical. We went on walks, cooked dinner together in the tiny kitchen and played Sequence at night.

These words came to me at 2 AM on the second day of our stay.

Bold, Bodacious and Beautiful

> *I am a jealous God, one who shares you with no one. Do not fill the empty spaces with vain and empty pursuits. Fill it with me. Fill it with prayer. Fill it with the study of my Word. Speak to others about me. Speak to me about others. Don't let days go by— or even hours. Tell others of me and my love and saving grace. Show others my love and saving grace. The bar is high. Move up to the bar. Do not coast.*

There it was again, "Do not fill the empty spaces with vain and empty pursuits."

> *…Be a light in the darkness. A candle gives a tremendous amount of light on a dark night…. I will light your way. My yoke is easy, [and] my burden is light. [Matthew 11:30] Light the way for others. They are not "other;" they are brothers and sisters. Family. Part of my family. Welcome them in. Teach them to love me, themselves and the world. You are not of the world [John 17:16], but I made the world, and I love it [Genesis 1:12]. Take care of my creation. You did not create it, but you must care for it. Yes, it will pass away, as will you, but you must not destroy it. It's not yours to destroy….*

As I read these words now, I realize how easy it is for me to still see people as "other" rather than as brothers and sisters. Especially people who think, look and live differently from me. This is a weakness of mine, seeing the "other" rather than a BRother. Fortunately, God's spirit, the Holy Spirit, loves to help me (and you) in our weaknesses. We don't even have to pray the perfect words; he prays and even groans for us when there are no words.

> Likewise the Spirit helps us in our weakness. For we do not know what to pray for as we ought, but the Spirit himself intercedes for us with groanings too deep for words.
> Romans 8:26

Interestingly, the quote on this page of my journal read, "You alone are enough. You have nothing to prove to anybody." -Maya Angelou

19

A few nights later, I awoke and these words came to me.

> *You are fearfully and wonderfully made. [Psalm 139:14] I knew you in the womb; I knew you before the womb. You are of infinite value. Don't compare yourself to anyone or anything. You devalue yourself and others when you compare. You devalue my beautiful and unique creation…. Believe I make no mistakes. You are who you are meant to be. I will perfect you. Don't try to perfect yourself. That is perfectionism—a trap. Allow me to fill and perfect you. Then you will be who you were meant to be—who I made you to be.*

These were the perfect words to prepare me for the coming year, but they mostly went in one ear and out the other. Yet God didn't give up on me. He

Bold, Bodacious and Beautiful

kept chiseling away at my insecurity and telling me the same things over and over again. "You are loved. You are enough with me by your side. Trust me."

> *...Go where I ask you to go. Every moment is a gift; use the moments well.... See them as gifts, and be grateful.... The javelinas were gifts. You asked to see them up close, and I provided that. Think of what else I can and will provide....*

I come from a family of hunters, and although I had seen mounted javelinas, I had never seen a live one up close. One evening, I prayed and asked God to show me a javelina while we were on the deck. I didn't really believe he would, but I thought it wouldn't hurt to ask. Several of them did pass by with their young, and I was even able to capture some videos on my phone. It was exciting to observe them up close and from the safety of the deck. I was thrilled that God had answered such a strange and trivial request, and I was reminded of this verse.

> Until now you have asked nothing in my name. Ask, and you will receive, that your joy may be full.
> John 16:24

20

During my last few days in Arizona, these words came to me.

Bold, Bodacious and Beautiful

> *I am the light of the world. A city set on a hill cannot be hid[den]. [Matthew 5:14] I am blinding light, light that illuminates the way. Cleansing light. My burden is easy and light. Be my light to a dark world—a world that doesn't even know it is in darkness. Eyes can adjust to the dark, but they can also adjust to the light. Be my light. It may be uncomfortable for some, but only for a short while as their eyes adjust—their spiritual eyes.*

I loved this part: "Eyes can adjust to the dark, but they can also adjust to the light."

It reminded me of the many times I had walked into a dark movie theater, and had to take a moment for my eyes to adjust before I could find my seat. These words begged the question: Had I grown used to spiritual darkness? Was I "being God's light" and if so, how?

> *…I am the Alpha and the Omega—the beginning and the end. [Revelation 21:6] All things begin and end with me and me alone…. Keep your eyes on me— your spiritual eyes. Many can see and hear and many can't. Be the salt [Matthew 5:13] and the light in this world. Show it it's darkness, and bring a flame of light to those who need and want it…. I will show you the way and empower you to do things you never thought you could do…. Don't look too far ahead, just far enough to see the next step. I've said it many times, but stay the course. I long to use you, and I long for you to know me deeply and to deeply love me.*

Bold, Bodacious and Beautiful

I longed to know and love God. I had prayed to have this type of relationship for a long time, and I wondered if it would happen soon. Perhaps it was already happening. I assumed God wanted to use me in our Connect Group, and I hoped our group would double, triple or even quadruple in size with women coming from near and far and growing into a deeper relationship with the Lord. It didn't occur to me that God might want to do a mighty work in my family too, since he gave me these words when I was visiting them.

Even though I knew I would see my family again during the holidays, I felt deep sadness as I boarded the plane. However, in her usual way, New York City had some surprises up her sleeve.

On my first day back, I ran into a friend from spin class who told me a new version of *West Side Story* was being filmed a few blocks from my house, on the same street where my old Catholic church was located. Sure enough, as I walked home with my groceries, I could see the entire street was lined with a colorful array of 1950's cars, taxis and trucks. That evening as a scene was being filmed inside and outside the church, the soulful tune of "Maria" filled the humid night air. Onlookers such as myself tried to catch a glimpse of the actors and set. The entrance of the church was hidden behind screens, so it was hard to watch the filming. However, I did see Steven Spielberg drive by and wave to the crowd.

As I stood with my friend from spin class who was there with her elderly mother and teenage

Bold, Bodacious and Beautiful

son, I thought to myself, this is another magical New York night. My sense of desolation had evaporated, and I felt content and even delighted to be back home in New York City.

> ...then you shall take delight in the LORD, and I will make you ride on the heights of the earth…
> Isaiah 58:14a

***

21

A few nights later, I woke up in the middle of a steamy night, window open and the occasional siren blaring. These words came to me.

> *The power of the word of God was the word made flesh and dwelt among us. [John 1:14] It is sharper than a double-edged sword—a needle. [Hebrews 4:12] It is fire and water and love and mercy and judgment and grace. It dwells in you—in your heart and mind. Feed on my word [the Bible] daily. Memorize it. Let it become you—who you are. My words bring life, and they will make you wise. Feed on my words and my Word. It is not boring. It is not dry. It is full of blood and life and death. It is your food—as my body is your food. [John 6:55] It is for you and everyone. Take my word to others. Feed my sheep. [John 21:17] Feed them. Be with them. Love them.*

Bold, Bodacious and Beautiful

Had God just made a reference to the sword named "needle" in the *Game of Thrones* or had my subconscious added that in?

> *…See the good in all people…. Stay out of politics. They change hourly, daily, yearly. What is dire right now won't be in five years. It may even be forgotten. Don't let politics divide you from those you love and those you don't love. Stay the course. Move neither to the left nor to the right. Stay with me and in me. Feed my sheep and those who aren't yet my sheep.*

These words were not exactly what I wanted to hear because I was passionate about my political views. I often posted about them on social media, yet it had been a point of contention within my family and between some friends. I had even unfriended some people who challenged my opinions.

I took this advice to heart and stopped posting about political topics. The change made a difference. I did not feel as angry at what was going on in the world and at people whose political views differed from mine. My political opinions hadn't changed, but my emotions regarding them had. Additionally, I had been putting the occasional uplifting Bible verse on my bathroom wall, but I hadn't memorized very many of them for decades. I decided I would try to memorize 1 Corinthians 13, the love chapter, while I was in Scotland. If I wanted to have more love in my heart, perhaps I could begin by "cementing" this chapter in my mind.

Bold, Bodacious and Beautiful

> If I speak in the tongues of men and of
> angels, but have not love, I am a noisy gong
> or a clanging cymbal.
> 1 Corinthians 13:1

***

22

Taking a trip to Europe was not an everyday
occurrence for me. I was nervous about traveling
overseas by myself as well as spending what to me
seemed like a good deal of money. Several of my
friends traveled extensively, but I generally opted to
visit my family in Arizona on my holiday breaks.
Several days before my trip to Scotland, I awakened
multiple times to words that I felt were from God.

> *I am the God of yesterday, today and tomorrow. I
> hold your days in my hand. Trust me, and do not fear
> the future or that which may never happen….*

"Trust me and do not fear the future…" such
as my credit card not working or not having access to
cash; my phone not working or my blow dryer and
the outlet adapter not working; my friend deciding
two weeks was too long for me to stay; having trouble
getting through customs, plane delays or my friend
missing me at the airport. My list of fears wasn't
short.

> *I long to be known by you. I long to use you in great
> and mighty ways. Don't let fear and regret consume
> you…. Don't be flattened by an unkind or*

> *unthoughtful word. Forgive easily, love much and hold others loosely....*

"Is there anything else, Lord?" I asked.
I will be with you as you travel to Scotland and reconnect with [your friend]. Let me do my work. Watch me work....

I had no idea what God intended to do on this trip, but his words calmed my worries.

> And which of you by being anxious can add a single hour to his span of life?
> Matthew 6:27

23

A few days before I was to leave, a colleague and friend on my fourth grade team fell and broke her leg as she was leaving the symphony. A day or so later, a blood clot caused a stroke that paralyzed her on one side and left her unable to talk. The news was devastating. She was just a few years away from retirement. When I visited her in the ICU, I didn't know what to say, except to express that I was so deeply sorry the stroke had happened. She knew I went to church, but as far as I could remember, in two decades of working together, I had never shared anything about my faith with her. I wanted to pray with her, but instead I told her I was praying for her.

Bold, Bodacious and Beautiful

The next day when I was praying, I asked God if there was something he would like to say to me.

> *I always have something to say. How infrequently you ask. I dare you to put aside the other distractions, the phone, your books, your fears and [social media]. I dare you to focus on me for one full day. One day. Not five minutes or thirty here and there. Not an hour or maybe… two. Focus on me. I have so much to share and now that you can hear it more clearly—why not? Why not take full advantage of my favor and my presence?… Let me into the secret places of your soul. You will not be disappointed. I know you fear where I may take you and where and when your life will end. Leave it to me. Let me "take the wheel"….*

I was surprised by God's sense of humor when he asked to "take the wheel." At least, I *thought* it was his sense of humor. I decided to spend the morning before my trip with the Lord, reading and praying. Then I went to spin class and was mindful of Jesus being there with me. It made me smile when I thought of him on the bike next to me or even just standing beside my bike. I did several errands and imagined him walking right with me on Broadway's busy sidewalk. In my imagination, he was wearing shorts and sandals. That also made me smile. When I ate, I visualized him at the table with me. The day wasn't as difficult as I had imagined, and I didn't feel a bit lonely or bored. I didn't have the vaguest idea that this day would prepare me for a difficult season to

Bold, Bodacious and Beautiful

come, but later I would look back and be grateful for it.

> And the disciples were filled with joy and with the Holy Spirit.
> Acts 13:52

***

24

A year earlier, in 2018 when I was visiting my dad in Arizona, I found a Bible study book that had belonged to my mother. It was called *A Heart That Dances* by Catherine Martin. Catherine had been a part of my parent's Young Life Club when she was in high school, and I remembered them mentioning her. When I opened the book, I saw that my mother had answered the first question with very shaky handwriting. She must have attempted to do the study when she had dementia, but couldn't complete the first page. The thought filled me with grief at the time, partly because I was still mourning her loss from the previous year, and partly because she had lost so much, including her ability to read and write, during her ten year decline into dementia.

I decided to continue the Bible study where my mother had left off as a way to remember and honor her. I loved it, especially the section on Moses. I didn't realize it then, but Catherine Martin would later become a key figure in my spiritual development. I would complete several of her online Bible studies

Bold, Bodacious and Beautiful

and become a part of her online community. As I sat down to spend time with God before my trip, Catherine Martin's chapter about Moses came to mind.

I wrote in my journal, "Before God spoke to Moses in the burning bush, Moses had to first <u>look</u> and then <u>turn aside</u> from what he was doing. Then God spoke to him. God, help me to look and then take the time to turn aside from my plans or my agenda and spend time with you." Then I wrote this verse from the Bible. "When the Lord saw that he [Moses] turned aside to see, God called to him out of the bush, 'Moses, Moses!' And he said, 'Here I am.'" Exodus 3:4

After that, these words came to me.

...You worry about so many inconsequential things. What if? What if? What if? What if one or all of those things happen? Am I still your God? Will you rely on me to see you through? Will you breathe my breath of peace to sustain you? Will you grasp hold of my hands to pull you up and out? Or will you shrink into yourself and panic and be filled with doubt and envy and bitterness?...

I wasn't sure what this had to do with Moses, but God was speaking to me, so perhaps that was the connection. I wanted to breathe his "breath of peace" but I didn't know how. How could I grasp hold of his hands so he could pull me out of my worry? I didn't know, but spending time with him was a start. And having his Word in my mind.

Bold, Bodacious and Beautiful

> *Allow me to be your boat and your bridge from one adventure in me to the next…. You allow your mind to wander down twisting alleyways of fear and destruction. Don't go there. As Christine Caine says, 'Get off the [fear] train.' Get off and step into the life I have for you. It is full and completely different from the way you live now. Open your heart. It's time…. Be the beautiful and gorgeous woman I've made you to be. Be bold and bodacious and beautiful. Yes, bodacious. Look it up.*

There was that phrase again: bold, bodacious and beautiful. I looked up the meaning of bodacious —outright, unmistakable, remarkable, noteworthy. Well, that definitely wasn't me; I was the opposite. I was the type of person who would enter a room, and no one would notice. Or people would be describing an event, and I would tell them that I had been there, and they would look at me blankly. I often thought that I would make a good spy.

> *…Get your house in order—your spiritual house, mental house and physical house. When I call, I hope you will come. It will be your choice. Yours alone. Do it. Be bold and bodacious and beautiful—and do it all for me and with me and in me…. I will refresh your spirit. I will refresh your soul. You will go forth in my spirit…. You will be uncomfortable, but I will be your comfort. Find your comfort in me and me alone. Only me. Always me. Only me. Amen….*

Bold, Bodacious and Beautiful

This was the third time the phrase "bold, bodacious and beautiful" was used to describe me. It occurred to me that even though those adjectives didn't describe who I was now, or who I felt like, perhaps they described who I was becoming? Or who I *could* become? I didn't understand, but I thought maybe I would know in time. I decided that when I returned home from Scotland I would go through my books and give away the ones I didn't love. That would be a start on "getting my physical house in order." After that, maybe I could get rid of some clothes and then tackle a closet or two. I didn't have time to consider my mental and spiritual houses. My main focus was getting to Scotland. I was, indeed, worried about many things. Meeting my friend after not seeing her for thirty years and getting to her small town an hour away from the airport were my top worries.

On the flight, my worries were replaced with excitement, and when I arrived at the Edinburgh Airport, my friend was there waiting for me. We had met at a small church in Manhattan when she was a nanny to three children, and I was a student at FIT. Later, when I worked on staff at the Episcopal church, she was also a part of that community. When she went back to the U.K. to live, we lost touch for about a decade. We reconnected on social media. It was such a gift to be able to visit her in Scotland after all those years. We took a car service to her home and then had tea in her charming seaside town of Broughty Ferry. Both my credit card and phone

96

Bold, Bodacious and Beautiful

worked. After lunch, we walked to the River Tay and continued catching up as we sat by the water with Broughty Castle—a castle!—in the distance.

> A friend loves at all times, and a brother is born for adversity.
> Proverbs 17:17

***

25

During my two week stay, I developed a routine of taking early morning walks along the shore and gathering sea glass. There was more sea glass on the beach than I had ever seen in my entire life. The locals thought it was funny to see the American gathering bits of glass, but to me it was a treasure.

Regular broken glass is trash. It's sharp and dangerous and carefully handled when disposed of. I googled sea glass and learned after seven-to-ten years of being tossed around the ocean—banging and rolling against sand and rocks—it emerges jewel-like, cloudy with smooth edges and a pleasure to hold. I also discovered that the sea glass made a lovely clinking sound as I walked. Trash had been transformed into something rare and treasured— sought after. I thought this could be an apt metaphor for life. When I am banged around and pummeled by life, I might emerge jewel-like with soft edges, sought after and rare—someone who is a pleasure to hold. The thought made me chuckle.

Bold, Bodacious and Beautiful

As I walked along the shore, I began to memorize 1 Corinthians 13. This chapter of 1 Corinthians is often called the "love" chapter, and many of the verses are quoted at weddings. It was written by the Apostle Paul, and it is actually the second letter that he wrote to the Church in Corinth, but the first letter was lost, so this one is called First Corinthians.

> [1]If I speak in the tongues of men and of angels, but have not love, I am a noisy gong or a clanging cymbal. [2] And if I have prophetic powers, and understand all mysteries and all knowledge, and if I have all faith, so as to remove mountains, but have not love, I am nothing. [3] If I give away all I have, and if I deliver up my body to be burned, but have not love, I gain nothing.

> [4] Love is patient and kind; love does not envy or boast; it is not arrogant [5] or rude. It does not insist on its own way; it is not irritable or resentful; [6] it does not rejoice at wrongdoing, but rejoices with the truth. [7] Love bears all things, believes all things, hopes all things, endures all things.

> [8] Love never ends. As for prophecies, they will pass away; as for tongues, they will cease; as for knowledge, it will pass away. [9] For we know in part and we prophesy in part, [10] but

Bold, Bodacious and Beautiful

> when the perfect comes, the partial will pass away. [11]When I was a child, I spoke like a child, I thought like a child, I reasoned like a child. When I became a man, I gave up childish ways. [12] For now we see in a mirror dimly, but then face to face. Now I know in part; then I shall know fully, even as I have been fully known.
>
> [13] So now faith, hope, and love abide, these three; but the greatest of these is love.

1 Corinthians 13, ESV

I worked on memorizing the passage for several weeks over that summer, and then I got distracted by teaching and life, and it got pushed to the bottom of a pile of things to do. However, as I began to write this manuscript, I began working on committing it to memory again.

***

26

Scotland was wonderful. I enjoyed cooking dinners with my friend, exploring her nearby childhood city of Dundee and catching up for hours, but I also found time to spend with God. These words came to me late one night.

> *I will pour out my spirit on you as I pour rain from the heavens—thick and unrelenting.*

"Is there anything else, Lord?" I asked. I loved the image of God's Spirit pouring out on me like rain.

> *I am your God, and you are my child…. Don't forget me as you go about your day. Keep me in the forefront of your mind and heart. Let my love pour out of you to a broken and lonely world…. Open your eyes and <u>see</u> the people around you. I have given you the gift of seeing their pain. It isn't up to you to heal them. I will do that. Point them to me….*

He had given me the gift of seeing other people's pain, but I had never considered it a gift. It was a relief to hear that I didn't have to try to fix anyone. That was God's job. All I had to do was point people to Jehovah Rapha, The God Who Heals. I didn't internalize this concept all at once; in fact, it took many reminders throughout the coming months and years for me to stop trying to fix people, situations and myself.

> *…I will fill you with love—just share it…. Welcome my family into yours. Welcome the outsider, the doubter, the invisible ones. Welcome them all….*

As I read over these words, I thought about our Connect Group, and I assumed the words referred to the many people that would be joining our group. I now believe the meaning was broader and far reaching. I worried about how to help so many friends, students and family members, but my job was simply to love them and welcome them.

Bold, Bodacious and Beautiful

35'For I was hungry and you gave me food, I was thirsty and you gave me drink, I was a stranger and you welcomed me, 36I was naked and you clothed me, I was sick and you visited me, I was in prison and you came to me.' 37Then the righteous will answer him, saying, 'Lord, when did we see you hungry and feed you, or thirsty and give you drink? 38And when did we see you a stranger and welcome you, or naked and clothe you? 39And when did we see you sick or in prison and visit you?' 40And the King will answer them, 'Truly, I say to you, as you did it to one of the least of these my brothers, you did it to me.'
Matthew 25:35-40

***

27

Early one morning during my stay in Scotland, I awoke to the sound of a fly bashing itself into the window. My friend had large, long windows that opened at the top, angling in toward the room and open on the sides. The fly kept circling around and zooming full speed into the glass when all it had to do was escape around the sides or over the top of the window. Eventually, it bashed itself to death. I knew there must be a metaphor for life in that stubborn fly, and it occurred to me that I could look to God more consistently for the way out of my difficulties. I may

Bold, Bodacious and Beautiful

only see one possible "escape," but God could see openings that were invisible to me. As I reflected on my summer, I realized the tension that had brewed between my New York friend and I had mostly gone away. It felt like a miracle. My morning walks along the coastline were providing time with God and the simple joy of nature. I was well rested, and I felt blessed.

> [7]How precious is your steadfast love, O God! The children of mankind take refuge in the shadow of your wings. [8]They feast on the abundance of your house, and you give them drink from the river of your delights.
> Psalm 36:7-9

***

28

My friend surprised me with an excursion to Stirling, Scotland. It was pure magic walking up the steep narrow streets and exploring the Old Town jail and the Church of the Holy Rude at the top of the hill. We spent a rainy day wandering around medieval Stirling Castle, taking in the history of the place and enjoying an incredibly delicious meal in the cafeteria.

On our last day, I took a bus to the National Wallace Monument, a 220 foot tower that commemorates the patriot and martyr, Sir William Wallace. I was intrigued by the life of the man I knew

Bold, Bodacious and Beautiful

from the film *Braveheart*. The lush green countryside took this city girl's breath away.

The visit to Stirling was a blessing. From the staff at one landmark who stored our luggage and offered to drive us to our Airbnb to our gracious Airbnb host who made us tea in her kitchen and drove us to the castle in the pouring rain, the residents of Stirling had shown us so much kindness time and again. An elderly gentleman named Finlay helped us find our way home after our day at the castle. As he led us down a winding path to the bottom of a hill, he told us about his life. When we reached the bottom, my friend asked him if he wanted her to pray for him and he did. I was impressed by her boldness and a little envious.

During our stay in Stirling, God spoke these words to me.

> *Why are you so surprised when I stop the rain or help you open a lockbox or help your phone to work? Why don't you ask for my help and guidance more often? If I can help you in these instances, just think of what else I can do. Nothing is too difficult for me. I am stronger than the walls of Stirling Castle, [and] I shield you better than those ancient stone walls.... I'm not planning your harm or to hurt or destroy you. My goal is to raise you up and place a crown of blessings on your head.*

I still didn't completely believe God's intentions for my life. Perhaps it would take a lifetime

Bold, Bodacious and Beautiful

to learn how to truly trust in God and learn that his best interests were my best interests.

> *Today when [your friend] prayed for Finlay, that was to model for you how to love and pray for others. Be bold. Be bodacious. Be beautiful. Be the person I created you to be. Right now you are only a fraction of who you could be. Learn to trust in me and "ride out" the uncomfortable moments, minutes, days, years. They too shall pass. Trust me to see you through to the other side…. Trust me to fill you with my abounding supernatural love and joy, spilling over and blessing all those around you….*

A few years later, when a friend asked me to sum up the theme of the words I felt I heard from God, I told her the overall message boiled down to two words, "Trust me." A lesson I am still learning today.

> Who among you fears the LORD and obeys the voice of his servant? Let him who walks in darkness and has no light trust in the name of the LORD and rely on his God.
> Isaiah 50:10

29

A few of my days in Scotland were spent exploring Dundee's restaurants, parks, museums and, most notably, the Verdant Works Jute Mill. Several members of my friend's family had worked in the jute mills, so she had a strong connection to the restored

Bold, Bodacious and Beautiful

mill that was now an interactive museum. I had taught my fourth grade students about immigration to America through Ellis Island, so I was intrigued by the stories of the Dundee textile mill workers. Their stories mirrored those of immigrants who came to America seeking a better life but ended up working long hours in sweatshops.

On one of the last days of my trip, we traveled by train and then bus to St. Andrews. I was charmed by its beauty, especially the rather ghostly remains of St. Andrews Cathedral and St. Andrews Castle. But the ongoing highpoint of my trip, besides spending time with my old friend, was taking long morning walks along the shore and gathering sea glass. I would typically walk for a half hour and then retrace my steps home. On some days, I even made it as far as Broughty Castle. I was repeatedly surprised by the sea glass I discovered when I headed back to my friend's house. I thought I had already collected all the beautiful little gems of glass to be found, but there were so many more I had missed and couldn't see them until I turned around. As I reflected on another metaphor for life, I wondered if I could be more open to changing directions in order to see new possibilities and blessings that I had perhaps missed the first time around. "Help me to grow from these life lessons I learned in Scotland," I wrote in my journal.

I said goodbye to my old friend, wistful for the time spent together. Who knew if I would see her again, at least on this side of heaven? But I was filled

Bold, Bodacious and Beautiful

with gratitude for the opportunity to renew our friendship and experience such an enjoyable adventure in Scotland. After being detained several hours in customs for two apples in my backpack, it was a relief to finally step into my steamy New York City apartment.

> You make known to me the path of life; in your presence there is fullness of joy; at your right hand are pleasures forevermore.
> Psalm 16:11

***

30

The summer wound down with another subway trip to my beloved Brighton Beach and a visit to a friend's bucolic home in upstate New York. I continued to hear from God even in my busyness. These words are some that came to me.

> *I have also missed my time with you… I am still with you here. Don't squander the weeks and hours. Spend them with me; let me be your companion and guide. Don't fill your time with social media, movies and books. Some are good and fine but not hour upon hour…. Stop spending so much time on [social media]; it is a meaningless void you can never recover. Spend it with people and with me. Your time with [your friend in Scotland] was also time with me. It isn't mutually exclusive. Be mindful of my presence in your daily life….*

Bold, Bodacious and Beautiful

I was not surprised by the words about social media, but I was astonished by the comparison of time spent with my friend in Scotland to time spent with God. How could it be one and the same? I was reminded of the words in Matthew 25 which spoke about whatever we do for a person is like doing it for God. Did that mean that spending time with people was the same as spending time with God? It felt like a slippery theological slope to me.

> *…Enjoy this life I've given you. Bring joy [to your friend who had the stroke and is paralyzed]. Read her funny books. I will show you. Enjoy your time with her. I am with her….*

I regret to say, I never really laughed with that friend. I couldn't. The sorrow of her situation felt too overwhelming to me. I did buy some books to read to her, but as I began reading one, it really wasn't funny at all. In fact, it was kind of grim, so I stopped. I also never really talked to her about my faith except to ask her if she wanted me to pray for her. She did, so I prayed for her during a few of my visits.

Control your tongue. Keep quiet when you want to gossip….

And as for gossip, in the coming year I contributed to more than my share of it with friends.

> Death and life are in the power of the tongue, and those who love it will eat its fruits.

Bold, Bodacious and Beautiful

Proverbs 18:21

31

A week later, this came to me.

I am the One, the only One. I am the first. I am the best. I am the front and the back. I am All. All in All.... I cannot be fathomed or understood or contained. Don't even try. The moment you think you know who I am, I will become bigger, grander, [and] more immense than you knew before. I go before, I surround, I envelop. I can find anything, do anything, be anything. Don't rely on saints. They are grains of sand, and I am the ocean and the universe that contains the ocean. I Am. I Am that I Am. I will be and I am—all at once. Just be in me, and I will do the rest....

I had never prayed much to the saints when I was Catholic, but I enjoyed learning about their lives, and I definitely had my favorites including St. Francis and St. Joan of Arc. The only exception was when I lost things, then I would pray to St. Anthony, and I have to say, I usually found what I had misplaced. But the point was well taken.

Show love you may not feel, and the feelings will come. Say love. Do love. Be love—and you will feel it. Be first. Do first, and then feel.

This advice to love first and then feel love was so practical; it made perfect sense to me. In fact, I thought it was brilliant advice. In actuality, though, I

Bold, Bodacious and Beautiful

rarely showed the love I didn't feel, especially in the coming school year.

> *...You are not insignificant; do not be fooled by the feelings you've always felt. They are lies, and they come from the liar. Learn to spot lies and rebuke them. Learn to see the lies. Learn to thrust the Sword of the Spirit [the word of God, also called the Bible] through lies. [Ephesians 6:17] Don't speak lies or listen to them. Tune them out. Tune in to me and my frequency. Listen to my music, watch my movies, read my books. Teach others to do the same.*

I had listened to a top 40 radio station for decades. When I became a teacher, I thought that knowing what my students were listening to would help me relate to them, and in some ways it did. I could stop them before they said something inappropriate because I knew all the lyrics to every popular song.

During the last summer my mother was alive, while I was visiting my family in Arizona, I began to listen to a Christian radio station while driving back and forth to the memory care facility where she was living. I found that the music assuaged some of my grief. She died a few weeks later, and I continued to listen to the same radio station in New York City during the ensuing months as I mourned her passing. The songs would play in the back of my mind and had a way of buoying me as I trudged through those melancholy days. One of my friends in our Connect Group had a keen interest in Christian music, and she inspired us to go to Christian concerts. Some of my best memories of my last years in New York City were when I saw King and Country on my birthday and Lauren Daigle at Radio City Music Hall *and* Carnegie Hall. I also discovered Crowder, another band I grew to love.

> *...You have filled this book with me and my words. Now fill another and another. Amen. Let it be so. Amen. Amen. Amen.*

It seemed fitting that the completion of my first journal would coincide with the ending of my fabulous summer. I couldn't believe it. I had a whole book filled with words that I felt were from God. God! The God of the universe was speaking to me. I thought back to that day in April when I wondered if I would ever hear from him again, yet I found that whenever I made time for him *always* showed up. It had been one of the best summers of my life, and I felt blessed by friendships, my church and especially the words that came to me early in the mornings. However, *hearing* the truth wasn't the same as internalizing it and actually *living* it. I wanted to hear from God, but I often didn't want to do what he asked me to do. Or I thought what he said was a good idea, but then I completely forgot about it. I now realize I had a long way to go on my spiritual path, but God was with me every step of the way, reminding me of his greatness and majesty. Reminding me that I could trust him. And reminding

Bold, Bodacious and Beautiful

me that because of his love for me, I could love
others.

> [7]How precious is your steadfast love, O God!
> The children of mankind take refuge in the
> shadow of your wings. [8]They feast on the
> abundance of your house, and you give them
> drink from the river of your delights. [9]For
> with you is the fountain of life; in your light
> do we see light.
> Psalm 36:7-9

Bold, Bodacious and Beautiful

3
SEASON OF STRIFE
(FALL 2019)

1

My first journal was filled, and I was ready to begin another. Who would have thought such a thing could happen? Certainly not me. I was about to begin my twenty-fourth year of teaching which was astounding because in many ways I didn't feel like a master teacher. There were still so many things I did not know, especially in the area of technology. I remembered when I was a fledgling teacher, and I wished I had the life and teaching experience of the older teachers. Why didn't I feel more confident now that I was a veteran? Shouldn't my final years of teaching be a breeze?

That summer had been phenomenal, and I was not eager to let it go. Yet, I was looking forward to seeing my colleagues, meeting my new class, setting up my classroom and beginning a new school year. These conflicting feelings were mixed with anguish over my colleague who had suffered the stroke and was partially paralyzed. She was still unable to communicate, except by pointing to "yes" and "no" and letters of the alphabet on a chart. We would begin the year without her on our team, and the loss of her presence weighed heavily on me.

Early one morning at the end of August, these words came to me.

Bold, Bodacious and Beautiful

> *I am your God…. The one to turn to in times of trouble. Your peace. Your joy. Your love. Your true love and your only love… Watch with me in the hours of the night when you can't sleep. I am great and mighty and too awesome to behold, but I also care for the wounded sparrow, and I care for you and your days…. You are my dearly beloved, cherished child. I am teaching you how to walk and run and ride a bike. When you don't feel my hands it is because I've "let go of the bike," and I'm teaching you to ride. I'm still there—close by and watching—ready if you should fall, but you most likely won't….*

The image of a loving father letting go of the bike not because he didn't care, but because he was enabling his child to learn a new skill as well as a new form of independence and fun was beautiful to me.

> *[Your friend who had the stroke] isn't alone. She has people, and I am with her. Show her peace and joy and love in the midst of pain….*

I faithfully visited my friend that Fall. She had been moved from the hospital to a care facility that happened to be next door to my apartment building. What were the chances of that? In some ways, it didn't surprise me at all. As an added blessing, I was able to visit her with one of my other colleagues who also lived on the Upper West Side.

> *This year is a final year; your time at [your school in New York City] is almost over…. Cherish each moment—don't try to get through them…. <u>Be</u> with*

Bold, Bodacious and Beautiful

> *people. Listen to them…. Be in the conversations.*
> *End your time well, and end it with love.*

To be honest, I didn't believe that this would be my final year in New York City. How could it? Life was wonderful and anyhow, I couldn't afford to retire. It didn't make sense to move.

> *Be the joy. Be my joy. Show my fruit of the spirit*
> *[love, joy, peace, patience, kindness, goodness,*
> *faithfulness, gentleness, self-control] to those you work*
> *with. [Galatians 5:22, 23] Be my peace to a worried*
> *world. Be my joy to an anxious and lonely world. But*
> *most of all, be my love. You are learning to love, as*
> *you asked. You are learning to show [love] when you*
> *don't feel it…. Feelings are not love—they are*
> *byproducts of love. Love is an action—patience,*
> *kindness, self-control, giving of yourself even when you*
> *don't feel it…. The "difficult" people need it the most.*
> *They don't feel loved even when it is right there before*
> *them. Be patient with their bumbling ways and*
> *unkind words. Let them [the words] pass over you.*
> *Do not grasp them and examine them. Let them fly*
> *over you and away. You only need the love and*
> *kindness of me. All else is icing on the proverbial*
> *cake.*

"Love is an action." I still need to remind myself of that almost daily; it still doesn't come easily or naturally to me.

> *I am your food. Eat of me and only me. Spend all*
> *four days [before school starts] with me. Retreat with*

115

Bold, Bodacious and Beautiful

> *me. Speak [of] me. Read [about] me. Stay with me*
> *[and] in my presence. Don't fill your days with vain*
> *and empty things. Some are okay; keep it to a*
> *minimum. Keep to me. Keep with me. Keep me in your*
> *heart and by your side. Be mindful of me. Always,*
> *only, ever me. Amen. Amen. Amen. Let it be so.*
> *Amen.*

As usual, I didn't quite know what to make of these words. I don't remember if I spent all four days with the Lord. I might have. As I look back on that year, I wish I had posted these words somewhere where I could often be reminded of them. Once the year got underway, and I was faced with a change in my teaching expectations, several new colleagues, and tension with a colleague who I liked, I tended to forget that my motivation for teaching and interacting with my peers was supposed to be love. Forgiveness flew away. So did my sense of humor. Instead, insecurity, anxiety, and, more often than not, anger were my taskmasters.

> Beloved, if God so loved us, we also ought to love one another.
> 1 John 4:11

***

2

Bold, Bodacious and Beautiful

During the previous year, I had discovered a handful of speakers and pastors that I loved and continued to feel the benefits of the wisdom they shared. I listened to Dawnchere and Rich Wilkerson, Priscilla Shirer and Christine Caine. T. D. Jakes had been around for years, but he was new to me, and he could preach like no one else I'd ever heard. Additionally, Michael Todd burst into my life with his "Crazy Faith" sermon series, and his passion absolutely took my breath away. These men and women, along with my own pastor, encouraged and inspired me during this season of my life.

I enjoyed listening to their sermons as I began clearing papers, books and other items out of my closets and bookshelves. In all, I gave away over a dozen bags of books, and it felt great to lighten my load. Later, when I was packing up my life and giving away so many of my belongings, I was incredibly grateful that God had encouraged me to start the process of purging over a year and a half earlier.

I awoke at 4 AM on the first of September and asked God if he had a word for me.

> *I do. You have a lot on your mind. Many thoughts roaming here and there…. Read and listen and meditate on my Word [the Bible]. [Pastors] bring you to my Word. Now come directly to my Word…. Read about Jabez and David and Solomon. Read about them yourself. Continue to listen to [the sermons of your favorite pastors on YouTube], but don't substitute them for me. Your relationship is with me not them….*

Bold, Bodacious and Beautiful

I had to admit, I enjoyed listening to a fabulous sermon more than reading the Bible.

> *I am molding you into the woman I want you to be.... Be bold, bodacious and beautiful. Be the woman I made you and called you to be. Be my love to those around you. Be my love when you are weary and depleted and when you are rested and calm. Be my love when you know you aren't feeling loving....*

There it was again. Be my love when you aren't feeling loving.

> *Be bold and bodacious and beautiful. Be who I've called you to be. Be me to a hurting world. The world may hate you, and it may love you. Love it regardless. Love people.... Don't compete. Competition is for insecure people, and you have no reason to be insecure.*

I wanted to be bold, bodacious and beautiful, but instead I tended to look around at what other people were doing, what they were wearing, how they were teaching and even how they were worshiping at church. Did I measure up? Did they measure up? It was a constant ping-pong game of feeling insecure, then superior and back to feeling insecure. My go to frame of mind was one of anxiety inspired by insecurity.

> *You long for your sister. If you want her, [then] you must move. Do you want to? It will come at a price, but the payoff will be your family. Enjoy the bustle*

Bold, Bodacious and Beautiful

and luster of New York City while you are there. Enjoy the museums and shows. Enjoy church and your friends…. Make your choice and make it with a clear head. The time in New York City will go quickly….

I didn't think living closer to my sister was possible. I also wish I had relished "the bustle and luster" of New York a bit more. I enjoyed my church and friends. I even made it to one museum. But that fall and winter, I was too busy to see any Broadway shows or concerts.

The more time I spent with God, the more I heard words that I felt were from him. It was such a phenomenal feeling. All of this time communing with him should have transformed me into a calm and confident version of myself. Instead, my anxiety increased. In the past, I had heard pastors and strong Christian friends say the closer they got to Christ, the more the enemy attacked their vulnerable places. Their explanation made sense, but I was dismayed and even distraught by my reactions to people, situations and even myself that fall.

A few days later, these words came to me.

You are anxious about many things. Which books to read? Are you smart enough?... Will you be as good as the other teachers? What is your reputation? Why is that student not in your class?... Will you know what to teach, and will it be enough? Are you enough? Are you enough? Are you enough?

Bold, Bodacious and Beautiful

Was I enough? I didn't know.

I will empower you to love, teach and laugh this year. Control your mouth. You have the power to set the tone. Control what you say about [people].... I am with you; you are not alone. I will give you ideas; be sure to heed them. This year will be easy and tough as they always are.

Why didn't I heed more of his ideas? I don't fully know. I suppose life got busier. My teaching schedule was too full to add more "God inspired" activities, and even though I received these words almost every day, they didn't quite sink in. As more time went by, they started to, a trickle at a time. One of the best parts about writing this book has been revisiting them over and over again.

Embrace love. Embrace joy. Embrace peace. Grasp onto me; I am your lifeline.... Joy is the key and, of course, love. Seek it. Speak it. Speak both. Amen.

You are altogether beautiful, my love; there is no flaw in you.
Song of Solomon 4:7

***

3

I was now back at school setting up my classroom, which I loved. I enjoyed transforming a dusty room full of boxes into a warm and exciting place of learning. I also enjoyed planning the first few weeks of activities that would, hopefully, set the foundation for a vibrant, kind and respectful classroom community. I hoped my new students would have a great year, and they would love being in fourth grade. I desired the same thing for the new teacher who was replacing my colleague as well as the new math teacher who would be teaching my students this year. I anticipated our fourth grade team would work well together.

I hoped our Connect Group members would all get along, too, and we would be inspired to grow in our relationship with the Lord. Would we all like each other? That was my prayer.

These words came to me early the next morning.

> *Stay patient with those who question your methods and motives. It is iron sharpening iron. [Proverbs 27:17] Don't take it personally—even if it is meant as a personal attack. You don't know; it might not be. Expect the best of people. Answer questions briefly and simply. Don't be defensive. People are busy and they forget. You are busy and you forget…. No one really knows what they are doing. Be patient with one another. Forgive. Love. Take it easy with each other. Give people some "slack." Stay positive and loving. I am birthing a new thing in you…*

Bold, Bodacious and Beautiful

I had no idea I was about to walk into (and cause) some of what I would later refer to as "a season of strife."

> When you pass through the waters, I will be with you; and through the rivers, they shall not overwhelm you; when you walk through fire you shall not be burned, and the flame shall not consume you.
> Isaiah 43:2

4

A few days later, the words continued.
...You did well to wait until morning to answer those texts. You prayed and sought me first; make a habit of that…. Dedicate large amounts of time to me, and spend each day with me by your side.

One habit I had wanted to cultivate for years was practiced awareness of God's presence beside me during my school day. More often than not, I completely forgot about God the moment I walked in the building. I hoped this year would be different.

Do you want to live in Arizona?... Your family will not always have time for you, and you will wonder why you made the effort…. I will be by your side; I will help you. Be ready.

"How can I be ready?" I asked.

Bold, Bodacious and Beautiful

Prepare your mind and heart. Treat this time as the end. Spend time with people you don't always see.... Spend time with your Connect Group friends.

I couldn't quite believe the words I was writing, but in hindsight, it really was my last year of "regular" in-school teaching in New York City. I wish I had taken the time to savor things like eating lunch in the cafeteria, walking around the classroom and casually interacting with my students, sitting close together on the rug with them as I read aloud, passing out hard copies of assignments and students being able to hand them directly back to me. I also had no idea what a gift it was to be with my colleagues in person and, of course, teach without a mask. School had always been pretty much the same from year to year, and I took those simple moments, people and tasks for granted.

As I was thinking about school and leading the new fall season of Connect Group, I asked, "Lord, how should we proceed?"

This was what I felt I heard.
Invite new women in....

"Anything else, Lord?" I asked.
...Invite in. Embrace. Make time. Be bold, bodacious and beautiful. You will do it in my strength and power.

I had to trust him for *all* of that.

Bold, Bodacious and Beautiful

In school, open up and do poetry. You know it. Allow children to create poetry. You've wanted to do it—now do it. Allow them to express themselves through many forms…. Do it with joy.

I had always loved teaching poetry, but with each passing year I felt I had less and less time for it. There were other skills that had to be taught such as narrative and expository writing. In hindsight, I regret not making the time. Reading student poetry was like peering through a window into their souls. Children who struggled to write a paragraph often expressed themselves clearly and freely through poetry. Maybe they enjoyed writing without "rules"? In the past, some of my most prolific poets disliked most other types of writing. I gave my students the option of memorizing a weekly poem, which many did eagerly, possibly because they received a prize for every poem they memorized. I didn't care why they did it as long as they were memorizing poetry.

Speaking of my students, I loved them! They were such an eclectic and fun mix of personalities; they gobbled up projects and jumped head first into each new unit. They were kind to each other and to me and compassionate in their responses to the suffering of people, both past and present. Again, I wish I had savored our time together instead of being so concerned about covering all the curriculum.

And I will lead the blind in a way that they do not know, in paths that they have not known I

> will guide them. I will turn the darkness
> before them into light, the rough places into
> level ground. These are the things I do, and I
> do not forsake them.
> Isaiah 42:16

***

5

In the busyness of the new school year, several days went by before I realized I had not made time to hear from God. For me, making time meant turning on my light and grabbing my journal and pen in the early morning hours when I woke up, usually between 3:00 and 4:00AM. I found that when I got up earlier, it would be difficult to fall asleep again. And if I got up later, I couldn't "hear" the words as well.

After turning on my light, I would write whatever came to my mind. I often only had one eye open. At times, these nighttime sessions involved stopping writing to pray for people. When the words stopped, I would close my journal, turn off the light and go back to sleep. I rarely remembered what I had written down. Sometimes I prayed that God would expand my sleep and the hour I had left would feel like three. I must have slept through several of these opportunities because this is what I heard on this particular morning.

> *It has been a long time. We can do this every day, you know. I wait on you. I await your attention…. Be the leader you were when you were thirty, and grow beyond*

Bold, Bodacious and Beautiful

> *that. Step into the light. Step into forgiveness. My armor also protects you from human attacks—unkind words, lies and all manner of hostility....*

God's armor was something my Connect Group and I had learned about in Priscilla Shirer's Bible study. We took our time, focusing on one or two days of work each week. We each took turns leading the discussions, too. We spent most of the previous winter and spring engaged in a study designed to take seven weeks. I like to think that we savored it, and we did. I loved it.

The apostle Paul wrote about the Armor of God in the Bible in Ephesians 6:10-18. He used the image of a Roman soldier's armor, a familiar sight at the time, as a metaphor for the spiritual practices that serve to protect Christ followers. First, we need salvation, faith and the word of God [the Bible]. We also must proactively embrace the righteousness of God and right living, as well as truth. Then it is essential that we walk in the gospel of peace. And finally, we are told to pray, or communicate with God.

> [10] Finally, be strong in the Lord and in his mighty power. [11]Put on the full armor of God, so that you can take your stand against the devil's schemes. [12]For our struggle is not against flesh and blood, but against the rulers, against the authorities, against the powers of this dark world and against the spiritual forces of evil in the heavenly realms. [13] Therefore

Bold, Bodacious and Beautiful

put on the full armor of God, so that when the day of evil comes, you may be able to stand your ground, and after you have done everything, to stand. [14]Stand firm then, with the belt of truth buckled around your waist, with the breastplate of righteousness in place, [15]and with your feet fitted with the readiness that comes from the gospel of peace. [16]In addition to all this, take up the shield of faith, with which you can extinguish all the flaming arrows of the evil one. [17]Take the helmet of salvation and the sword of the Spirit, which is the word of God. [18] And pray in the Spirit on all occasions with all kinds of prayers and requests. With this in mind, be alert and always keep on praying for all the Lord's people.

Ephesians 6:10-18 (New International Version)

6

I tried to remember to mentally "put on" the armor of God each morning when I woke up. It helped me to be mindful of what was truly important every day such as walking in God's peace and remembering my faith in him was like a shield of protection against the evil one. One day, several years later, I heard Bill Johnson, pastor of Bethel Church, say he never took it off and that was yet another deep revelation to me.

Bold, Bodacious and Beautiful

The words that I felt were from God continued.

> *Teach with love and care. Go at a brisk pace, but not a hurried and harried pace. Be bold and be beautiful and bodacious at school. Don't second guess yourself. You can teach math when [the math teacher] is away....*

"Lord, I pray for wisdom in math," I answered.

This was the first time in twenty-four years of being a teacher that I wasn't in charge of teaching math. I had never thought of myself as much of a mathematician, but after meeting with the math specialist every week for a year when I was new to the school, I discovered that I enjoyed teaching it. So twenty years later, when the school hired math teachers who only taught math, I felt that I was viewed as not being good enough to teach this subject any more. This was not the intent, but I couldn't quite shake the feeling of being the "old dinosaur" who didn't have much relevance in a modern classroom. I wonder how I would have reacted to this shift in responsibilities if I had been more mindful of God's unwavering love and approval, as well as the metaphor of his armor?

The math specialist who taught my class was brilliant and technologically adept. On the first day of math class, I couldn't wrap my mind around what she was teaching, and my self-esteem took a deep plunge. On top of that, I spoke some careless words to her all

Bold, Bodacious and Beautiful

the while thinking I was being upfront and direct, but she felt attacked. It was a misstep I deeply regretted, and it took us some time to figure out how to best move forward.

After praying for wisdom in math, I felt like this was the response.

> *You will have it. Try [the math specialist's] way. Try it and learn from it. Interject some skills that can be taught.*

The advice was so simple, but regaining my self-esteem that term, unfortunately, was not.

> *Now onto bigger things. Your future. You will choose between two very different paths. Both blessed, both difficult and joyful. There will be a sense of gain, loss and peace when you choose. <u>Be</u> in the moments. <u>Be</u>. Enjoy your time in New York. Don't hide away. Come out and come on. Date. Laugh. Have fun. Follow me. Talk to me. Imagine me by your side all day—because I am. Right there—closer than you can fathom. Trust me. Trust me. Trust me. I Am that I Am. What you imagine now is only a ray of the sun. What John saw in his vision was a dimmed down glimpse of what is to come. What you will experience and dwell in forever.*

I loved the vision that Jesus's disciple, John, had of heaven. This passage was mentioned in our Connect Group's Bible study book called *Crazy Love* by Francis Chan, which I was beginning to preview.

Bold, Bodacious and Beautiful

My mind kept returning to John's description of heaven.

> [1] After this I looked, and behold, a door standing open in heaven! And the first voice, which I had heard speaking to me like a trumpet, said, "Come up here, and I will show you what must take place after this." [2]At once I was in the Spirit, and behold, a throne stood in heaven, with one seated on the throne. [3] And he who sat there had the appearance of jasper and carnelian, and around the throne was a rainbow that had the appearance of an emerald. [4] Around the throne were twenty-four thrones, and seated on the thrones were twenty-four elders, clothed in white garments, with golden crowns on their heads. [5] From the throne came flashes of lightning, and rumblings and peals of thunder, and before the throne were burning seven torches of fire, which are the seven spirits of God, [6] and before the throne there was as it were a sea of glass, like crystal.
>
> And around the throne, on each side of the throne, are four living creatures, full of eyes in front and behind: [7] the first living creature like a lion, the second living creature like an ox, the third living creature with the face of a man, and the fourth living creature like an eagle in flight. [8] And the four living creatures, each of them with six wings, are full

Bold, Bodacious and Beautiful

of eyes all around and within, and day and night they never cease to say, "Holy, holy, holy, is the Lord God Almighty, who was and is and is to come!"
Revelation 4:1-8

7

I had never given heaven much thought probably because I imagined lots of clouds and harp playing. To be honest, it sounded boring. But John's description was anything but boring. I imagined my mother there, and I wondered what she was experiencing.

The words continued.

In the meantime, love and love well. Love unabashedly. Forgive, embrace and accept. Accept all people. I am the judge. Not you. Not you. You have discernment, but don't let it run to judgment. You are not a judge.

This was good advice for me.

Don't be afraid of [leading] your Connect Group.... Be direct and loving. You will be okay.... You will be blessed to overflowing.... [Your coach] will help and guide you.... Don't "go it alone"....Collaborate and share the load with [your co-leader]. I will bless you all. I already have. I love you so much. More than you know. More than you feel. More than you imagine. Amen.

Bold, Bodacious and Beautiful

I felt extremely supported by my Connect Group co-leader (and our coach) as we planned the Fall semester. I was also excited about beginning the book *Crazy Love* because Francis Chan's interpretation of what it meant to be a Christian both challenged and inspired me. He wasn't satisfied with just going to church on Sundays. Francis was passionate about giving his whole life to the Lord by being generous with his time and money, as well as living simply. And all of it was motivated by his love for God and his desire to love others and share Jesus' love with them. For instance, he and his wife had sold their home which they felt was too big, so they could move into a much smaller home and live more simply and economically. This was not easy to do since he had a rather large family, and people told him he was crazy. His words caused me to take stock of my life in a way I never had before. His life inspired me to "love unabashedly" as well.

> Do not work for the food that perishes, but for the food that endures to eternal life, which the Son of Man will give to you.
> John 6:27a

***

8

Early one morning, these words came to me.
> *You are learning about me [as you prepare for leading the Crazy Love Bible study with your Connect*

Bold, Bodacious and Beautiful

Group]. This is just the first step—a big one, I'll grant you, but the first step. Keep going. Be faithful. This is material more people need. Keep doing it. Even after this season. Maybe some of the women will also step out and lead—in spite of their shortcomings. I fill all voids and shortcomings. Stay the course. How many times must I say this?

Apparently many times.

… Be the woman of me I made you to be. Be a warrior with your armor…. I have bigger things in mind for you and [your co-leader]…. You are needed in this moment—this season. You have practice; you have resilience; you have love even though you don't feel like it. I will give you strength and health. Fill your mind with me and my Word [the Bible]. Nothing else matters….

I wondered what these "bigger things" were?

You exist for me and only me. I will be your joy and laughter and rest…. Rest in me and my spirit, and I will take you [to] places you've never been. Yes, some will be difficult and scary, but my strength will be enough. Some will be joyous and light and refreshing —beyond belief. Take both. Experience my joy in both…. Don't hide "behind-the-scenes." Be center; be a leader. I will lead you and be your center. Rely on me and only me as your parents did when they moved to the West Side [of Phoenix]. They were only in their late twenties, and I used them in so many lives. Now I want to use you. Be ready. Go. Amen.

133

Bold, Bodacious and Beautiful

When I was in second grade, my parents had moved from a nice part of Phoenix on the East Side to a less desirable neighborhood on the West Side. They were going to host and lead a Young Life club at our house, and they wanted to live close to the high school students with whom they would be working. I had always admired them for making that sacrifice, but I don't think they considered it a loss.

A few days later, I asked God if he had a word for me, and this is what came into my mind.

I am with you in the going in and the coming out, in the rest and the toil, in the joy and in the sorrow.

"Is this me or you?" I asked.

It is me. I am speaking to you. Your hearing is imperfect but good enough. I long to be with you all day, throughout your days and all night. You are awakening to me and my presence. I've always been with you—even when you were developing in the womb. I was holding your hand as a toddler. You felt my presence. You may not remember, but you did. I spoke to you in Amsterdam and at [your church in New York]. Both those times were when you were doing full-time ministry. You were closer to me and thoughtful and mindful of my presence in ways you haven't been until now…. You are beginning to revere me, and you must continue down that path. Do not come to me lightly or flippantly. Come to me often….

Bold, Bodacious and Beautiful

Sometimes I lost sight of the realization that I was communicating with the God of the universe, and it was a good reminder.

> *Don't compare. I have shown you what to do for school; now do it. Do it and watch your students thrive. Watch them grow. Allow them fun and joy in their days; allow them laughter. Allow them space to be. Allow the same for yourself. Go on a date or two. Enjoy the fall and winter. Enjoy your group. Enjoy leading; relax control…. Rest now…. You are not feeling well after eating all those chicken [strips]. Amen.*

I had the distinct sense that God was smiling or even chuckling when he mentioned the chicken. I loved breaded chicken strips, and I always ate too many when the cafeteria served them at our school meetings. I had never really considered that God might have a sense of humor, and I was surprised as I began to catch glimpses of it here and there when he spoke to me.

As for his directives, I had a hard time relaxing control with my students and even more difficulty with our Connect Group. It seemed to spring from my insecurity and fear of doing something "wrong" or not as well as someone else.

I also did not go on any dates during this season, which I later regretted when I couldn't go on any at all. I had experienced online dating for years without incident, but several months earlier, I had had a strange and unsettling experience. It was enough to

135

Bold, Bodacious and Beautiful

give me pause, and I began to seriously rethink my methods of meeting men. So instead of trying something else, I went on a couple of more dates, and then I stopped altogether. I didn't mean to; it just happened. One month led to another and then another, and all of a sudden a year had passed by. The experience had frightened me more than I realized at the time, and as much as I wanted to be with someone, I didn't feel up to getting back out in the dating scene.

> 7Be patient, therefore, brothers, until the coming of the Lord. See how the farmer waits for the precious fruit of the earth, being patient about it, until it receives the early and the late rains. 8You also, be patient. Establish your hearts, for the coming of the Lord is at hand.
> James 5:7-8

***

9

Several days later, I thought I would try a new approach to asking God if he had anything to say to me. Instead, I used the words of Eli in 1 Samuel 3:9 in the Bible. "Speak Lord, for your servant is listening." Earlier, I had asked God to speak to me as I walked through the park.

Bold, Bodacious and Beautiful

I felt I heard this response. *I have a lot to say to you. You asked me to speak to you while you walk. Is this not enough?*

"Yes, it is, [but] I thought we could speak [in] a different way," I responded. I was surprised by his response. Why wouldn't he want to speak to me as I walked home through Central Park? Now I realize, I wouldn't have been able to record his words, and I would have forgotten them very easily.

You will hear differently in time, but you must crawl, walk, run, then fly. Do not be too eager to push ahead of my way and my speed for you....

This made sense to me.

...Take my hand and walk quietly with me through the park. Enjoy my beauty—the beauty of autumn, the sadness of death and the encroaching darkness. Dark days are beautiful, too.... Embrace the darkness of winter. It may be your last.... Be bold, bodacious and beautiful.... You will have to trust me to leave and trust me to stay.... What if you stayed and left? What if you left and returned? There are many options—many ways to achieve the same goals.

"The beauty of autumn, the sadness of death and the encroaching darkness..." These words were so hauntingly lovely. I had finally made peace with the short winter days in New York City, but it had taken a long time—decades. These words helped me to appreciate this dark, cold season even more. I also took note of the words about staying *and* leaving.

137

Bold, Bodacious and Beautiful

> *Be in the moment. You become overcome with fear of failure and anxious about many things. Stop it. Stop it now. Trust me to catch you and guide you and save you....*

I didn't know how to stop it.
You can't seem to trust that I am not the enemy. I am the divine friend and lover and guide and spouse.... Carve out large chunks of time with me. Don't fill your weekends with vain and empty pursuits....

Did I really think God was my enemy? Of course not. But the question wouldn't leave me alone; it just kept poking at me. After thinking about it for I don't know how long, I realized that deep down I believed if God knew what I *truly* wanted, he would take it away from me. Like the story of Abraham and Isaac [Genesis 22: 1-19]. God didn't take Isaac away in the end, but he came pretty close. He wanted to know Abraham was willing to let go of his most precious gift: his son. I was afraid God would do that with me. He would make me give up my dreams of living near my family, being married, having a home, the list went on and on. Maybe he was right. Maybe I did think of him as a sort of enemy I had to outwit. It made me think of a friend who told me his older brother tormented him when they were children. My friend would put on a poker face and pretend the abuse didn't bother him. Eventually, his older brother would give up and leave him in peace. That was when I

Bold, Bodacious and Beautiful

realized I had my own version of a poker face with God.

> *I caused your plans [this weekend] to fall through—both of them. I want to spend that time with you…. Focus <u>hard</u> on me in this season [and] run the race with me by your side….*

I wanted to think of God as my friend and protector, someone who would run alongside me, not as the unkind, even masochistic, older brother.

> *…Keep your mind on me…. Keep planted in me like a tree with deep roots…. I am yours, and you are mine…. Amen. Let It Be So. Amen.*

It was a lot to digest, and frankly, I couldn't take it all in at the time. I did, however, begin to internalize the idea that God was *not* my enemy. Maybe I could truly trust him *without* the poker face? During the following months, I very slowly began to open my heart to him and experience his faithfulness in my day to day life. Then after experiencing his faithfulness, a foundation of trust began to be built, brick by brick. This was the foundation upon which my relationship with God rested.

> [5]The apostles said to the Lord, "Increase our faith!" [6]And the Lord said, "If you had faith like a grain of mustard seed, you could say to this mulberry tree, 'Be uprooted and planted in the sea,' and it would obey you."
> Luke 17:5-6

Bold, Bodacious and Beautiful

10

A few nights later, I had a rather disturbing dream about a large crow the size of a small airplane flying around Times Square. It had red eyes and was peering into the windows of the buildings, one of which I was in. Then the scene changed, and I was in my apartment. There were three smaller crows attempting to break through the screens on my windows by bashing against them, but I was able to close the windows. Each crow was about two feet tall. Then the dream ended.

I woke up feeling shaken and uneasy, and I asked God about it.

The crow in your dream was [a metaphor for] the evil one, but you closed the window and kept it out—kept them out. Do not fear the evil one who lurks outside your door [and] peeks into your windows. What you did not see was the army of angels that encamp around you. The armor I give you is strong—strong [enough] to defeat and oppose the evil one. My heavenly army is [even] stronger.

So yes, the large crow was out in the city flying around and peeking in the windows—but that is all. Be on your guard. Guard your tongue. It has the power to wound.

It was not lost on me that God had compared this huge crow, which was a metaphor for evil, with my tongue. I knew my words had the power to wound, and as a teacher, I needed to be mindful of my tone of voice as well as my words.

Then I asked a question about one of my students, and I felt God answer back.

...Be steady in your love and acceptance of your students…. I will use [those students], and they all need you. They need your acceptance and love. Don't fear the evil one, but also don't forget it. It lurks and looks for an opening. Anytime love is lacking, there is an opening….

"Anytime love is lacking, there is an opening" was sobering to think about. There were plenty of times in my life I had inadvertently given an opening to Satan. If as an adult, I needed daily acceptance and love from the people around me, I couldn't imagine how much my young students needed it. It was a good reminder that I tried to heed that year.

The days ahead will be unsure and unsteady at times, but your surety and steadfastness comes from me and only me…. I am far more loving and accepting than you know or than you imagine…. Be me to an empty, confused and bleeding world. Bind up their wounds with my love. Smile. Laugh. Love. Amen. Amen. Amen….

The dream felt creepy and slightly terrifying to me, but the words from God put my mind somewhat at ease. How wonderful it would be to "bind up the world's wounds with love."

Bold, Bodacious and Beautiful

> The Spirit of the Lord GOD is upon me,
> because the LORD has anointed me to bring
> good news to the poor; he has sent me to
> bind up the brokenhearted, to proclaim liberty
> to the captives, and the opening of the prison
> to those who are bound...
> Isaiah 61:1

11

A few days later, I had a three day weekend for Rosh Hashana. I rested and spent time with God. I still didn't know how to ask God to speak to me in a way that seemed natural, and I was experimenting with using different phrases. On this day, I combined the words of Lana Vawser with the prophet Samuel [1 Samuel 3:10] in my journal. "What is on your heart, Lord? Speak for your servant is listening."

> *I have much to say to you—always. What do you want to hear?... You are becoming aware of patterns that need to change. Don't hang on to misery or self-condemnation. Don't replay mistakes or unkind words over and over again. Acknowledge the sin and then move on…. Every day be mindful of stepping in my steps, loving large and living with loving abandon. Living with loving abandon. Just think of it. You can't even begin to imagine it…. Don't entertain fear…. Don't get on the "fear train" when it pulls into the station. [From a sermon by Christine Caine.] Let it depart without you.*

Bold, Bodacious and Beautiful

"Loving large and living with loving abandon" was so beautifully expressed, the words inspired me even more to want to live that way. I wanted to "love large" rather than focus on all the ways I had failed or others had failed me.

The Greek word *hamartia* which is translated into the English word "sin" means "missing the mark." This was an archery term that was used when an archer missed the bullseye with an arrow. Sin is an unpopular concept these days, but focusing on how we or others have failed or "missed the mark" is not unpopular at all. We simply don't call it what it is.

This is a quiet growing season—but not for long. Grow and learn of me, and hear my voice as much as you will or can. Do not be overwhelmed by people. Instead, embrace and enjoy them….

How I wished I was better at embracing and enjoying people. I hoped the more time I spent with God, the more I would be filled with his love for everyone who came across my path.

Know this, my beloved brothers: let every person be quick to hear, slow to speak, slow to anger…
James 1:19

***

Bold, Bodacious and Beautiful

12

October had begun, and it didn't feel much like a "quiet season." My fourth grade students were busy finishing the final edits on their peer interviews and writing autobiographies for their 1900 immigrant personas in preparation for the annual Ellis Island simulation. Our fourth grade team was also focused on preparations for transforming our hallway and classrooms into The Great Hall and Ellis Island. Our first Connect Group meeting of the fall season was also just around the corner. I would be leading our Bible study, and our co-leader would be handling many of the administrative duties.

In the midst of it all, these were the words I felt I heard.

> *You are worried about many things: your group members, Are you "lukewarm"? [from Revelation 3:15 -16], Open House, curriculum, the teachers you work with, the teacher who had the stroke, your friends, your sister's foot, and your family. So much to carry. Let me carry it, all of it. Give it all to me, for my yoke is easy, [and] my burden is light—like a backpack [Matthew 11:30]. I have it all….*

I believed God had it all, at least I hoped he did. I had no idea how I could let him carry all of my worries, though. Now I know more about the power of talking to God about my worries, and even doing a physical act such as opening my hands and visualizing him taking them. The Bible tells us to hold every thought captive—our thoughts don't hold us unless

Bold, Bodacious and Beautiful

we allow them to. We can control whether or not we obsess on them. If worries come into our minds, we can tell them to leave. [2 Corinthians 10:5]

> *Don't focus on "Am I lukewarm?" Yes you are—but I am bringing you out, and you are willing.... Keep praying. Don't think of the evil one... or demons. Focus on me, but be mindful—aware—of "it".... You did well with [your student].... Help him be a better version of himself. [Speak] kindly to him....*

I was astonished by how detailed this advice was, especially regarding my student who I couldn't seem to get through to. I feared I was either being too hard on him or not doing enough to motivate him. Additionally, Francis Chan's book *Crazy Love* was convincing me that I was living a lukewarm life— neither hot nor cold—and reminding me that God doesn't enjoy lukewarm Christians any more than most people enjoy lukewarm coffee, and he says he will spit them out of his mouth. These words shouldn't have surprised me at all, because God already knew everything that was on my heart.

> 15 "'I know your works: you are neither cold nor hot. Would that you were either cold or hot! 16So, because you are lukewarm, and neither hot nor cold, I will spit you out of my mouth.'"
> Revelation 3:15-16

***

Bold, Bodacious and Beautiful

13

Our Connect Group met on the third floor of a South Korean bakery in Times Square. We would typically chat and eat for about half an hour. After catching up, we would discuss whatever Bible study we were using and close our time by praying together. These ladies encouraged me in my faith, made me laugh and over the years they had grown to be close friends.

During the summer, about fifty people had inquired about our group, and on that first evening of the Fall semester not one of them showed up. It was still the six of us. I tried not to be disappointed, but deep down I was. I had worked hard to meticulously follow up on each inquiry, and I was looking forward to meeting at least some of these new ladies. It was interesting being on the "other side" of leadership. In the past, I rarely felt that I was noticed or that I mattered in group settings. I was learning how challenging it was to lead a group, and a good leader noticed each person who showed up—or didn't show up. Eventually, I learned to relax and not take it so personally when people came and went or seemed dissatisfied.

The following day, the morning of my 56th birthday, these are the words that came to me at 4:40 AM.

> *Numbers are not what matters; what matters is your willing heart. You did what I told you to do; you were faithful. Well done…. Keep moving on and forgiving.*

Bold, Bodacious and Beautiful

You don't feel nice feelings all the time—but act kindly, speak kindly and smile, and the feelings will usually follow, but not always. There will always be difficult ones—you have been difficult too. Think of [how you treated your high school English teacher] and your mom and your friends. You were and are difficult. Iron sharpens iron. Love [others] unconditionally.

When I was a freshman in high school, a new English teacher joined the faculty. It was his first year teaching, and we students were onto him like sharks on entrails. One day we all decided to make loud jungle noises in the middle of his lecture. I still remember the look of bewilderment and frustration on his face as he tried to get us under control, and I can only guess we made the first several months of his teaching career miserable. And guess who was one of the ringleaders?

The words continued.

The ladies are guarded. Show them they can put down their guard around you and in the group. Model the behavior you want. It will come. They will come. I didn't overwhelm you last night. Think of your mom and her campaigners. Some came and many didn't, but the ones that did, forge mighty paths for me now.... They are strong women. Powerful warriors. It is not the numbers—it is the individual. The one lost lamb—the one son or daughter I desire to bring back to me.

Bold, Bodacious and Beautiful

Many years earlier, when my parents were Young Life leaders and I was in grade school, my mother had led a Bible study for high school girls called Campaigners. I remember her putting extensive preparation into their weekly early-morning meetings. From what I remember, one or two girls generally joined, but on a few occasions, no one showed up. I felt heartbroken on behalf of my mother when I saw her discouragement. However, those few women who did show up are now strong Christians and mentoring their own groups of young women. That memory encouraged me to look at the individuals rather than the numbers.

> *...Be not afraid. I will move your lips and mind tonight [at Open House].... Happy Birthday.... Be joyful in me today. Be glad you are alive and well and happy. Be glad you have ears to hear and a heart that is changing from stone to flesh, from flesh to fire, from fire to me.... I guide you. I protect you, and I love you....*

I would like to say I had a wonderful birthday that year, and part of the day *was* joyful. But in all, I felt inadequate and anxious about my teaching skills. My wonderful team took me out to dinner before Open House, and I'm sorry to say I cried during part of it. I seemed to have completely forgotten every word I had heard that morning. Fortunately, after having a good cry and eating delicious food with my colleagues (who were also friends), I felt much better, and I was able to enjoy Open House. I had taught

Bold, Bodacious and Beautiful

some of the older siblings of my current students, and it was wonderful to see their parents as well as meet new ones.

The feelings of anxiety and inadequacy continued to plague me through that fall season more than they had in the past. Thankfully, my therapy group was a godsend. Not only were they thoughtful and unafraid to call me out now and then, but many of the members knew me quite well, and I trusted their insight. As I look back, I wish I had savored the time with everyone in this group. I didn't realize that meeting together in person was a gift that would disappear in the spring, and I would not see most of those dear people in person again.

> Abide in me, and I in you. As the branch cannot bear fruit by itself, unless it abides in the vine, neither can you, unless you abide in me.
> John 15:4

***

14

The morning after Open House, I felt I heard these words. I must have asked God if it was really him speaking to me.

> *You know I am speaking to you. I come through you —so it's partly you but it is me. You are strong in me —even at your weakest you are strong. When you feel overwhelmed, come to me…. Rest in me and see what*

Bold, Bodacious and Beautiful

> *I do…. Now rest this weekend. Love. Laugh. Have fun….*

A few days later, these words came to me. *You are comfortable, but will you step into this seemingly discomfort of my will? Will you trust me with your good?*

I didn't know the answers to those questions. I wanted to, though.

> *Watch your mouth. Watch your heart. Watch your mind. Fill it all—fill yourself with me and only me. Your mother knew the importance of this—she modeled how to love and follow me….*

My mom showed her love for God in different ways. She spent time reading the Bible and praying daily, and she participated in weekly Bible studies for years. She also volunteered in several ministries in her lifetime including Young Life, Stephen's Ministry (lay counseling), the marriage ministry at her church and she taught Sunday School and Vacation Bible School. Mom helped people when they needed it, even if it meant cleaning their houses, cooking a meal or just lending a listening ear. She was also never a gossipy person, and that was one of the many character traits I admired about her. One that I hoped to emulate.

> [25]Strength and dignity are her clothing, and she laughs at the time to come. [26]She opens

Bold, Bodacious and Beautiful

her mouth with wisdom, and the teaching of
kindness is on her tongue.
Proverbs 31:25-26

***

15

In the morning, I had started saying "Good Morning"
to God, and one morning this was the response I felt
I heard.

*Good Morning. I love it when you greet me each
morning. Yes, really….Go into the world with my
love in your heart, and I will give you my words to
speak. Speak love. Smile. Spread my joy….*

Speaking of joy, I felt so much of it when I
went to church, and I was surprised by the elation
that filled me when I worshiped. I had heard the
words "spiritual high" thrown around in my lifetime,
but I had not imagined I would experience it for
myself. Dawna DiSilva, a pastor at Bethel Church
says, "Worship gets you out of your mind and on to
God." I couldn't have agreed more.

You make known to me the path of life; in
your presence there is fullness of joy; at your
right hand are pleasures forevermore.
Psalm 16:11

16

Throughout October, I continued to wake up early in the morning, turn on my light and write down what I felt were words from God that came to my mind. Afterward, I would typically fall back asleep, but not always. Then when my alarm went off, I would read the words I had written earlier. After that, I would read my daily devotional called *Jesus Calling,* and then I would spend some time talking to God (praying). I also tried to read a portion of the Bible, but I didn't always have time. Additionally, I was mindful of God's presence with me when I was walking to work through the park or to the bus stop. I was growing closer to God in ways I had never fathomed, and it was exhilarating. But there was a cost, and as I said earlier, it was loss of sleep. I almost never *wanted* to turn on my light at 3:00AM, but afterward as I read the words, I was glad I had taken the time to write them down. And now, as I write this book, they continue to bless me.

Meanwhile, at school, I was working to repair certain relationships. One colleague and I were finding a way forward after a rocky start at the beginning of the year, and it felt like a huge weight had been lifted off of me. But conflict with the other colleague seemed to drag on. Every time I spoke to that person, I became annoyed. I didn't know how to fix my annoyance, and for that matter, I didn't know how to "fix" myself. Maybe there was no "fix", and I just had to walk through it. I couldn't drum up the love that I was lacking. I knew that God could,

Bold, Bodacious and Beautiful

though, and I prayed he would fill me with love for that person. To be honest, I never felt it and never showed it like he asked me to. Perhaps if I had *shown* love first, the feelings would have come next. I think they would have, so this lack of love was a failure on my part.

> For the whole law is fulfilled in one word: "You shall love your neighbor as yourself." Galatians 5:14

17

In early November, these words came to me. *I am the Alpha and the Omega—the beginning and the end, the first and the last and the one that is to come [Revelation 1:8]. My words to you are a gift. It will not always be like this, like it is now, but it is your choice whether or not you go deeper in me. Follow me through the tall places and the low places, through the sunlight and the gloom. I am your light—the light of the world [John 8:12]….*

I wondered what "It will not always be like this" meant? Did God mean the words would stop at some point? Did he mean the world would change? Or did he mean something else?

Accept others as they are—as I do…. I will do the deep work in their hearts….

Maybe that was part of the "fix"—accepting others as they were. Definitely easier said than done.

Bold, Bodacious and Beautiful

> *Be bold, bodacious and beautiful…. Keep your beauty and reclaim it. Wear it…. Stay with me through good times and bad; as you've seen, they often go hand-in-hand. See the gold shimmer in the darkest cave…. Look up to the mountains from which will come your aid. [Psalm 121:1]*

At the time, when I read "Look up to the mountains from which will come your aid," the phrase reminded me of the scene in *The Sound of Music* when Maria is talking to the Mother Superior about wanting to become a nun rather than follow her heart into a relationship with a man. Now, when I think of looking to the mountains, I think of one of the names of God, or El Shaddai. El Shaddai has several meanings including, "God Almighty" and "All-sufficient One," but another possible meaning is "God of the Mountains." These days, when I see a mountain, I often think of God.

> [11]And he said, "Go out and stand on the mount before the LORD." And behold, the LORD passed by, and a great and strong wind tore the mountains and broke in pieces the rocks before the LORD, but the LORD was not in the wind. And after the wind an earthquake, but the LORD was not in the earthquake. [12]And after the earthquake a fire, but the LORD was not in the fire. And after the fire the sound of a low whisper. [13]And

Bold, Bodacious and Beautiful

when Elijah heard it, he wrapped his face in
his cloak…
1 Kings 19:11-13a

Bold, Bodacious and Beautiful

Bold, Bodacious and Beautiful

4
SEASON OF SURRENDER
(FALL AND WINTER 2019)

1

Francis Chan's *Crazy Love* Bible study was intense, but I was enjoying it. It felt timely and right for this season in my life. Perhaps it was the way Chan didn't sugarcoat his words or ideas. He challenged me to think deeply about the way I was living my life, especially with regard to my relationship with Christ. One part of the study that especially spoke to me was his explanation of the "good soil" from the Parable of the Sower.

> [3]And he told them many things in parables, saying: "A sower went out to sow. [4]And as he sowed, some seeds fell along the path, and the birds came and devoured them. [5]Other seeds fell on rocky ground, where they did not have much soil, and immediately they sprang up, since they had no depth of soil, [6]but when the sun rose they were scorched. And since they had no root, they withered away. [7]Other seeds fell among thorns, and the thorns grew up and choked them. [8]Other seeds fell on **good soil** and produced grain, some a hundredfold, some sixty, some thirty....
>
> [18]"Hear then the parable of the sower: [19]When anyone hears the word of the

kingdom and does not understand it, the evil one comes and snatches away what has been sown in his heart. This is what was sown along the path. [20]As for what was sown on rocky ground, this is the one who hears the word and immediately receives it with joy, [21]yet he has no root in himself, but endures for a while, and when tribulation or persecution arises on account of the word, immediately he falls away. [22]As for what was sown among thorns, this is the one who hears the word, but the cares of the world and the deceitfulness of riches choke the word, and it proves unfruitful. [23]As for what was sown on **good soil**, this is the one who hears the word and understands it. He indeed bears fruit and yields, in one case a hundredfold, in another sixty, and in another thirty."
Matthew 13:3-8 and 18-23

Francis Chan wrote one sentence that hit me over the head: "Don't assume you are **good soil**." I had *always* assumed I was the "good soil" in the parable. Weren't Christians generally considered the good soil? What *did* it mean to be good soil? I would discover the answer in his Bible study.

Because of the study, I was beginning to enjoy leading our Connect Group, too. I found some short videos of Francis Chan speaking about the material covered in each chapter to help facilitate discussion, and the book culled each chapter down to two

Bold, Bodacious and Beautiful

discussion questions, which made leading much easier. For me, coming up with good discussion questions was one of the most difficult parts of leading a Bible study. With the extra material to help me lead, the group was engaged and settling into a positive rhythm, which allowed me to feel more calm and confident in my new role.

As November got underway, these were some of the words I felt I heard.

> *You must follow me with your whole heart—just as Francis Chan says…. It will be impossible and easy at the same time….*

The words "impossible" and "easy" were not synonymous. How could something be impossible and easy? It made no sense to me.

> *Your trust in me is growing. Let it flourish like a beautiful garden in your soul… a place of refuge and peace. A place with the brook of bliss. [Psalm 23:1-3] A place where I will come and sit with you in silence and in conversation. A refuge from the chaos of the world.*

I wanted my trust to flourish like a "beautiful garden in my soul." What a lovely image! I could also imagine a cool, shaded, grassy place next to a bubbling brook with Jesus and I sitting there in "silence and conversation." In fact, in the coming months I recalled that image multiple times.

Bold, Bodacious and Beautiful

I've healed you from anxiety. You asked. Can you feel the difference? Learn to live an anxiety free life. It's a beautiful gift, isn't it?....

Was I really healed from anxiety? I had lived with it for so many years that it had worn deep grooves into my thought processes that affected how I responded to situations and people. Anxiety was, after all, my "go to" response. I decided to claim the healing even though I still felt anxious plenty of times. Perhaps it was something to grow into or learn —new ways of responding and new ways of thinking. Sort of like growing into becoming bold, bodacious and beautiful? I didn't know the answers, but I felt curious and hopeful.

Several days later, this is some of what I felt I heard.

> *I am your God. High above the heavens I dwell, and I also do dwell in your heart.... Make me a deep and lasting part of your day and routine. Your routine will soon change, and I will still be a part of it.*

Of course, I had no idea that Covid was coming, and I would be teaching on Zoom. Had I known, my anxiety level would have skyrocketed. I'm grateful God doesn't often let me know details about the future.

The next day, I stayed home because I was sick, and the message continued.

> *You fear sickness—now fear me. Fear me as the Almighty God of the Universe—yet the one who lives*

Bold, Bodacious and Beautiful

*in your heart and whispers to it in the early morning
dawn.*

I did tend to fear missing work when I was
sick. Would one day be enough? Would the sub be a
good one? Would the school administration be upset?
*Open your heart to those who think differently. They
don't need to be your bosom friends, but they, or most
of them, aren't your enemies either.... I will fill you
with love and change your heart [of stone] to flesh and
then fire. [Ezekiel 36:26]*

I hoped I could and he would. The message
seemed to continue on the following day.
*Your time on earth is brief, and eternity is forever.
[Ecclesiastes 3:11] Eternity is for all time. Live this
life wisely because it will be over all too soon. Cherish
every moment with me and with others.... Live with
laughter. Be in the final moments of New York City.
Close the doors, but don't burn any bridges. End with
kindness and love. Let each person know they are
important to you.*

As beautiful and sobering as these words
were, I still doubted their veracity. I did not see how
this could be the end of my time in New York City. It
just didn't make sense, especially financially speaking.
I still had several more years of teaching to
accomplish before I could afford to retire. Also, I was
enjoying my life and not feeling a pressing need to
move. Yet, at the same time, I felt a continual pull to

Bold, Bodacious and Beautiful

live closer to my family. As usual, I didn't know what to make of any of it.

> And your ears shall hear a word behind you,
> saying, "This is the way, walk in it," when you
> turn to the right or when you turn to the left.
> Isaiah 30:21

2

The next day, these words came to me.
You have a long road to travel; travel with me by your side. I am your walking staff and your shoes. I am your strength and fortification. There will be bright sunny days along the path and windy rainy ones. I am your umbrella and shield and buckler. I am your all.

I didn't know what a buckler was, so I looked it up. Buckler: 1. A round shield, 2. Any means of protection.

> *I gave you rest, and you took it with very little anxiety. Embrace this anxiety-free way of thinking and living. [Philippians 4:6] It is how you will travel the next path. You resist decisions. Why must you be told what to do? I've told you [that] you may choose. Why don't you choose? The most convenient path isn't always the best one—nor is the toughest one.*

I wanted God to tell me to leave or stay because moving across the country seemed like such a monumental decision, especially just a few years before retirement.

Bold, Bodacious and Beautiful

A couple of days later, these are some of the words I felt I heard.

> *You did well to rest…. I have healed your inability to sleep through the night—because you asked. [Matthew 7:7-8] You never thought to ask. There are other areas you haven't asked for. Now ask as you think of them. I will bring them to mind…. Let me heal the deep places, and health will likely follow more naturally.*

"Let me heal the deep places, and health will likely follow more naturally." This was such a profound idea; something to which I had never given much thought. I was focused on eating properly and exercising to maintain my physical health, and I went to my therapy group each week to cultivate my mental health. I hadn't given much attention to the relationship between mental, spiritual and physical health, though. How did my spiritual health figure into the mix? I now know that worshiping God increases my feelings of joy, and I believe joy not only boosts my spiritual health, but also my mental and physical health.

> And the ransomed of the LORD shall return and come to Zion with singing; everlasting joy shall be upon their heads; they shall obtain gladness and joy, and sorrow and sighing shall flee away.
> Isaiah 51:11

Bold, Bodacious and Beautiful

**

3

It was the eve of the full week before Thanksgiving break, and the fourth grade curriculum was in the creative and fun phases of several long term assignments. Students had each read and written about two books by E.B. White, and now they were completing boxes based on the work of artist Joseph Cornell that reflected one or more motifs of White's writing such as life and death, friendship, and change. They were also creating Oral History scrapbooks after transcribing and editing their immigrant interviews. Additionally, I was introducing our Cinderella unit with a discussion of "What is a fairy tale?" and "What is a Cinderella story?" I had been doing these projects with my students for over twenty years, and I loved them all.

As I was thinking about my students, these words came to me.

Open your students' [understanding of their] lives with love. Do it all with love. The idea is from me:

Your sphere of influence: Classroom

Where do you fall in your sphere of influence? Do you add to it in a positive way, are you neutral or do you add to it in a negative way?... Share about self-awareness and the ability to grow and change. [Say] "Harness the good—don't let it run wild like a

Bold, Bodacious and Beautiful

> *stallion." Use it for your good and the good of others....*

I took what I felt was God's advice and made a chart with my class. I introduced it exactly as I felt God had described it. We brainstormed different scenarios where students could influence the classroom community in positive, neutral or negative ways. Then I asked my students to think about how they individually impacted our community, and we had a fruitful discussion. I may have asked them to write me a letter about where they felt they were on the chart and where they wanted to be. Later, I noticed real growth in some students who habitually called out, chatted and played around rather than focused on completing assignments.

Over the next few days, these are some of the words I felt I heard.

> *You spoke of me yesterday in [your therapy] group. What if I brought you there for them? To share me with them? What if you spoke freely to them about me? What if you pushed through your fear and insecurities and spoke of me naturally? The more you do it, the easier it will be.*

The members of my therapy group seemed genuinely interested in hearing about my spiritual life; they were accepting, curious and asked me questions. I never felt judged by them, far from it. In fact, I felt encouraged and affirmed after sharing my experiences.

Bold, Bodacious and Beautiful

The next day this came to me.

Be still and know that I am God—today and always. [Psalm 46:10] Take shelter in my wings. [Psalm 61:4] Let me lead you to the high places away from the fear, chaos and noise, into the midst of my glory and fearsomeness. Take refuge in me, and rest under the warmth of my wings. [Psalm 91:4]

I loved the metaphor of God as a mother bird sheltering her young. One day during the previous spring, as I was walking home along the reservoir in Central Park, I saw a mother goose gathering her goslings under her wing. They were completely hidden until one small gosling popped out. She stretched her wing a bit, and it scurried back underneath the wing's expansive protection. It was an image I have since recalled many times.

Be the person I made you to be: bold, bodacious and beautiful…. Let me grow you…. Grow deep in the soil of my love—even in the midst of the noise and chaos of the world. Your roots are protected in the soil of my grace. They are nurtured there as you grow up into the sunshine of my love. And you, in turn, will provide shade and shelter for others. [Jeremiah 17:7,8] Let me nurture and grow you into a mighty oak, a baobab tree, a mountain, a refuge, and I will be your fortress. [Psalm 31:3]

Years earlier, I had put up images of baobab trees in our classroom when I was reading parts of

Bold, Bodacious and Beautiful

Sundiata: An Epic of Old Mali to my students. Baobab trees were humongous and gorgeous, and I loved the idea of being like one of them.

The following day I heard this.

...Be of few words. Remember, your words carry weight.

> The words of a wise man's mouth win him favor, but the lips of a fool consume him. Ecclesiastes 10:12

***

4

Finally, it was the weekend before Thanksgiving, and I was thrilled about the upcoming two-day work week and my trip to Southampton, Massachusetts to spend Thanksgiving with a dear friend and her family. She was my first "New York friend." Our mothers had met when we were moving into the dorm at The Fashion Institute of Technology, and then they introduced us to each other. Who would have guessed that we would still be so close over thirty years later?

In the meantime, I was off to Brooklyn for a Hallmark Christmas movie marathon with some friends from my Connect Group. I couldn't wait.

As I was contemplating my plans, I asked God if he wanted to speak to me.

You do well to ask if I wish to speak to you. I do. Always. I have much to say and little time to say it. Keep my words close to your heart—in your heart, in

167

Bold, Bodacious and Beautiful

> *your mind. You stopped listening to [and memorizing] 1st Corinthians 13. Continue to do so until it is lodged in your heart, and then move on to another passage. Be relentless in your memorization….*

Even with another nudge from God, I still didn't do it. In the midst of the upcoming holidays and the busyness of life, I forgot. In fact, years later, as I write this book, I'm still working on it.

> *I will help you sort your photos. Begin now. Continue weeding out the books….*

I still had way too many books, especially if what God said actually happened, and I would be moving soon.

> *Be generous with [your friend who had the stroke]. You did well to visit her. Be consistent with your visits…. Bring her [something] from her classroom.*

I inquired about getting a few things from my colleague's classroom, but everything had been packed up and stored away. I was disappointed about not being able to bring her at least something from her teaching days.

The next day the words continued.

> *Thankfulness is the key to praying without ceasing. [1 Thessalonians 5:16-18] The "Jesus Prayer" is rote memorization and not bad—but not alive and vibrant and "in the moment." It's not directly interacting with me. I desire a relationship with you, to know and be known by you. I desire <u>all</u> of you—your whole being,*

Bold, Bodacious and Beautiful

> *all of your attention and all of your focus. I desire a conversation with you—not just mumbled words spoken over and over like mumbling clamor. There is a time and place to repeat prayers, my name or groanings over and over—but not always.*

I loved the "Jesus Prayer." I discovered it in college when I read the book *Frannie and Zoey* by J.D. Salinger. In the story, Frannie wants to learn to pray without ceasing, and along the way she discovers a book about a Russian pilgrim, who possibly lived in the sixth century, and wanted to do the same thing. The pilgrim travels throughout Russia asking people he encounters along the way how to pray without ceasing, and eventually he discovers a way to pray this verse from the Bible. "But the tax collector, standing far off, would not even lift up his eyes to heaven, but beat his breast, saying, 'God, be merciful to me, a sinner!'" (Luke 18:13) The pilgrim begins to say the prayer as he inhales and exhales. Inhale: "Lord Jesus Christ," Exhale: "Son of God," Inhale: "have mercy on me," Exhale: "a sinner."

This story can be found in the book called *The Way of a Pilgrim*. There is also a condensed version of the prayer. Inhale: "Jesus Christ," Exhale: "have mercy on me." As I said, I loved the Jesus Prayer, but I could understand that being the recipient of it might be somewhat monotonous.

> Continue steadfastly in prayer, being watchful in it with thanksgiving.

Bold, Bodacious and Beautiful

Colossians 4:2

5

Over the next few days, these are some of the words I heard.

> *[Time] is going by fast…. Inspire your children to do their best today. Inspire them with praise. Challenge them. Do it all with kindness and without criticism. Ask yourself [why some students] aren't performing at their peak…. Have patience; the journey is more important than the product.*

I believed with all my heart that the journey was more important, but I also wanted the product to be fabulous.

> *Let thanksgiving rule your heart—not resentment, anger or complaining. Let thankfulness become your language—your go-to emotion. [1 Chronicles 29:13, Ephesians 5:20] Let your thankfulness be heard, and others around you will also be thankful. Amen. Amen. Amen.*

The words about thanksgiving felt especially appropriate for that weekend.

> And they sang responsively, praising and giving thanks to the LORD, "For he is good, for his steadfast love endures forever toward Israel." And all the people shouted with a great shout when they praised the

Bold, Bodacious and Beautiful

> LORD, because the foundation of the house
> of the LORD was laid.
> Ezra 3:11

6

It was the morning before Thanksgiving, and whatever sickness I had been fighting a few weeks earlier had returned. I don't remember what I had, but it was common for me to get sick when the temperature dropped in November. For weeks, I had been looking forward to visiting my friend in Massachusetts, but my body was telling me I should probably stay home and rest. My desire to lie down outweighed my disappointment.

This was what I heard.

Let go of the deep sense of insecurity you feel.... I approve of you, and that is all that matters....

I dreaded telling my friend I wasn't coming as much as I dreaded spending the long Thanksgiving weekend alone. I also felt guilty for canceling at the last minute. Who did that, and why couldn't I just "power through" being sick like so many people I knew?

Ask for my help and guidance before every task.... I am here by your side, surrounding you.... I long for you to know my presence and practice it.... Trust me on the path, and I will guide your steps [and] decisions and be with you in crisis. [Psalm 73:23-26] The crises are the tests and the blessings and the times of felt grace. Do not fear them....

171

Bold, Bodacious and Beautiful

After reading these words, I didn't have quite as much guilt and dread as I climbed into bed and fell asleep.

Later that morning, this came to me.

Stay home and rest. Let go of guilt. Your body is fighting the flu. Rest well and rest with me....

Rest in the LORD, and wait patiently for Him.
Psalm 37:7a, New King James Version

7

The next day, I watched the Macy's Thanksgiving Day Parade on TV while sorting through my many photo albums, and I also spent much of the day sleeping. It wasn't how I had envisioned spending the day, but I felt surprisingly peaceful and content. What I feared would be a lonely long weekend, actually felt like a blessing. God was keeping his promise, and I felt him "by my side and surrounding me."

The day after Thanksgiving, this is what came to me.

...Keep thanking me in every situation. [1 Thessalonians 5:18] You are becoming mindful of not fixing others. Let go of the desire to fix—even in your teaching. Guide, question and love, that is your goal and aim. [1 Thessalonians 5:11] Amen.

Continue steadfastly in prayer, being watchful in it with thanksgiving.

172

Bold, Bodacious and Beautiful

Colossians 4:2

8

On the following day, I felt I heard words about two friends. Up until this point, I had generally shared the words I heard about others. However, this time the words for one friend were unsettling. They were mostly positive, but there was a dire warning at the end, and I didn't quite know what to do. I thought about the implications of *not* sharing an important message or warning versus going ahead and letting the person know what I felt I had heard. I decided to share them. This friend was understandably upset, and she let me know. I felt terrible.

I didn't know that when sharing words I felt I heard, it is a good idea to wait for a while and ask God what to do with them. If God gives the "go ahead" then ask the person if they want to hear them. I now know that if they *are* interested in hearing them, I stress that they are words I *felt* I heard from God. If they resonate, then great. If not, then the words can be "set on a figurative shelf" to be thought about and perhaps returned to later, or they can simply be thrown out or "flushed" like refuse. The truth is, though, that difficult words are never easy to share, and, thankfully, I haven't heard many of them.

I definitely had a lot to learn, and I realized that the results of misusing this new gift could be devastating to both the giver and the receiver. Had I lost a dear friend? That was when these words came to me.

Bold, Bodacious and Beautiful

> *Always ask me before you share my words. You felt compelled, and that was enough in the past. Now ask me. Tell your friend you are sorry for the way you did it and that you love her....*

I apologized, and eventually (thankfully) we were able to repair our friendship.

> ...this is God, our God forever and ever. He will guide us forever.
> Psalm 48:14

***

9

On the first day of Advent and the last day of the long Thanksgiving weekend, these words came to me.

> *You have spent the last four days with me. You have not felt alone or felt a sense of regret, for I have been with you. Even when you felt terrible about [your friend], you did not entertain shame, grief or anxiety —even though all came powerfully upon you. You praised and focused and prayed and "got on with the next thing".... Most importantly, you are mindful of me with you.... Enjoy your tree and the Advent season.*

The next day, it occurred to me that it had been eight months since I had first heard from God. Eight months! I couldn't believe it.

Bold, Bodacious and Beautiful

> *Yes, it's been eight months since I began speaking to you—eight months since you began to listen. I spoke to you in other ways, though, and shouted a few times [in the past].... Now remember to ask me before sharing these words.... Keep them close to your heart and in your mind....*

God had spoken to me through other ways, most notably and most reliably in his Word, the Bible. But he also spoke through friends, sermons, and the beauty of nature. In many ways, he is constantly speaking to those who have ears to hear. "Keep [the words] close to your heart and in your mind" was another admonition I didn't take as seriously as I wish I had. After a few years of hearing from God, I now read the words in the morning *and* in the evening. This helps to keep them in my mind, as does making an occasional list of tasks I feel he is asking me to do.

> *For now, focus on this week and entertaining your guests. Even if only two or three come—make them feel blessed and loved. Make dinner. Make something you love. Amen. Amen. Amen.*

I had invited my Connect Group friends over to dinner, and I couldn't wait! My tree was decorated, so by default, it was a Christmas dinner and we were also celebrating the birthday of our co-leader. When I was in my 20's and 30's, I entertained quite frequently. But at some point, I got fed up with all the work and didn't enjoy my guests as much as I wished to because I was so busy serving them. I stopped inviting people

Bold, Bodacious and Beautiful

over for meals and instead met friends at restaurants. People had me over for dinners, but I rarely reciprocated. Eventually, I realized there had to be an easier way, so I began to buy disposable plates and cups and even ready-made food, and it made entertaining so much more enjoyable for me.

That night, I bought delicious wonton soup from the Chinese restaurant around the corner, crusty French bread and homemade chicken noodle soup from West Side Market, and I made a salad. We had all chipped in to buy a delicious chocolate birthday cake from Silver Moon Bakery. My friends laughed when they realized I had bought the soup, but I didn't care. This was the way I was able to entertain, and anyhow, how different was it from catering a meal? We ate dinner next to my Christmas tree, and I had so much fun with everyone that night.

A few days later, I felt I heard this.

I have been with you each day this week, but I've been with you each day of your life. Just because you aren't aware of it or it is an "easy" day doesn't mean I am any less present.

Why did I tend to remember (and rely on) God's presence only in difficult situations? I wanted to be mindful of his companionship and guidance throughout each and every day, so I began praying earnestly for this (again), along with the ongoing prayer that he would fill me with love for himself and others.

Bold, Bodacious and Beautiful

> *I am your mother and father. I am more than that:*
> *your God, your Provider [Jehovah-jireh, Genesis*
> *22:13-14], the Alpha and Omega, [beginning and*
> *end, Revelation 22:13], I Am, Yahweh, Prince of*
> *Peace [Isaiah 9:6], I Am that I Am [Exodus 3:14],*
> *Jehovah Rapha [The Lord Who Heals, Exodus*
> *15:26], The Good Shepherd [Psalm 23:1], The*
> *Holy One of Israel. I am All. I long to show you*
> *Heaven and the storehouse I have there. Will you*
> *grow to that point?*

I deeply desired to see Heaven and God's storehouse, but I couldn't imagine how. Recently, as I began writing this book, I felt led to memorize some of the names of God, and it is a wonderful way to magnify (or show great respect) to his name when praying.

Then the words took a turn.

Lana [Vawser] is right—there is a spirit of offense. Don't fear it. You will feel it if you speak out my words. Don't fear it.

This wouldn't be the last time I heard about "the spirit of offense" or how it affected my life. However, in the busyness of the holiday season, and in my usual manner, I forgot all about it.

> Oh, magnify the LORD with me, and let us
> exalt his name together!
> Psalm 34:3

***

Bold, Bodacious and Beautiful

10

Several days later, these are some of the words I heard.

> *Hundreds of years of fighting can be resolved in a moment with my power and in my power. So think [of] what I can do between friends, colleagues and strangers who have only known each other for minutes, months and years? Be of few words…. A hug can communicate what words can't. It communicates love, acceptance and forgiveness. It communicates restoration and restored communication…. Be a woman of forgiveness. It will free you in so many ways. Forgive.*

In a sermon called "Let It Go," I recently heard TD Jakes say that unforgiveness hurts *you*, not the person who hurt you. He went on to say that unforgiveness is like drinking poison and waiting for the person who wronged you to die. Those words resonate with me and convict me. How many times have I drunk the poison of unforgiveness?

> *Learn to "ride through" the difficult emotions that crash upon you like a tidal wave but then recede…. Feelings of being overwhelmed aren't the same as actually being overwhelmed—by bandits, war, displacement or hunger. You face none of this—yet— but you may. The world is a perilous place, but with me beside you and in you, it can be a glorious adventure.*

Only God could make me feel less terrified when comparing the perilousness of war, displacement and hunger to a "glorious adventure" with him by my side.

Try not to waste food, time or other precious resources. Be more frugal with yourself but generous with others. Give more money away.... Be generous. I will provide....

I loved the words, "Be more frugal with yourself but generous with others." I tended to think about money, but did God also mean intangible things like forgiveness and love? I assumed so. I had experienced God's provision when I was generous in the past, but I still struggled to truly and readily trust that he would provide for me.

Whoever brings blessing will be enriched, and one who waters will himself be watered. Proverbs 11:25

11

Early the next day, this is what I heard.
Focus on your students' strengths. They are tenacious, creative and loving. See those gifts and encourage them. Model the behavior you hope to see in others.... Show them you approve of them. Be vocal with your love of others. Be showy. Be effusive in your love—as [your math specialist] is. It feels good to be loved.

I was beginning to see that the more time I made for God, the more he spoke to me. I loved

Bold, Bodacious and Beautiful

reading these words. Even so, it was still a struggle to turn on my lamp and *write* them so early each morning.

That night, I had a dream that I lived in a small, broken down house, but I loved it. Then I realized there was a door I had never noticed before, and I opened it. Several more beautiful rooms with gorgeous furniture opened up before me, and it was all mine. The house was on a beach which frightened and thrilled me.

Then these words came.

I have much for you. In my house there are many rooms [John 14:2-3] for you—large and airy and light. Lots of outdoor space, too. In me there is a profusion of good things. Things just for you—places, experiences, people, relationships, knowledge, homes, family and most of all, love. You live sparsely in New York City. I long to give you more. Much more. Ask, seek, knock. [Matthew 7:7] I long to give you a multitude of good gifts. They wait in my storehouse. Ask. Ask. Ask.

In response, I asked God for everything I wanted. It felt strange, but also wonderful to freely write about so many things that I hadn't even realized I wanted. Once I started writing a few things, deeper desires floated to the surface of my consciousness, and it felt wonderful to "put it all out there" before God.

Bold, Bodacious and Beautiful

> The LORD will open to you his good
> treasury, the heavens, to give the rain to your
> land in its season and to bless all the work of
> your hands. And you shall lend to many
> nations, but you shall not borrow.
> Deuteronomy 28:12

***

12

The holiday break was just over a week away, and
everyone in the school building was counting down
the days with exhausted (teachers) and frenzied
(students) anticipation. But in the meantime, I was
eager to enjoy some of the magic and excitement of
the holidays in New York City. The festive lights and
holiday windows were always a treat. I met a dear old
friend for our annual trip to the Metropolitan
Museum of Art to experience the Christmas tree and
the charming Neapolitan nativity scene set beneath it.
I never got tired of walking around the tree and
seeing Mary, Jesus and Joseph as well as more than
sixty additional figures that were created in 18th
century Naples, Italy. Even with the crowds, I was
quickly drawn into the holy miracle of Jesus' birth
taking place beneath the branches.

Then on Friday, the thirteenth of December, I
heard this.

*There is no such thing as a bad luck day. All days
are blessed with me….*

Bold, Bodacious and Beautiful

I wasn't superstitious, or at least *super* superstitious, but it was, after all, Friday the 13th. I couldn't help but wonder in the back of my mind if it would be a doomed day of bad luck. God said it wouldn't be, and I believed him.

Over the next few days, this is some of what I heard.

> *Go forth in me today. Wear my armor of truth, peace, righteousness and salvation with the sword of the Spirit and the shield of faith….* [Ephesians 6:10-18, see Season of Wondering section at the end of the book]

> *Continue to <u>let go</u> of anxiety. It has no place in your new life…. You walk with a posse surrounding you: me, the Holy Spirit, and my son and angels. You are fully and completely surrounded. Impenetrable. Walk like it. Be bold, bodacious and beautiful. Remember who you are in me and [in] my power. My power permeates your being—your steps, words and actions. Operate in me and my power today…. Show my love. Smile. Laugh. Show my joy.*

I loved the idea of a posse surrounding me, and I thought of that image many times during the coming year. I still do. But how was I supposed to "let go" of anxiety? I simply kept offering it up to God, rebuking it in his name and asking him to replace it with his peace, joy and love, and even physically offering it up to him with open hands. It was a start.

182

Bold, Bodacious and Beautiful

> And [Jesus] told them a parable to the effect
> that they ought always to pray and not lose
> heart.
> Luke 18:1

13

Later in the week, I joined two friends at a worship and prayer service downtown that was sponsored by a ministry called The Ark. The singing was powerful, as always, but this evening was even better. I felt such deep joy that evening, and especially when I prayed for a family member who was battling glaucoma. The person who prayed with me, prayed that my family member would have 20/20 vision in 2020. Clever. I was filled with renewed hope. And the icing on the cake (literal and metaphorical) was when we stepped out of the church, it was snowing outside. It hadn't snowed much during the past few winters, and a few inches of snow now covered the streets. The festive red, yellow and green lights of Little Italy glowed through a haze of white. Even the life-sized nativity outside of the church was coated in snow— something I had never seen. My friends and I jumped and spun around like laughing children.

Another magical New York City night, I thought as I crunched through the snow on my way to the subway. It was a gift I hadn't even anticipated, much less asked for.

Bold, Bodacious and Beautiful

> If you then, who are evil, know how to give good gifts to your children, how much more will your Father who is in heaven give good things to those who ask him!
> Matthew 7:11

14

The following morning, these words came to me as I was thinking about a dear friend and her son.

> *I actually have [your friend's son], thanks to your prayers, although he does not know it. He thinks I hate him—because of who he is and what he's done. He doesn't realize I love him, and I made him…. He will find me because I will surprise him at every turn. He will find me even though he does not seek me….*

It filled me with joy to know that God was looking out for my friend's son. In fact, I had several friends with sons who fit this description, and I had prayed for all of them.

> *As for you, don't stay in your feelings. Stay in me. Love can feel heady and light and heavy and burdensome. Let the feelings come and go…. What is it you truly seek? Do not make anyone or anything an idol over me. [Matthew 6:21] Make me your idol, and I will give you all else…. Consider all I've said when you are in Arizona….*

I had been thinking about relationships, and I had a crush on a man I had barely spoken to, but I admired from afar. I believe God told me on multiple

Bold, Bodacious and Beautiful

occasions, however, that his path was not in Arizona, so I never pursued him.

On the final day of school before the holiday break, I received these words.

> *You have many decisions ahead, and I am with you in each one. I will make you a firm decision maker—not one who tarries and wavers, not knowing whether to go to the left or to the right. When you follow me closely, I guard and guide your steps. When you ask, I answer....*

> I was still amazed that God *did* answer me!
> *Be with your family. Don't try to figure everything out. Just be with them. Enjoy them; smile with them; laugh with them....*

I tended to miss the present moments while trying to figure out the future, but I took this advice to heart. Was I more serious than God? He was constantly reminding me to enjoy my days, smile, laugh and *be* in the moment.

> *I have a sense of humor. I created humor. I AM joy. Full joy. Joy is better than humor. Joy builds up, and humor is a dark and sometimes cutting shadow of joy. In me, your joy will be complete.*

There it was again, Joy. These words were so profound to me. "Joy builds up, and humor is a dark and sometimes cutting shadow of joy." I had never thought of this before, but perhaps it was why I didn't enjoy listening to many comedians.

Bold, Bodacious and Beautiful

> A joyful heart is good medicine, but a crushed
> spirit dries up the bones.
> Proverbs 17:22

***

15

While I was waiting for my flight at JFK Airport, I picked up a small book by Joel Osteen called *2 Words That Will Change Your Life Today*. It was a quick read, and it had a deep impact on me. One of the ideas Osteen wrote about was that we become like the words we speak. If we are always complaining about being tired and broke, we are "calling in" exhaustion and poverty. However, we can do the opposite. We can speak blessings over ourselves and others. Additionally, when we say "I am…" we are actually saying "God is…" because "I Am" is one of God's names. It was a lot of food for thought. I got a cold during Christmas, but instead of saying "I have a cold," I tried saying "I am getting better and better." I did feel better a few days later, which was a small miracle since my colds generally morphed into sinus infections, strep throat or bronchitis. I wondered if speaking life affirming words had helped? I thought the book was profound, and, in fact, I read it two more times over the course of the next few months.

These are some of the words that came to me during the first few days of my stay in Arizona.

Bold, Bodacious and Beautiful

You have arrived safely in Phoenix…. Speak "I am" words to yourself daily. I am strong. I am healed. I am a child of God. I am a friend of God. I am strong in the Lord. I am bold, beautiful and bodacious…. You are also speaking of me, for my name is "I Am." I Am that I Am. This is a deep concept that can be pondered for years, centuries, ages….

I felt God had already said my words carried weight, yet I had trouble believing it. However, the idea that *all* people's words carried weight was much easier for me to digest.

My birth was only the beginning—yet it was also the middle because we did much in the centuries before my birth. Think about Moses, David and all the saints who came before me. Yet they were all forerunners of me, pointing to me and my coming. They heralded my arrival on earth.

I realized this must be Jesus who was speaking. The idea of the trinity, three persons but one God, was difficult for me to comprehend. Was it Jesus who was always speaking to me or God the Father or the Holy Spirit? I didn't know.

…Keep to my path with your hand in mine. Nothing or no one can replace our relationship—only compliment it…. I will work through you and give you my words. You are just the vessel, but the power is mine.

Bold, Bodacious and Beautiful

> My foot has held fast to his steps; I have kept
> his way and have not turned aside.
> Job 23:11

***

16

In the midst of reconnecting with sweet friends, hiking in the desert at sunset and preparing food for our Christmas Eve festivities with the family, these words came to me on December 24th.

> *It is impossible to know what a situation will be like until you step into it. It will be one way at the beginning and another six months later and another six years later. My hand is upon you in each "place" and time. Trust me in this. You don't know what Phoenix will be like; it will be better and worse than you imagine. Trust me [Psalm 62:8]…. Keep asking for my direction and help. I am here to guide you….*

Christmas Eve night at my sister and brother-in-law's house was filled with family, delicious food and drinks as well as a plethora of gifts. It was my great niece's first Christmas, and as such, we lavished her with toys and books. In contrast, Christmas day was a quiet day spent with my dad at his house. It felt a bit anticlimactic, but also peaceful. My mother had passed away two years earlier, and my father and I felt the emptiness of the house without her in it. Dad made us a "family pancake" and we enjoyed a bike ride around a rather rural section of his neighborhood where some people raised cows, pigs, chickens, horses and goats. I worried about my dad being all alone in the house, but I knew God was asking me to put aside all worry, including this one.

Early in the morning these words came to me. *You had great plans for yesterday—and some happened and some didn't. Isn't that how life is?…*

It was.
Spend the day enjoying the presence of me and your dad…. Enjoy my presence today. It was my gift to you to come to earth. [Luke 2:11-14] Accept it, enjoy me and pass it on to others….

As 2019 was winding to a close, people with the gift of prophecy were calling the next decade the "roaring" 20s. Dancing flappers drinking champagne and wearing cloche hats and long strands of pearls came to my mind, but they often mentioned the image of a roaring lion. The lion of Judah. I wondered what it meant.

I spent my final days in Arizona with my sister, taking her dog for long walks in the desert, going on hikes on a nearby butte and praying together. When we said goodbye, we assumed 2020 would be a year like every other. She would most likely visit me in New York City for a few days during Spring Break, and I would visit the family in July for a week or so. I would go on a few other trips during the summer, including Maine which I had missed this summer, teach fourth grade in my classroom on the

Bold, Bodacious and Beautiful

9th floor and visit my family again at Christmas. It was the familiar rhythm of the past thirty-five years.

> And one of the elders said to me, "Weep no more; behold, the Lion of the tribe of Judah, the Root of David, has conquered, so that he can open the scroll and its seven seals."
> Revelation 5:5

***

17

When I returned to New York, I had a lot on my mind and missed my family. I still felt tension with a few people at school but less so than in the fall. I also wondered what our Connect Group should study next.

These words came to me during the first few days of the year.

> *Keep an open mind. Lead without controlling…. Lead lightly…. I will show you how. Leaders do need to exercise some control—but not excessively so….*

Leading our Connect Group with finesse was something I had not yet mastered. I tended to want to get through every point, rather than allow space for conversations to take us "off topic." It was difficult for me to redirect conversations without feeling heavy handed. Was it more important to chat or to cover the material? I thought a bit of both, so "leading lightly" was a good reminder—and goal—for me.

Bold, Bodacious and Beautiful

> *You do well to thank me in <u>every</u> circumstance. When you do this, I will show you deep and hidden truths, and you will know me in a more profound way. Continue to thank me for the uncomfortable situations; I am there and working my good 'behind-the-scenes'. Trust me implicitly. Trust that I have your <u>best</u> interests in mind. Do not be afraid, but draw nearer and nearer to me. Sit at my feet and gaze into my eyes. Look upon my face. Be with me and in my presence…. Keep your hand in mine, your eyes on me and your steps with my steps.*

These words gave me hope as I stepped into 2020 with God.

> Beloved, we are God's children now, and what we will be has not yet appeared; but we know that when he appears we shall be like him, because we shall see him as he is.
> 1 John 3:2

***

18

The dear friend with whom I was supposed to spend Thanksgiving was coming to town with her family, and I had to write reports all weekend. It was a familiar feeling to be torn between what I wanted to do and what had to be done.

These words came to me early that morning.

Bold, Bodacious and Beautiful

> *Be mindful of my presence always.... I will enable you to do far more (and less) than you hope or imagine. [Philippians 4:13] I am your strength and health and joy....*

It felt miraculous that I was able to see my friend and her family as well as finish the reports that weekend, and maybe it was.

> *See what I will do tomorrow for your friend and her family. Get up early and secure good seats for them [at church].... Let me be preeminent in you this decade. Look it up.*

I looked it up, and this was the definition. Preeminent: Having paramount rank, dignity, or importance: outstanding, supreme. (Merriam-Webster Dictionary)

> *Let me be first in your thoughts, actions and life. Let me move to the forefront of your mind. Be aware of my presence with you each day. Take my hand and run, walk and rest with me by your side and in your heart and all around you. I am The God of the Universe and I am calling to you—seeking you, desiring you. Say yes to me today and always....*

I wanted The God of the Universe to be "first in my thoughts, actions and life." In fact, I still couldn't quite believe he was speaking to me. *Was* it really him? I thought it was, but how could it be?

I was able to save seats for my friend and her family on the ground floor near the stage of The Hammerstein Ballroom where my church met. It was

Bold, Bodacious and Beautiful

wonderful to have them there with me. Afterward, we had lunch and took a photo in front of The Fashion Institute of Technology where we had met over three decades earlier. I didn't realize it at the time, of course, but I wouldn't see my first New York friend again until a year and a half later when she and her family came to help me pack up my apartment.

On the following day this is some of what I heard.

> *...Continue to do the work of welcoming women into your group and shepherding the ones you have. You don't know when they will wander back in—or out for that matter. Do not take any of it personally. You do not know what I am doing in others' lives. Hold people lightly and lovingly. Fight for them if need be.... Embrace the iron sharpening iron. [Proverbs 27:17] Embrace the ones who hold you accountable.*

It was all excellent advice, especially "holding people lightly and lovingly" and not taking people's comings and goings personally. I kept these words in mind as people came and left, but I wasn't always able to separate myself from the excitement when people joined and the disappointment when they left.

> *I will go with you as you begin this new season at school. Be mindful of my presence with you. Be thankful in every circumstance. Embrace the difficult to love people—all of them. Be sure you are loving and kind and accepting of others. Smile. Love. Laugh. Welcome. See what I will do. Amen....*

Bold, Bodacious and Beautiful

I was more mindful of practicing love and thankfulness, but I was definitely a work in progress.

> A new commandment I give to you, that you love one another: just as I have loved you, you also are to love one another.
> John 13:34

***

19

The new year began with the suicide of a member of our school community. My students and I quietly talked about wanting to make sense of it, and not for the first time, I wished I had answers that would assuage their confusion and sorrow. So it was with a heavy heart that I walked through the motions of beginning a culminating Cinderella themed writing project, celebrating the accomplishments of my students' Oral History interviews and continuing to write student reports on the weekends.

These words came to me early that week.
I do have a word for you. No, it is not you "making it up." You are the imperfect filter—but I am the Perfect Word. You had a rather loving word from [your colleague].... You have more in common than you think. Watch and see. Be open to me and my presence today. Keep your eyes open.... Be my light to a dark world. It grows darker, and you grow lighter. Be prepared. The darkness hates the light.

194

Bold, Bodacious and Beautiful

The "rather loving word from my colleague" was from one of the people with whom I had gotten off to a bad start at the beginning of the year. She gave me a note that was so kind. Who would have thought?

> *I heard your prayers for [your student], and I will act. Trust me in this. Reach out to [your administrator]. I brought her there for a purpose. Talk to her; share with her. Be my light….*

God did act, and I felt that the meetings went well with my administrator and later with the parent of my student.

> Over the next few days, the words continued. *Yes, I gave you joy in the midst of sorrow…. Show my joy and peace to your hurting community. Show them love even when you are irritated and tired. Be kind to your students. Inspire them with love. Inspire them with joy today. Be kind and gentle—even when you don't feel it. Be kind to yourself and lean on me…. Rest in my arms, and let me carry you today…. Don't rush ahead of me—like a toddler into traffic. Stay by my side, and hold my hand. Let me guide you at my pace. Rest in my timing….*

I was exhausted physically from my friend's visit, mentally from writing reports and emotionally from the suicide.

> *Today is a day to celebrate [your students' Oral History Projects], so celebrate well. [Your student] will be grateful for your call. He does not see your*

Bold, Bodacious and Beautiful

> *weaknesses—only his own. Tread lightly with him, and be sensitive to him. Be sensitive with all your students. They work hard and desire your approval. Be kind and gentle even when you feel terrible and without patience.*

It felt wrong to celebrate when we were all grieving. However, I remembered my students had begun their Oral History Projects in October, and they had spent three months working assiduously to interview their subjects who had immigrated to the United States, transcribe the interviews, and then revise and edit the text (being mindful of adding brackets to words they added and ellipses to words taken out). After that, they gathered and designed images to complement the text and then created colorful interactive scrapbooks that cleverly told the immigration stories of their interviewees. They deserved a celebration along with their parents and interviewees, and to be honest, so did I. For a few hours we applauded the children, laughed, talked and enjoyed delicious food from around the world. I didn't realize then that it was the last time all of us would be gathered together in one small, stuffy, yet loving and joy-filled space.

> Clap your hands, all peoples! Shout to God with loud songs of joy!
> Psalm 47:1

***

Bold, Bodacious and Beautiful

20

That week felt like a month, and thankfully, we teachers had Friday off to write reports. These are some of the words I heard that morning.

> *See what I do in the midst of imperfection, chaos and uncertainty?... You need to rest.... Let me refresh your spirit.... The reports will practically write themselves.... Wait and see what I will do....*

The weekend was wonderful, and as usual, I was able to finish the reports.

> *You did well to go to your friend's Dream Planning Party.... I desire you to spend more time with those ladies.... They seek me, but they are freer than your group.... They also come from a dispossessed culture, and they can teach you more than you know. You have very few black friends, and you need more....*

That was true. The Dream Planning Party was given by one of the previous leaders of our Connect Group. We rarely saw each other now that she wasn't leading our group, but every time I did, I felt deeply blessed and encouraged by her.

> *Do you not see what a gift it is for a white woman to be a part of a group of women of color?... Learn from your friend; learn from the younger women.... You venture into their territory. Don't fear them or their passion. You didn't recognize [one of the ladies].... Try again. She feels disrespected by you because you don't remember her name or recognize her.*

197

Bold, Bodacious and Beautiful

> *Keep this in mind—black people often feel disrespected by whites, and this is one of the ways….*

I wish she knew that remembering names and faces of *all* people was (and is) challenging for me. Perhaps because I have so many student names and faces in my memory? I don't know.

Stay the course. Do you know what that means? Look it up.

I looked it up, and these were a few of the definitions I found. "Stay the course" is a phrase used in the context of a war or battle meaning to pursue a goal regardless of any obstacles or criticism (Wikipedia). To continue to do something until it is finished or until you achieve something you have planned to do (Cambridge Dictionary). To continue with a process, effort, even though it is difficult (Merriam-Webster).

I didn't know if "stay the course" meant that I was to put more effort into honoring people by remembering their names, or that I was to finish the reports, or get more rest, or continue to seek to walk closely with God, or something else. Perhaps all of it?

> Love one another with brotherly affection.
> Outdo one another in showing honor.
> Romans 12:10

Bold, Bodacious and Beautiful

21

The words continued the next day.

"I will never be far from you…. You wondered if I would "speak" to you [today]. What if I didn't? Would you still love me? Would you still trust me? See how long [your friend] hasn't "heard" from me? But I still love her, bring her through hard times and give her good gifts. She still loves and trusts me—even in the dark. All of my mature (and immature) followers go through dark times. Much of your life has been hidden in shadows—yet I was there.

This was true. In fact, I tended to seek after God more consistently and passionately during the "desert" seasons of life, especially the times when I felt exhausted, lonely, sorrowful and confused, yet God *was* always there.

Let me guide you…. Step into the newness of the same. Step in with a smile and a prayer. Step in with trust in my guiding hand and, ultimately, my deliverance. Amen. Amen. Amen.

All the paths of the LORD are steadfast love and faithfulness, for those who keep his covenant and his testimonies.
Psalm 25:10

***

Bold, Bodacious and Beautiful

22

During the next week, my students and I continued to feel the same bleary-eyed grief the whole community suffered. Combined with report writing on the weekends and daily obligations, I continued to feel depleted.

These are some of the words I heard during that week.

> *Stay the course. Now you know what it means. These aren't your thoughts. It's all me, given through an imperfect vessel, you. Keep listening for my voice throughout your day. It's a small voice. You used to think it was your intuition—but it's me…. Listen to me and heed me. I give you hints about where to go and what to do….*

I recently heard someone say that you will know you are hearing from God if that voice draws you closer to him. Satan's whispers draw you farther away.

> *…Yes, time certainly "flies" when you live it with me. Ask me to slow it down when you wish, and I will. I can also speed it up when you go through difficult times. I am the author of all time, The God of Time, The Keeper of Time….*

Even before I heard these words, I began asking God to make each vacation day feel like a month, and I felt he did.

> *…Be bold. Be bodacious and be beautiful. Pray that I will use you in great and mighty ways. Pray for*

Bold, Bodacious and Beautiful

> *discernment and temperance. Pray for protection and blessing and favor. Pray to be used mightily of me. Pray for strength and endurance—joy in the midst of chaos and confusion. Pray for peace. Pray for the anointing of my spirit upon your life and marriage. Pray for your future and your [future] husband. Pray for the city I've brought you to. Don't be fearful. You are bold, bodacious and beautiful—walk in this knowledge.*

I wrote this list of prayer requests on an index card, and that card became my prayer for that year and into the next. I had to look up the word "temperance" several times to remember its meaning. This was the first time I had written God's words on a card with the intention of returning to it many times. The timing and content of the list felt weighty and important. All of the prayer requests required ongoing prayer. Since it was still January, and I hadn't made any New Year's resolutions, the words God gave me felt like the perfect prayer "resolution" list.

> *Your prayers avail much. I love you more than you know. More than you fathom. Tell yourself that daily….*

22The steadfast love of the LORD never ceases; his mercies never come to an end; 23they are new every morning; great is your faithfulness. 24"The LORD is my portion," says my soul, "therefore I will hope in him."

Bold, Bodacious and Beautiful

> [25]The LORD is good to those who wait for him, to the soul who seeks him.
> Lamentations 3:22-25

***

23

During this time, I continued to use the daily devotional *Jesus Calling*. My sister had the same book, and I felt a connection with her knowing that she was reading the same inspirational words and verses from the Bible that I was reading each morning. I later realized that two of my cousins were also reading the book, adding to my feeling of being with God in a long distance community. My morning "quiet time" consisted of spending time with God by reading the Bible and the devotional, praying, and hearing these words. These practices built up my reservoir of strength and even joy during these months.

Another place that gave me strength and encouragement was the prayer ministry called The Ark Healing Rooms. About a year earlier, a friend in our Connect Group had invited all of us to join her at one of their "Encounter Nights." I loved the worship as well as the opportunity to go forward for individual prayer, and had since attended a few more. For some reason, I had difficulty asking for prayer; it was hard for me to summon up the courage. However, I was consistently and deeply blessed every time I did. I even saw miracles happen. In December, I had prayed

Bold, Bodacious and Beautiful

for my family member with glaucoma at the Ark, and over the course of the year, his vision returned.

> Heal me, O LORD, and I shall be healed; save me, and I shall be saved, for you are my praise. Jeremiah 17:14

24

One Saturday in January, I met a friend from my Connect Group for brunch before heading to The Ark for prayer. I enjoyed catching up with her over coffee and Mideastern food in the crowded, steamy and bustling cafe.

Later, when we walked around the corner and entered the church where the healing rooms were housed, there was a peaceful hush upon the place. Quiet worship music played in the background. A stillness came over me and my nervousness vanished. A woman with big hoop earrings came to pray with me, and I told her about receiving words from God. She wasn't surprised in the least. I also shared the list of prayers I had written on the index card. When she began to pray for me, she seemed to have supernatural insight into my life. I have since learned that such insight is typical for people who have the gift of prophecy. The basic definition of "prophecy" is "a message from God."

Afterward, she told me as she prayed for me, she had seen a mental picture of me sitting on a beach, and a gigantic tidal wave was about to wash over me. In her vision, I looked up at it and said,

Bold, Bodacious and Beautiful

"Bring it on." She sensed I was powerful and unafraid of anything that could come at me when I was relying on the Lord. I couldn't imagine saying "bring it on" to an approaching tidal wave, but I felt deeply encouraged and heartened by her vision and prayers. Perhaps, I would "grow into" this vision too?

Later when my friend and I exited the church, everything was covered in white, and the usual noise of the city was muffled by the snow. It was another magical (and spiritual) New York moment.

> [1]Pursue love, and earnestly desire the spiritual gifts, especially that you may prophesy. [2]For one who speaks in a tongue speaks not to men but to God; for no one understands him, but he utters mysteries in the Spirit. [3]On the other hand, the one who prophesies speaks to people for their upbuilding and encouragement and consolation.
> 1 Corinthians 14:1-3

***

25

I heard about a class at The Ark called "Exploring the Prophetic" that was scheduled to meet over the course of several weeks in February and March. However, the class was downtown on Sunday afternoons while my church now met in Washington Heights in the morning. That meant my Sundays would be spent traveling on the subway uptown to church, downtown to the class, and back uptown to my home. Losing time on Sundays meant I would have to complete most of my school work and planning on Saturdays, which would take time away from relaxing and seeing friends. I really wanted to take the class, but I also didn't want to overcommit myself.

This is what I felt God said to me.

Yesterday was my gift to you: brunch with [your friend], the light snow, meeting [that lady at the Ark] and my words to you given through her.... They were my gifts to you. Today is my gift, too.... This prophetic class could be just what you need for the next step of your growth. Count the cost, [but] the cost will be worth the sacrifice.

I decided to take the class, and three friends from my Connect Group joined me, which made the experience fun as well as spiritual. We would meet downtown for delicious steaming ramen in a tiny restaurant that only held a handful of people, or sometimes we went to an equally tasty burger place. Then we would pick up a coffee or tea as we walked the few blocks to class. I had no idea at the time that those joyful meals with my friends or the ability to travel freely around the city were precious gifts that would soon vanish.

These are some of the words I felt I heard from God as I pondered my future.

Be clay in my hands, and I will mold you into an intricate vessel and fill you to overflowing with my

Bold, Bodacious and Beautiful

> *perfect, profuse and abiding love…. You were once a "cracked pot" as [your friend] Mrs. Buckley taught many years ago, but I have reformed and [I] am reforming you into a beautiful vessel. My vessel….*

In my world, Mrs. Buckley was one of the giants of the faith, as was (and is) her entire family. I worked with her younger son on the staff of an Episcopal church when I was in my late twenties and early thirties. During that time, she taught a Bible study at the church, and I loved soaking in her incisive insight and humorous stories. When she was teaching about being a vessel for the Lord, she laughed and shared how we were all "cracked pots." We had all been broken in one way or another by life, and God was the only one capable of repairing and filling us with his healing, power and love, filling us with himself.

> *Let yourself be honored and loved and cherished…. Let yourself be my love to a hurting world—a closed-off world—a broken world. It starts with the people in your sphere; it begins with the ones who hurt your feelings and neglect you. Love them.*

I wanted to, but the question was could I or would I? Perhaps as God filled me with his love, there would be more than enough to share with others.

> ¹The word that came to Jeremiah from the LORD: ²"Arise, and go down to the potter's house, and there I will let you hear my words."

Bold, Bodacious and Beautiful

> ³So I went down to the potter's house, and there he was working at his wheel. ⁴And the vessel he was making of clay was spoiled in the potter's hand, and he reworked it into another vessel, as it seemed good to the potter to do.
> ⁵Then the word of the LORD came to me: ⁶"O house of Israel, can I not do with you as this potter has done?" declares the LORD. "Behold, like the clay in the potter's hand, so are you in my hand, O house of Israel."
> Jeremiah 18:1-6

26

And the following morning the words continued.

> .....*I also enjoy these times. I know you so well, and I love that you desire to get to know me. Reach out to me throughout the day as you would to your sister in a quick phone call. I desire you to feel the loss when you "hang up" and go on with your day…. Stay mindful of me by your side and surrounding you.*

I didn't feel a sense of loss when the words stopped in the early morning hours and I went back to sleep or when I closed my devotional book or Bible and began to get ready for the day. But I did feel a sense of sadness when I said goodbye to my sister on the phone. I wanted to grow to the point where I felt a deep sense of loss when my time with God came to a close each day. It became part of my

Bold, Bodacious and Beautiful

ongoing prayer for God to fill me with love for himself and others.

> *Continue to grow. Don't think you have ever "made it" because [growth] can be compared to a Kindergartener, or a child who learns to read, or a college graduate. Each feels a sense of accomplishment for having "arrived." But __do__ enjoy your growth and [the] seasons [of life].*

Recently, I read in "The Call To Celebrate" in the YouVersion Bible app, that instead of focusing on how far you have to go, it is better to reframe your thinking and focus on how far you've come and *celebrate* it.

> *…Don't worry about my love leaving you.... Be mindful of your love leaving me. It is always my children who "walk away"—never me.*

I had never thought about that before, but the words resonated with me.

> *Stay patient and loving with your colleagues and class. __Listen__ to them and be with them. Talk up your lessons. Get them excited. Yes—maybe have them write poetry. Use the senses…. Get them excited about incorporating senses into their stories. Enjoy your calling as a teacher.*

I loved these words for so many reasons. God valued language, and he was once again suggesting I write poetry with my students. I wanted to, but we were so busy with other work that had to be

208

Bold, Bodacious and Beautiful

accomplished, and I didn't think we had the time. I also appreciated, but didn't always heed, his encouragement to enjoy my life more fully.

Later that evening, the words continued.

Yes, the end of your day was tough: the desire to call your mom [who had passed away], difficult students who don't do what you [ask them to do] and criticism by [your colleagues] implying you grade too easily.

When my mother was alive, and before dementia had gripped her mind, I was in the habit of calling her about halfway through my walk home through Central Park. I had decided to stay off my phone for part of the walk so I could walk in silence, mindful of God's presence with me. During the other half, however, I loved to talk to my mom. Now that she was gone, I often found myself wanting to talk to her, and I missed those conversations we used to have. Earlier that afternoon, a meeting with my colleagues after school had been rough for me, and not being able to call my mom afterward felt like the rotten icing on a moldy cake. God's words spoke to my inner gloom.

But look on the bright side—the day was good. [Your friend] sought you out with good news, you gave [another friend] a gift, and you were honest with [another colleague]. The class seems interested in the Arrivals from China [unit] and [writing] Cinderella stories. You also got [to eat] lunch in the cafeteria…. What a gorgeous gray day it was, [and] you got to decompress with [your sister].

Bold, Bodacious and Beautiful

All of that was true. So maybe the "cake" wasn't that moldy after all. As I look back, I could have had a thicker skin when my colleagues critiqued my teaching. A meeting about how to teach paragraph writing really shouldn't have left me feeling utterly devastated, but it had.

> *My blessings are plentiful if you have eyes to see. See your life with my eyes. See yourself with my perspective. Ask me to remove your critical spirit to[ward] yourself and others. Fight for grace in grading [your students]. Be graceful; be full of grace…. Be my grace….*

Decompressing with my sister and hearing these words that I felt were from God helped me to refocus and recover from the day. Life sometimes felt like such an unexpected combination of pain and joy. It was challenging, at times, to process all of it, but one strategy that was helpful was to write all the things I was grateful for in a little book a colleague had given me. About once a week, I would recount all the people, events and blessings for which I was thankful. This practice helped me to remember, refocus and thank God for the many, many blessings that filled my life. I never would have guessed how much joy such a simple practice could bring to me, but it did.

> 9And Nehemiah, who was the governor, and Ezra the priest and scribe, and the Levites

Bold, Bodacious and Beautiful

who taught the people said to all the people, "This day is holy to the LORD your God; do not mourn or weep." For all the people wept as they heard the words of the Law. [10]Then he said to them, "Go your way. Eat the fat and drink sweet wine and send portions to anyone who has nothing ready, for this day is holy to our Lord. And do not be grieved, for the joy of the LORD is your strength."
Nehemiah 8:9-10

***

27

The next day was Friday. We had been back to school for only three weeks, and I had enjoyed a three-day weekend for Martin Luther King, Jr. Day, but I was still anticipating sleeping in on Saturday. These were the words I heard early that morning.

...it is in the difficult, sorrowful and lonely times that you truly seek me…. It's easier to hear my voice and sense my presence in the stillness…. Few people treasure solitude, but my cousin, John the Baptist, did and so did I. [Mark 1:4] So did Moses. [Exodus 3:1-5] It is the mark of a friend of mine. Even gregarious David found me in the wilderness caves. [1 Samuel 22:1-2] Be a woman after my own heart…. Remember I came first, and I will be there at the end….

Bold, Bodacious and Beautiful

I had not grasped the connection between treasuring or practicing solitude and being a friend of God. It seemed that Moses and David were led or forced into the desert by their circumstances, but it was where they met God.

> *I will give you protection as you face your day. Give grace to your students. You fear you are not academically rigorous enough—but it is a gift to make difficult tasks easy, and you have that gift. You have the ability to hone in on the important, and clear away the dross. This is a gift I've given you, so you must cherish it....*

I was feeling better and better.

> *....Accept all my gifts—even the gifts of adversity and strife. They come and go as you have experienced. A friend can become an enemy and an enemy a friend. Stay the course with me by your side....*

Adversity and strife did not seem like obvious gifts, any more than solitude, but they must be if God said they were. How different my life would be if I could see them as such.

> Every good gift and every perfect gift is from above, coming down from the Father of lights, with whom there is no variation or shadow due to change.
> James 1:17

***

Bold, Bodacious and Beautiful

28

On Saturday, which was also the Lunar New Year, this is a bit of what I heard.

> *You must forgive without hesitation…. [Colossians 3:12, 13] Speak your feelings and stay in relationships.*

It was simple, but not easy, as author and speaker Elisabeth Elliot liked to say in her sermons.

And the following day:

> *…The path is rarely smooth and straight—only in books and movies. Don't fill your head with too many books and movies. They become a part of you as do your friends. Be selective with what and whom you spend a lot of time.*

I had learned to lose myself in books when I was young. During our hot Phoenix summers, I spent hour upon hour curled up with a book and eagerly disappeared into the different worlds of New York City or the Midwest in the 1800s or Narnia and other worlds and stories. It was a way of escaping sadness, boredom and even myself. Now, decades later, I was not very selective about what I put into my mind, and I saw the wisdom in the advice to be more discerning.

> *I see your trust is growing and reshaping itself. Trust is an entity—as are fear and anxiety. Embrace trust. Embrace grace. Grace for all people and yourself. Be patient. Show love. Enjoy the sweet moments and stay present and loving in the difficult ones. Smile. Praise*

Bold, Bodacious and Beautiful

and laugh. Love. Love others well…. Show kindness.
Be my kindness to those around you—the ones you
love and the ones you don't.

Simple, not easy.
Be patient with your students. They are young and
growing; they only know what they've been taught.
Model the behavior you wish to see, and teach them
well.

Again, the advice to model the behavior I wished to see was so simple, yet so challenging. I sometimes thought about God's words as I walked to and from work across Central Park. Having grown up in the desert, my tolerance for cold weather was not very high, even after living in New York City for so many years. However, I quickly discovered that a good coat and warm waterproof shoes were essential in winter. Once I bundled up, the walks through the park were fantastic. Very few people were out on weekday afternoons around 3:30, so my walks home were generally peaceful and quiet. When there was any kind of precipitation, only a handful of runners, walkers and people with their dogs were willing to brave the snow, sleet and rain. I loved experiencing and photographing the change of seasons, and January and February were sometimes the most visually stunning times of the year, especially after a snowstorm.

During the last week of January, these words came to me early in the morning.

Bold, Bodacious and Beautiful

> *I take joy in your joy of nature. The trees, moving clouds, blue sky, crisp yet sunny air and the floating and swooping hawk were my gifts to you [the other day]. Do you remember how you felt when you saw [your great niece's] room at [your sister's] house with all the unused toys [after Christmas]? That is how— just a fraction—of how I feel when my creation goes unnoticed. I feel desolate and angry. Why did I create such a beautiful and intricate world when so few take the time to notice, appreciate and enjoy it—much less take care of it? It is my gift to you—one of them. One of many. I have given you an appreciation of it. Let that wonder and appreciation grow. Take delight in my spectacular world….*

I was thinking about Christmas and all the toys and books my baby great niece had received. Because her family lived in an apartment, they left most of her gifts at my sister's house in one of the spare rooms, which had become my great niece's "room." While keeping some of her things at her grandparent's home was a good idea, when I saw the gifts that had been left behind after Christmas, I couldn't help but feel a deep pang of grief that she wouldn't have them. I had never considered that God might feel the same way when we humans don't enjoy and care for his beautiful world.

Bold, Bodacious and Beautiful

> And God saw everything that he had made,
> and behold, it was very good. And there was
> evening and there was morning, the sixth day.
> Genesis 1:31

29

Over the next few days, these are some of the words I felt I heard.

> *Yes, I always long to speak with you—more and more each day. Stay close to me. Stay in my word, and I will be a lamp unto your feet and a light unto your path. [Psalm 119:105] I will guide you…. Hold my hand in trust.*

The lamps used in Biblical times were not like our powerful flashlights. They were tiny little lamps that only lit the way for the next step and then the next and the next. God was so much like that, letting me know the next step when I wanted to know the next ten thousand steps.

> *You do know what you truly want….. Even though you have never had some things—you know "things" cannot produce the joy and fulfillment you seek. Even experiences can't. They are a byproduct of joy—not the cause.*

This went against the mainstream thinking of our culture. Even people who had discovered the emptiness of owning lots of possessions still believed experiences brought joy.

Bold, Bodacious and Beautiful

> *You learned when you were twelve that you were still yourself, with all your weaknesses, in Hawaii. That came as a shock to you—to be yourself in "paradise." It is the same for marriage. You will still be you—so become the best "you" now, and bring that person into your marriage. It makes sense doesn't it?*

When I was twelve, I remember thinking I would be perfectly blissful in Hawaii. It was, after all, paradise. However, when I arrived, I discovered that I was still annoyed by my family, bugs and the plethora of large and small annoyances that nettled me at home. My twelve-year-old self was utterly astonished by this discovery. In some ways, I still held on to similar fantasies about being married. I imagined if I were married I would not be lonely on holidays and would automatically have a partner to do fun things with, so I would be perfectly content. I knew from dating experience that this way of thinking was a lie.

> *I delight in giving you the desires of your heart. I delight in your thankful spirit. I am removing the complaining spirit. I am giving you a grateful heart.... Walk with me moment-by-moment, hourly and daily. All of a sudden, you will realize a year has passed in my presence and then a decade and then a lifetime. Stay the course. Stay bold, bodacious and beautiful. Stay in my word....*

Imagine spending a lifetime in God's presence? I was down to the last page in my second journal when these words came to me.

Bold, Bodacious and Beautiful

Whatever you put in your body determines how you will feel and, ultimately, look. It is the same with what you put into your mind. What you put into your mind is what you will become. If you watch people behaving unkindly, unlovingly and selfishly, then how can you expect to remain fully kind, loving and unselfish? Keep this in mind as you choose movies and shows to watch. Keep your mind pure. That doesn't mean you have to remain ignorant about what is going on in the world. Just don't dwell on it. It's true what you dwell on becomes your idol. Don't have any idols except me: not your health, marriage, career, retirement, family—anything. Dwell on me and allow me to take full residence in your mind and heart…. Let me illuminate you and bring the deep beauty only I can give. Let me come to you in the night with dreams and deep rest. I long to guide you and give you rest….

This message about being mindful of how I spent my time and which ideas I put into my mind was finally taking root in my thinking. I began to try to choose movies and books that were life affirming even though my life had become so busy that I didn't have much down time.

You have filled your second book with my words. I long to have you use my words to reach many people who don't have this gift. See what I will do.

Two books! I couldn't believe it. Was I internalizing the words and changing? I really didn't know. I now see that I was beginning to reconsider

218

Bold, Bodacious and Beautiful

my choices. I stopped watching shows on Netflix just because they were popular and reading novels because they were bestsellers. My choices became more discerning, in line with God's words for me. It was a small shift in my thinking, but it served me well in the coming months.

Bold, Bodacious and Beautiful

Bold, Bodacious and Beautiful

5
SEASON OF ACCELERATION
(WINTER 2020)

1

I typically dreaded Februarys in New York. The days were short, dark and frigid, and even though February was the shortest month of the year, it felt endless. If I had known it would be my last opportunity to spend time with my students, friends and church in person, I would have savored every moment. But I didn't, so I didn't.

These are a few of the words I heard early in the month.

I desire to accelerate you in ways you never imagined. Keep the faith, stay the course. Laugh when you are tired. Look to me when you are confused....

"Laugh when you are tired" sounded like an excellent plan, and a far cry from my usual way of acting when I was exhausted.

You are in a season of acceleration. This would have frightened you at another time.... You have come far and will go farther still. Stay the course.

I had no idea what a "season of acceleration" was, but life did seem to be moving at a breakneck speed. In some ways, I felt like I was growing in leaps and bounds, and in others, I felt stuck. I continued to battle insecurity in my career, church and pretty much

Bold, Bodacious and Beautiful

every area of my life. I see now that "stay the course" was mentioned twice, but I'm not sure I noticed it at the time.

Several days later, these are some of the words I felt I heard.

> *You are very task-oriented—like Martha. She was a tremendous hostess and cook, and people loved to come to her home. Yet she tended toward bitterness and resentment—especially toward her sister Mary. Lean in and sit at my feet as [her sister] Mary did. Let others serve for now. Now is the time to lean in and be fed, saturated and adorned by my presence. Let my power adorn you with splendor and light. Let my light permeate your being....*

I naturally identified with Martha more than Mary. How many times in the past had I been distracted by my "to do" list? Mary seemed somewhat lazy, and it annoyed me that Jesus took her side. Now I can see that these words could have been meant for what was soon to come; I would be forced to "sit at God's feet," and others would do much of the work for me.

> [38]Now as they went on their way, Jesus entered a village. And a woman named Martha welcomed him into her house. [39]And she had a sister called Mary, who sat at the Lord's feet and listened to his teaching. [40]But Martha was distracted with much serving. And she went up to him and said, "Lord, do

Bold, Bodacious and Beautiful

you not care that my sister has left me to serve alone? Tell her then to help me." 41But the Lord answered her, "Martha, Martha, you are anxious and troubled about many things, 42but one thing is necessary. Mary has chosen the good portion, which will not be taken away from her.
Luke 10:38-42

2

It was the second week of February, and in school we were beginning two new units: historical fiction book groups and the history of the transatlantic slave trade. My students were also finishing final edits on their Cinderella variants and creating Valentine's bags for our exchange on Friday.

The Exploring the Prophetic class at The Ark had begun, and it was thought-provoking, uncomfortable, at times, and challenging. I learned that God wants to communicate with people, and no one is disqualified. Even children can prophesy. Joel 2:28 says, "And it shall come to pass afterward, that I will pour out my Spirit on all flesh; your sons and your daughters shall prophesy, your old men shall dream dreams, and your young men shall see visions."

I was surprised I had never noticed Moses' admonition of Joshua in Numbers 11:29, when Joshua reported that some men were prophesying in the camp. "But Moses said to him, 'Are you jealous for my sake? Would that all the Lord's people were

223

Bold, Bodacious and Beautiful

prophets, that the Lord would put his Spirit on them!'"

I learned that the purpose of prophesying was to strengthen, encourage and comfort others. First Corinthians 14:1-3 clearly states, "¹Pursue love, and earnestly desire the spiritual gifts, especially that you may prophesy. ²For one who speaks in a tongue speaks not to men but to God; for no one understands him, but he utters mysteries in the Spirit. ³On the other hand, the one who prophesies speaks to people for their upbuilding and encouragement and consolation."

After months of hearing from God but feeling insecure about the gift, I was relieved and affirmed to be with people who believed in modern day prophecy, many of whom had been operating in the gift for years. There were also plenty of people, such as myself, who were new to the gift or unfamiliar but curious about it.

During this busy week of teaching and learning, I felt physically drained, but also spiritually and emotionally energized. In spite of spending two hours on the subway traveling to church and class and back home, I was surprisingly chipper. These are some of the words that came to me.

> *...Why do you imagine a feeling about [an] event and then feel disappointed when that feeling doesn't exist in the actual event? Try not to imagine so much. Try to be open to the complexity of people, events and life in general.*

Bold, Bodacious and Beautiful

I wasn't sure what experience these words were referring to, but a past relationship did immediately come to mind. I had dated a man with two dogs and a truck. I had imagined us driving to all kinds of adventures with the dogs in tow. It turned out that the dogs were so smelly, I was secretly revolted every time they came near me even though I typically love dogs. The actual relationship with this man hadn't resembled anything close to my fantasy.

You contend with pushing people to a place of growth —seeking perfection. <u>Don't seek</u> perfection for you[rself] or anyone else. Seek only to love others. Let your <u>love</u> guide them, not your desire to make them more perfect which results in judgment…. Celebrate growth, but not in a condescending way. Celebrate your students, friends and family.

I didn't think I pushed my students to perfection, only myself, but maybe I did? I hoped not, but I had a sneaking suspicion that God had hit the nail on the head.

Make your expectations more nuanced—adding imperfection, fear and the other emotions, and I will exceed them. Let go of perfection. Let it go. Rebuke it…. It is a harsh taskmaster, and it creates harsh taskmasters. It is joyless—only producing judgment and insecurity and anxiety and shame.

I had never considered perfectionism being a harsh taskmaster or creating harsh taskmasters (ouch!), but it rang true. Was perfectionism also one

225

Bold, Bodacious and Beautiful

of the reasons I had experienced so little joy in the past?

> *Let go of perfection.... Be willing to stretch and bend and admit you are growing. You are not perfect. Is that such a surprise?... I wrought you in the depths of the earth. You knew me before you were born. I knew you. [Jeremiah 1:5] You have no recollection? Don't think back—<u>feel</u> back.*

I tried "feeling back," but I couldn't quite achieve it. I also couldn't imagine knowing God before I was born. The thought astounded and intrigued me.

> *Delight in your "uncut diamond in the rough" qualities. Embrace your flaws. The flaw, the irritant, creates the pearl. You are my pearl of great price [Matthew 13:45-46], but keep in mind what formed it—an irritant, an imperfection, a piece of sand. Let the "sand" come into your life to buff you and create pearls. Let other people and events "sand-off" your rough edges and make you smooth to the touch...."*

I couldn't imagine how I could "delight" and "embrace" my flaws, and I felt the familiar feelings of shame creep in until I read the following words.

> *[Your colleague] is truly a star, but you, my dear, are bedrock and many people rest upon your might and your steady and loving spirit.... Let me give you a backbone of steel. Let me make you strong enough not to let anyone's opinion of you but **mine** matter. Let*

Bold, Bodacious and Beautiful

> *me give you a soft heart. Listen to your heart with regard to your students. Listen to me....*

The comparison of me to bedrock heartened me. I also hoped God would give me a "backbone of steel" as well as a "soft heart."

> [19]And I will give them one heart, and a new spirit I will put within them. I will remove the heart of stone from their flesh and give them a heart of flesh, [20]that they may walk in my statutes and keep my rules and obey them. And they shall be my people, and I will be their God.
> Ezekiel 11:19-20

3

The next night, I awoke at 2:00 AM.
.... [Your team] saw you at a vulnerable time on your birthday. You feel the same feelings of unworthiness now. It is a spiritual attack, Gini. The spirits of doubt and fear, and to a lesser degree, anxiety, come upon you strongly. You feel hopeless. I am your hope. I am your strength. I am your ability to love others through it all. Be strong. I will give you a voice....

The idea of spiritual attack resonated with me. There were, after all, very few reasons why I would feel so inadequate as a teacher after teaching for almost twenty-five years.

Bold, Bodacious and Beautiful

> *Remember, [in the book of Acts and Philemon 1:10] Paul had people who were enemies and who sought to imprison and hurt him, but I provided for him. <u>I used them to put him where I wanted him</u>.... Paul knew my love—even in the dark depths of the cistern [prison]. Even when all humans left him, he felt <u>my</u> presence the strongest. [2 Timothy 4:16-18] Feel my presence now—when you feel attacked and alone. When you "feel" less than or you haven't measured up. Be <u>good</u> to yourself. Be <u>kind</u> to yourself. Be <u>loving</u> to yourself, and you will be loving to others....*

I was beginning to see how God had used hard situations, and even the unkindness of others, in the past to bring me out of one situation and into another.

> *...I am giving you "a thicker skin," but it only comes through strife and buffeting. Let yourself be buffeted a bit and see what it does to you. You only need to stand. Talk to me during it. Just call out for help....*

I did want to have a "thicker skin," but I didn't like what it took to attain it. After all, who wanted to go through strife and buffeting? Definitely not me, yet the idea of simply standing and not fighting the conflict seemed doable. I now realized I could call out for help too.

At the end of the week, on Valentine's Day, these words came to me.

> *You spent your evening reading a novel when you could have been with me.... See how loving and generous*

Bold, Bodacious and Beautiful

> *your class is? They love you. See the gift [your student] gave you and the note [the other student] wrote? They mean it. [Your student] did his best during the [introduction to the Transatlantic Slave Trade] slideshow. He felt overwhelmed. Give him a sticker [on his incomplete work]. Encourage him.*

God's kindness surprised me again and again.

God's kindness is meant to lead you to repentance…
Romans 2:4b

***

4

A week had passed, and early one morning I awoke at 3:00 AM.

> *See what I did between you and your colleague?… She notes your strengths and weaknesses, and she will play to your strengths if you let her. Play to hers. Play to hers. Keep giving her words of encouragement. Tell your class what they did well and how proud of them you are. Tell them….*

Unlike previous Februarys, this one was passing by in a blur. Waking up early to receive words from God almost every day, the prophetic class on Sundays, teaching, and co-leading our connect group during the week kept me continuously tired and busy. I also felt a constant, vague sense of unease about the

Bold, Bodacious and Beautiful

coronavirus that began in China and had now spread to Italy. The situation seemed to be escalating from a public health emergency towards pandemic status. I couldn't imagine living through a pandemic, and my mind immediately went to what I knew about the 1918 influenza pandemic. Could the world really be heading in that direction?

> There are many who say, "Who will show us some good? Lift up the light of your face upon us, O LORD!"
> Psalm 4:6

***

5

It was the last week of February, and I eagerly anticipated my sister's visit in three weeks during Spring Break. I couldn't wait to see her. I had purchased tickets for us to see the musical "Mean Girls" on Broadway, and we were going to play the rest of her visit "by ear." The plan was to relax, sleep late, eat leisurely breakfasts at my place, go for walks in Central Park, visit a museum or two, enjoy our favorite restaurants and maybe get tickets to another show at TKTS. We could always go to a movie as well. My unease regarding the coronavirus was increasing with every passing day, but I hoped it would not affect her visit.

These words came to me early on a Sunday morning

Bold, Bodacious and Beautiful

> *....Let people know you love them and care about them. Let them know you notice them…. [Your students] care about what you think of them. So do your Connect Group ladies. Don't be dismayed by small numbers. Each lady is worth ten, one hundred, one thousand [people]. They will all reach many people for me…. Be patient with everyone—especially and even yourself.*

It was difficult to ignore the small numbers in our Connect Group, especially since we went to a megachurch, but the words "They will all reach many people for me" heartened me. The words also stayed with me throughout the coming months, and I still think about them.

> *Stay the course. Be open to hearing from me in new (and strange) ways. I am out of the box—I am the box. I am all. I Am that I Am. Sometimes I whisper, or nudge, or trip you up. Sometimes I open doors, and other times I slam them. Still other times I allow you to walk through them or I allow you to see a new door you hadn't noticed before. I can nudge you with a word or look or sigh of a friend…. Look for me throughout your days…. Listen to me. You think it is your intuition—but it is often me whispering to you. Heed those whispers as you are beginning to do. Look for me in new ways. Remember I am the box.*

I loved "I am out of the box– I am the box." And later that morning:

Bold, Bodacious and Beautiful

> *… Face each new challenge as it comes—with me by your side to protect and help and guide you. Do not fear <u>anything</u> in the future. Fear is designed to drain your joy in the present moment and leave you feeling lifeless. I am your life—your joy and love and peace…. Now rest in my peace. Enjoy <u>every</u> moment of today….*

"Fear is designed to drain your joy in the present moment and leave you feeling lifeless." I felt the reality of this statement and I saw it in the faces of the people around me, that empty fearful look.

That evening the words continued.

> *Hang on to joy and don't let go…. Rejoice, Gini. Rejoice in me and what I'm doing in your life.*

It seemed completely counterintuitive to rejoice in the face of fear, but I tried it by listening and singing along to Christian music, worshiping at church, writing in my gratefulness journal and thanking God each day for the many blessings I enjoyed. Believe it or not, I felt deep joy even while I was feeling fear.

> But now thus says the LORD, he who created you, O Jacob, he who formed you, O Israel: "Fear not, for I have redeemed you; I have called you by name, you are mine."
> Isaiah 43:1

***

Bold, Bodacious and Beautiful

6

I started having strange and even troubling dreams almost every night, and I wrote them down in my journal. I don't know if I was absorbing the anxiety in the world or if it was simply my own anxiety. Perhaps it was a combination of both.

I had participated in two more Exploring the Prophetic classes with my friends, and much of what I was learning was extremely practical. I now knew that if I said, "God said this…" I didn't give others a choice to either accept, "shelve" (save for later) or "flush" the words. People needed to be given a choice of accepting them or not. Instead, I was encouraged to preface my message with "I feel" or "I think" God is saying….We were all acquiring and practicing new skills, and absorbing new information. I also enjoyed the extra time with my friends when we met beforehand for lunch.

As February wound down, I felt these words come to me.

> *Yes, you are being accelerated, and with that comes a certain amount of confusion and perhaps bewilderment and less sleep. I will provide the rest and help you need….*

Then, as they so often did, the words switched to a new topic.

> *You will live lightly and help others carry their gifts. You may move—so be ready….*

Bold, Bodacious and Beautiful

I didn't even know how to prepare for what seemed to be an approaching pandemic. How did one move in the middle of one? I supposed clearing out my things was a good starting point.

Your life has been full—three careers I carried you through. You will soon be moving into another one. Your last one. Be ready. I have used you at your church in a small but mighty way. You are a woman of integrity and grit, and you always have been. You became hard and angry for a period of time, but you are soft and loving again....

Was I? I wasn't consciously aware of being either "hard and angry" or "soft and loving."

Speak to your [therapy] group about me, and see what I will do. I long for all of them—even [your group leader]....

I did speak to them, and they asked me questions, encouraged me to keep sharing and seemed genuinely supportive of my journey with God.

Today will be long and short.... Thank me often, and ask for help. Your class loves you and loves this unit. Let them work at home later if they wish. Let them wonder and think deeply. Let them talk with each other. Let them take off and fly. They will and do embrace the challenge....

Teaching fourth graders about the transatlantic slave trade was not easy. It was

Bold, Bodacious and Beautiful

challenging to walk the fine line of sharing accurate information without overwhelming them.

> *I have guided you through this month…. Use your time wisely. Get rest when you can. Take naps this weekend and <u>slow down</u>. I will help you.*

Slowing down was advice I relished. I felt like a car engine that was running on empty.

It was difficult to slow down my mind, though, when so many opinions and feelings about the coronavirus were swirling around. New Yorkers were beginning to stock up on food and supplies which was challenging to do without a car. Report checklists were also due—again.

This is what I felt I heard on the last (Leap Year) day of February at 1:30 AM.

> *…Do not be afraid of what is to come…. Buy [some extra bottles of] water today…. Buy some rice and beans—things you like…. Listen to the words you told your class. Do not worry. Spend time in the present….*

Easier said than done.

> *Rest in me and in my Word [the Bible]. Stay away from rumors…. Use this time and what is to come to grow in me and my love. <u>This is a pivotal time for the physical and spiritual world.</u> Stay off your phone, and be aware of the time you are on it…. <u>Rest as you work</u>. Stay calm in me. I will use you to calm the fears of others. You [would] do well to stock up on supplies*

235

Bold, Bodacious and Beautiful

> *over the next few weeks. Be aware of others doing the same….*

I had cleared out a bookshelf, and it became my new food pantry, since my kitchen storage was rather limited. I tried to "rest as I worked" by closing my eyes for a few minutes on breaks, breathing deeply, praying now and then, and drinking enough water. I still haven't grasped the full meaning of resting while working.

> *…You are bold, bodacious and beautiful…. Do not embrace fear. It creeps outside your house and stalks your mind. Rebuke it. You no longer have anxiety. Now rebuke it's brother/sibling—fear. It is older, harder and more covert. It is setting up camp in New York City with its minions. It controls New York City in many ways. It desires to sabotage and overwhelm you—to undermine you and swallow you up as much as it can. Rebuke it. Wear my [metaphorical spiritual] armor. Focus on Psalm 91. Speak and pray with Christian friends. Do it often, and do it now. You are not alone….*

I felt a sense of dread that seemed to permeate the city, and God's words both comforted and scared me. I didn't relish the idea of an entity called fear "creeping outside my house" and "stalking my mind." I began telling fear to get out in Jesus' name and asking God to replace it with Love, Joy and Peace who were also spiritual entities.

> *Get water. And remember—I am your living water.*

236

Bold, Bodacious and Beautiful

I did buy several gallons of water which took several trips. It turned out that I didn't need them during that season, but I did use them months later when I was moving. They came in handy when my kitchen was all packed up, and I ended up giving the last one to my movers.

A few seasoned Christians I knew were memorizing Psalm 91, so I looked it up. Verses five through seven especially resonated with me. So did verse four. It seemed to be the perfect prayer for this particular season, so I decided to read it every day, and perhaps memorize it. I didn't end up doing either, though.

> [1]He who dwells in the shelter of the Most High will abide in the shadow of the Almighty. [2]I will say to the Lord, "My refuge and my fortress, my God, in whom I trust." [3]For he will deliver you from the snare of the fowler and from the deadly pestilence. [4]He will cover you with his pinions, and under his wings you will find refuge; his faithfulness is a shield and buckler. [5]You will not fear the terror of the night, nor the arrow that flies by day, [6]nor the pestilence that stalks in darkness, nor the destruction that wastes at noonday. [7]A thousand may fall at your side, ten thousand at your right hand, but it will not come near you. [8]You will only look with your eyes and see the recompense of the wicked. [9]Because you have

Bold, Bodacious and Beautiful

made the Lord your dwelling place—the Most High, who is my refuge—[10]no evil shall be allowed to befall you, no plague come near your tent. [11]For he will command his angels concerning you to guard you in all your ways. [12]On their hands they will bear you up, lest you strike your foot against a stone. [13]You will tread on the lion and the adder; the young lion and the serpent you will trample underfoot. [14]"Because he holds fast to me in love, I will deliver him; I will protect him, because he knows my name. [15]When he calls to me, I will answer him; I will be with him in trouble; I will rescue him and honor him. [16]With long life I will satisfy him and show him my salvation."

Psalm 91

***

7

The first week of March was a blur. The feeling of fear and uncertainty was palpable in New York City and among everyone I knew. My students talked about how they were feeling, and many said they were afraid. Some remained silent, and I worried about them. I shared that I had heard someone (Christine Caine) talk about fear and compare it to a train that pulls into the station of our minds. We have a choice of whether or not to get on the "fear train" when it

Bold, Bodacious and Beautiful

pulls into the station. We can get on and let it carry us to wherever it wants to take us, or we can watch it pull in and wait for it to leave without getting on. I encouraged them not to get on the "fear train." We also reviewed some of our mindfulness strategies such as PBS: Pause, Breath and Smile. It didn't feel like much, but I hoped it would help.

These are some of the words I felt I heard that week.

> *Yes my daughter, you do well to rebuke fear.... It knows it is ultimately vanquished, but for now it is having its moment.... Don't listen to its voice or give in to its whispers.... Keep hold of my hand.... Keep your eyes on me.*

I was learning to discern the voice of fear in my mind. Most thoughts that caused me to feel fear were from, what I believe is, an entity called "fear." However, I reminded myself that not all fear is destructive or evil. Some fear is meant to save lives or at least protect me from pain. The fear of being burned keeps you from putting your hand in fire.

> *There will be chaos and fear. People will go "crazy" for a short time. Fear <u>NOT</u>. Stay calm. Eat your good food.... It will be a sweet time for you. Use it well. Use it to grow and study and clear out stuff. Use it to spread my peace and love to a broken and frenzied world....*

Would it really be a sweet time?

Bold, Bodacious and Beautiful

> *Warn them not to go back to the status quo when things return back to normal. Warn them to remember me....You had another night of very little sleep. Do you feel better now that you are spending it with me?*

"Yes, I do, Lord," I replied in my mind, although I was tired, as usual.

> *You have been through a terrible and wonderful week. You were encouraged when [a student] asked if you would run for president and [another student] told you he thought about not getting on the "fear train" when he was frightened. Keep talking to your class. Ask if they tried any of the [mindfulness] strategies. Read them a book after you work a bit this morning.... Let them know you love them and are there for them.*

[29]Are not two sparrows sold for a penny? And not one of them will fall to the ground apart from your Father. [30]But even the hairs of your head are all numbered. [31]Fear not, therefore; you are of more value than many sparrows. Matthew 10:29-31

8

It was now Sunday—one more week until Spring Break. Normally, the week before Spring Break was chaotic, but fear of the coronavirus added an additional layer of confusion and uncertainty. We teachers had been copying and collecting work and books to send home with the students just in case school did not reopen after break. Our team stayed late one night and compiled everything into several take-home folders for each student. Would it be enough? What was going to happen? How would we teach? Could we possibly teach fourth graders online?

I didn't realize it at the time, but that Sunday was a day of "lasts." I don't remember if I went to church, but if I did, it was the last day everyone met in person for well over a year and the final time for me. I wouldn't see my Connect Group friends in person for over a year, and the prophetic class did not meet downtown again. Looking back, I was grateful I met a friend from my Connect Group for coffee on that day.

These were the words I felt I heard that weekend.

> *Spring break is exciting, and the coronavirus is terrifying. The combination is wreaking havoc on people. Let your students get away with inattention this week. This is not a typical year or time. Cut yourself a lot of slack, too. Be good to yourself today….*

Once again, God was looking out for me, and I felt encouraged.

> *…Be brave. Be brave with technology. See it as an adventure and a new way to learn. See it as a challenge—a good challenge. You are taking good care of yourself—but realize I also take care of you. I hold you no matter what happens around you, in you or to you. I have you, Gini….*

Bold, Bodacious and Beautiful

God took care of me. I knew this in my mind and believed it, but the reminder that, in the moment, God was *actually taking care of me* was an astounding realization.

> *Stay the course. Last week was tough, and this week will be tougher and easier. Stay with me. Keep focused on me and in my Word [reading the Bible]. Praise me and thank me often. Go to lunch and [the prophetic] class today. Be open to those around you. Smile. Be kind. Listen and see what I will do.*

[1]O LORD, my heart is not lifted up; my eyes are not raised too high; I do not occupy myself with things too great and too marvelous for me. [2]But I have calmed and quieted my soul, like a weaned child with its mother; like a weaned child is my soul within me. [3]O Israel, hope in the LORD from this time forth and forevermore.
Psalm 131:1-3

9

The final week of school was only two days. In hindsight, that was the "easier" part of a tough week.

On what would be the final morning with my students, I felt I heard this.

> *Be strong in me today. Focus on me. Keep your eyes on me. Seek my face. Linger with me. This is the first word that spurred you on [last year]. Linger.*

Bold, Bodacious and Beautiful

It was. Lana Vawser had spoken about "lingering with the Lord" and the idea took hold in my mind and spirit. I often read through Psalm 23 in the Passion translation when I was attempting to linger with the Lord. God was leading me (and many others, I discovered later) into a season of "lingering" with him.

That Tuesday was a day of small and large miracles. Thankfully, our team of fourth grade teachers had worked hard and stayed late to prepare almost everything our students would need in case we didn't re-open after Spring break. At the last minute, I added two poetry packets. I was cheered by the thought that I might finally be able to write poetry with my students! Something told me to gather together another packet of materials. I don't remember what it was, but probably the material for our geographical states study. I had about fifteen extra minutes to dig out all of the shopping bags I had collected over the year and put a stack of folders and books on each student's desk. It didn't make sense to pass out all the work on Tuesday when we had three more days of school, but that's what we did.

Then without warning, we were told to send our students home with all the materials they would need to continue school at home after Spring Break. The last class of the day was canceled so students could pack up their things. I don't remember how I said goodbye. I was so thankful everything had been compiled, and every student was able to take home

Bold, Bodacious and Beautiful

the packets we had so painstakingly assembled. No one lost anything. It never occurred to me that it would be the last time my class and I would be together in person.

That final afternoon after my class left, I gathered some books and teaching materials I might need in case school *actually* didn't reopen. We teachers were told that we could come in later that week to gather additional materials and clean up our classrooms, so I left my laptop at school. I was headed downtown to my therapy group (another last), and I didn't want to carry the additional weight. I later regretted leaving the laptop because we were not allowed to return to the building that week. It was being deep cleaned.

> [1]Yahweh is my best friend and my shepherd. I always have more than enough. [2]He offers a resting place for me in his luxurious love. His tracks take me to an oasis of peace near *the quiet brook of bliss*. [3]That's where he restores and revives my life. He opens before me the right path and leads me along in his footsteps of righteousness so that I can bring honor to his name. [4]Even when your path takes me through the valley of deepest darkness, fear will never conquer me, for you already have! Your authority is my strength and my peace. The comfort of your love takes away my fear. I'll never be lonely, for you are near. [5]You become my delicious feast even when my

Bold, Bodacious and Beautiful

> enemies dare to fight. You anoint me with the
> fragrance of your Holy Spirit;
> you give me all I can drink of you until my
> cup overflows. *⁶So why would I fear the future?*
> Only goodness and tender love pursue me all
> the days of my life. Then afterward, when my
> life is through, I'll return to your glorious
> presence to be forever with you!
> Psalm 23 (The Passion Translation)

10

The next few days passed in a blur while I prepared for my sister's visit. I was grateful to sleep in and catch up on some much needed rest in the midst of grocery shopping, looking up fun things to do online and preparing food. I wrote this in my journal. "God, should [my sister] come to New York City? I have mixed feelings. It's not really safe."

> This is what I felt I heard.
> *Cast your cares on me for I care for you. [Psalm 55:22] I care for you. Let me take care of you. Release your cares. [Your sister] will come, and she will be fine. I have reasons why I want her to come….*

I felt relieved, and somewhat guilty. Even though I wanted to see my sister, I still tried to talk her out of coming, but she was set on visiting. I wondered what reasons God could have for wanting her to come to New York at such a time? The governor declared a state of emergency for New York

Bold, Bodacious and Beautiful

City the next day. My sister was due to arrive the following morning.

> This is what I felt I heard from God.
> *Yes, all of the above is true, but fix your eyes on me. Always me, only me, only me. <u>I will raise you above your circumstances</u>. Keep your eyes on me. When you look away you become overcome by the cares of this world. Don't do it. Don't succumb to fear, anxiety and dread. Stay close to me, and I will fill you with joy, peace and love—the qualities you so desire.*
>
> *I will be with you and your sister. Rest in me. Laugh, remember and love…. Look to me every day she is with you. Don't worry about her getting sick or stuck in New York City. I am bigger than sickness or travel restrictions. Maybe watch a play. Walk a lot. Yes, [going] uptown to Hamilton Grange and Morris-Jumel Mansion would be fun and adventurous. See what I will do. I will do the unexpected. Leave your expectations "at the door" and see what I will do. You will look back on this time with much fondness.*

Thankfully, my sister arrived safely on Saturday morning, and I can't begin to describe how thrilled (and uneasy) I felt. That morning, these are the words that came to me.

> *Cherish the moments with your sister. They will pass quickly. Speak often of me, watch the online movies, walk, talk, laugh, eat and the time will be gone—If you wish for her to leave on time. Otherwise, she might*

Bold, Bodacious and Beautiful

> *be stuck for a long while with you. Which do you prefer?*

"I don't know. It doesn't seem right that she would be apart from her family," I answered.

> *You are her family, too.... I have brought your sister to be with you and comfort you and to teach her. Trust me.*

Oh yeah. I *was* her family, too. I tried to trust God with her visit.

> I have said these things to you, that in me you may have peace. In the world you will have tribulation. But take heart; I have overcome the world.
> John 16:33

11

The weekend my sister arrived, the museums closed. The Morris-Jumel Mansion was open, so we decided to walk uptown for a tour. After walking about twenty blocks and stopping for lunch, we opted to take the subway at 125th Street the rest of the way. I loved that elevated station, but as we rode the crowded train, I feared we had made a mistake.

The mansion was located in Washington Heights, and it always took my breath away when the huge white two-story edifice came into view. It had been built in the mid-1700s, and General George Washington had occupied the house with his officers

Bold, Bodacious and Beautiful

for about a month in 1776. We only saw one other person at the mansion, and we had a private guided tour of the house as well as the surrounding grounds that lasted all afternoon. That evening, we enjoyed homemade Ma Po Do Fu and rice while watching *Father of Lights* by Darren Wilson. We ended up watching all the movies in that free week-long movie fest partly because we loved them and they were fabulous, and also because almost everything was now closed except for a few neighborhood restaurants. Broadway closed down that weekend, so we didn't see *Mean Girls,* which was disappointing for both of us.

> The next morning, I felt I heard these words.
> *[The coronavirus] is <u>not to be feared</u>. Fear me…. Yes, I am your father, but I am also the holy and mighty Creator of the Universe….Love only me and all other people on the earth. Just like the movie [you saw last night], love others…. Make sure <u>all</u> you do points to <u>me</u>. I am All in All. Not only in moments of crisis, but always. Step in my steps. Let each step you take be one I've taken first…. I will take you to another level that far surpasses the "next level."*

I had no idea what the "next level" might be or one that surpassed it, but it sounded thrilling.

> *Enjoy this full evening and day with your sister. See every moment with her as a gift. Do you not feel encouraged and joyful? Seek out others when and if she leaves on Wednesday….*

Bold, Bodacious and Beautiful

After another delicious and leisurely breakfast, we joked, "Do you want to go for a walk in the park or would you rather go for a walk in the park?" We had fun walking by the pond up by my place as well as around the reservoir. Some of the trees were beginning to blossom, and we joked about keeping socially distant as we walked. Our favorite neighborhood restaurant was now closed, but thankfully a neighborhood bar that served food was open. I was still getting used to the new social distancing rules, and I sat at a table without being mindful that people were sitting very close by. Later, when they left, my sister told me they had given us a dirty look when we sat down. I hadn't noticed, but being a rule follower, I felt bad about offending them.

Later that evening, I heard these words.

I know these are fearful times for you, my daughter.... Keep your eyes on me. You can't run away from this virus. It is everywhere. Do you wish to be in Arizona? Your family is there, but your friends are not. Nor is your church or your work. Your life is here. I've brought you here. Do not run away.... Stay where you are, and I will use you mightily. I brought you to New York City for such a time as this. Be bold, bodacious and beautiful, my daughter.

And above all these put on love, which binds everything together in perfect harmony.
Colossians 3:14

Bold, Bodacious and Beautiful

12

The following day we had another lovely "sister" breakfast and read some old cards and letters my mother had written to me in the years before she passed. We had a sweet time remembering her, and it almost felt like she was there with us.

Earlier that morning, I felt I heard these words.

You will hear fearful things. Do not fear. Do not fear. Do not fear. I am above fear, chaos, all of it. I will give you peace and joy (and the love you desire) in the midst of chaos. I will give you all you need.

How in the world would I experience peace and joy in the midst of chaos?

Let your sister decide what she will do. I will be with you both, indeed, I am with you both—surrounding you and in you. I will provide ways and means and miracles. Let me use my power. Your power is small, but mine is magnificent.

Later that morning, there were rumors that the airports were going to shut down, so my sister had to decide whether or not she should change her ticket and fly home immediately rather than wait until the next day.

That is when I heard these words.

There are things you want or things you "need" to do —get things at school, shop, change [your sister's] ticket. Are you sure you need to do all of that? It is your vacation—your spring break. Do something fun

Bold, Bodacious and Beautiful

and light—a bike ride or another walk. It's chilly today. Keep that in mind and dress warmly. Have fun. Laugh. Sing. Eat and talk—but be sure to thank me for this time and pray, pray, pray.

After walking through the park, which was indeed chilly, we met an old friend and her husband at an Italian restaurant that was scheduled to close the following day. It almost felt like any other fun evening with dear friends except there was an underlying sorrow. Who knew how long everything would be closed up? We made the most of it, though, and had a feast—laughing, telling stories and eating delicious pasta. My sister and I both agreed it was one of the best memories of her visit.

As we walked home on Amsterdam Avenue, the streets were mostly empty even though it was still quite early. The emptiness was eerie. We stopped for groceries and some of the shelves were a bit sparse, but I found most of what I wanted. It was good to get home and watch another movie in my warm apartment. That night, I had one strange dream after another.

When I asked God what the dreams meant, I felt this is what he answered.

It means you have entered the unknown. Much of the world deals with war, famine and terror, but America never has—unless you count Pearl Harbor and 9/11. You've never dealt with a mass tragedy. You think by loading up on toilet paper and food you can "save" yourself. You are used to the best of everything—

251

Bold, Bodacious and Beautiful

organic food, good clean clothes and vitamins and hair care products. What if you didn't have any of it for a season—a "weekend"? What if you didn't have money? Would you rely on me? Would you trust me? Do you trust me now that your family—[your sister] —is leaving soon? Do you trust me? Do you trust me? Do you trust me?...

I didn't know. I wanted to.

Be sure you keep your eyes on the children. I will use them mightily <u>now</u>. I know you can't speak of me, but you can <u>model</u> my love and <u>show</u> me [to them] through your actions—patience, kindness, love and tolerance. In this time—don't feast on trash and refuse... fear and rumors, predictions of dire things to come and desolation. Don't feast on it in the days to come. If you hear it let it pass over you....

These words were scaring me.

Tell people I love them, and I am well pleased with them. I am love and justice and the Mighty God Who Reigns on High, but holds each one like a mother hen holds her chicks under her pinions [wings]. I am both. I am all. I am all in all. I Am. I Am that I Am. I am all, everything, the beginning and the end, the first and the last, Yahweh, Jehovah Jireh, Jehovah Rapha. Elohim.

I didn't realize this at the time, but it seemed that God was telling me he would provide (Jehovah Jireh), he would heal (Jehovah Rapha) and he was The

Bold, Bodacious and Beautiful

All-Powerful Creator (Elohim). Those are just a few of his names and their meanings.

> When my spirit was overwhelmed within me,
> Then You knew my path.
> Psalm 142:3 (New King James Version)

13

On my sister's last day, these are the words that came to me.

> *Your heart is heavy on this day that your sister is leaving, but thank me that she is able to fly home. I am allowing this as you asked.*

He was right. I had asked that she would be able to safely fly home.

> *You could have had it differently if you had asked. She could have stayed—but her place is in Arizona as yours is in New York. I allowed you to come together at a crucial and dangerous time for five days of fellowship and fun and blessings. You used it well; rejoice in it.*

He was right. I was extremely thankful for the time I had been able to spend with her, but I didn't feel quite up to rejoicing. Now I know I *could* have rejoiced even if I didn't *feel* like it, and I most likely would have felt a bit better.

> *...Don't be afraid; you are not alone.... This [next] week [of spring break] is a deep and lasting gift from*

Bold, Bodacious and Beautiful

> *me. Use it well…. Don't stay on your phone for long periods of time…. Feast with me, my love.*

We spent her last day walking through the North Woods and sitting on a huge rock next to an old stone building called the Blockhouse. This was the oldest building in the park, and it was built to defend New York during the War of 1812. Saying goodbye to my sister was always heart wrenching, but this time it was even more so. Her flight to Arizona was practically empty, and she safely arrived home. I didn't know this at the time, but God would indeed give me the "feet" to walk the path ahead of me.

> [31]For who is God, but the LORD? And who is a rock, except our God?— [32]the God who equipped me with strength and made my way blameless. [33]He made my feet like the feet of a deer and set me secure on the heights.
>
> Psalm 18:31-33

6
SEASON OF SOLITUDE
(SPRING 2020)

1

Our Connect Group was now meeting on Zoom. It had gone surprisingly well, and I was grateful to spend time with my friends, albeit virtually. These were some of the words that came to me.

> *You will never understand the virus, and when it is over it will be hard to remember this time. Keep a record of gratefulness—more than once per week to remember the faithfulness of God…. See things more and more positively. See me in a positive light, too. Enjoy a rest. Enjoy me. Ask your Connect Group about meeting virtually for a meal this weekend and see what they say.*

My Connect Group did decide to meet for brunch via Zoom. Each person described what they were eating, and I felt a sense of relief to be able to talk to my friends even if I couldn't be with them. That same day, on March 22, the governor's "New York State PAUSE" or shelter in place order went into effect. It meant that everyone had to stay home except for buying groceries and other essentials or getting a bit of exercise outside. During outdoor activity people were instructed to maintain a six-foot distance. All non-essential businesses were closed, and

Bold, Bodacious and Beautiful

sick people were instructed to stay home unless seeking medical help. Even though I thought of myself as an introvert, and I enjoyed spending some time alone, I was terrified at the thought of being by myself for days on end. A vague sense of doom descended on me.

During that spring, at the end of each day I began to write down all the things I was grateful for in my "gratefulness" notebook. I was surprised how quickly I could fill a page of the little book; as I thought of one blessing, another would come to mind and then another. Then, I took a few minutes and thanked God for them all. It helped me keep my "spiritual eyes" on God and all he was doing for me each day. It also helped transform my normally critical and complaining spirit into a much more peaceful and contented spirit. In some strange way, the more cognizant I was of his blessings, the more my mind was shielded from all the negativity around me. The sense of doom lessened and lessened and mostly disappeared. That little notebook also helped me write this book because I was able to leaf through it and clearly remember each day of that strange spring.

These words came to me that day.

Make this next week fun, restful, a time of learning and a creative time…. I will give you people to walk with, and you must walk with me, too. Explore new paths and places….

Bold, Bodacious and Beautiful

2

I wasn't sure what I would do to pass the time, much less have fun, but I felt a sense of hope. I was deeply grateful to go on two wonderfully long walks through Central Park with my friend who had joined my sister and me for dinner during the previous week. We didn't typically see each other often, so it was a joy to spend two afternoons in a row with her. Unfortunately, she strained a leg muscle, and that put an end to our walks together.

I reached out to a few friends in the neighborhood to see if they were interested in walking with me. One wasn't going out at all, and the other already walked with her family. It is difficult to describe the fear that descended on the city during those weeks when most people only felt comfortable being with their family members or a very close friend. I completely understood their caution, but I couldn't restrict myself to close relationships. My family lived across the country and my good friends didn't live in my immediate neighborhood.

I quickly realized that my walks would be solo, and I would need to make peace with my situation. These words came to me at this time.

> *Life has made an unexpected turn, and you hold on tightly—afraid to drop into sickness, starvation, loneliness, anxiety, oblivion. You "clutch your [metaphorical] pearls," but you, my dear, are the true pearl. I will keep you from falling, being without, being lonely. Yes, it may be many weeks, and I know the week of Hurricane Sandy was overwhelming for*

Bold, Bodacious and Beautiful

you. This is different. Trust me through this time, these days and weeks, my love.

The week of Hurricane Sandy had been lonely and frightening even though I had weathered other hurricanes on my own. My neighborhood was unscathed by the storm, but the wind and tidal surges destroyed parts of Brooklyn, Staten Island, Queens and lower Manhattan, not to mention New Jersey. I spent most of that week processing the loss by myself. Since I didn't have a car, I didn't volunteer at a shelter in one of the hard-hit places, and that added guilt on top of loneliness. If one week of Hurricane Sandy was that lousy, how would I endure another week or even possibly multiple weeks of being alone during a pandemic? I didn't know.

Fear not, nor be afraid; have I not told you from of old and declared it? And you are my witnesses! Is there a God besides me? There is no Rock; I know not any.
Isaiah 44:8

***

3

A friend had posted on social media a simple art project to do with children. Since the finished product looked so pretty, I thought I would try it. First, I would need to gather interesting leaves and then place them beneath a sheet of paper and rub the side of a

Bold, Bodacious and Beautiful

crayon over them. Then I would paint watercolors over the leaf rubbings.

These words came to me that morning.

Keep your eyes fixed on me…. Spend time in nature today. The park will be empty because of the rain. Gather leaves, and see what beautiful art you can make.

As I walked through the park, I found very few leaves since it was March. Some trees were in bloom, but the blossoms were too fragile to use. I had fun hunting for leaves and found a few that would withstand the pressure of the crayons. When I got home, I rubbed the white crayon over the leaves under the paper. I loved how the leaf pattern "magically" emerged when I painted watercolors on what looked like a "blank" sheet of paper. It was a fun and creative way to spend a few afternoons. When I got lost in a project, I wasn't worrying.

A few mornings later, these words came to me. I must have asked God if he had anything to say to me.

Yes, I do have more to say…. Be careful what you willingly put into your mind—endless hours of [movies and social media]. They are pits—pits of waste….

I decided that I wouldn't spend every evening watching TV, but instead when I did decide to watch a movie, I would choose ones that benefitted me or at least uplifted my spirits in some way.

Bold, Bodacious and Beautiful

This day is precious unto me.... Remember when once in a while you would spend a whole day with me? Now do it every day. This time is precious.... Enjoy my presence.... Enjoy me, Gini, as I enjoy you.

"People are praying for me, aren't they?" I asked God.

Yes, many people are praying for you—even people you don't know are "praying for New York." But many of your old friends are, too.... Remember people love you even though you don't always feel loved.

I could feel people's prayers. It's difficult to describe, but I knew I normally wouldn't be feeling this deep sense of peace if it hadn't been for the prayers of others. I felt "buoyed" in a supernatural way, and I knew it wasn't my doing.

> The prayer of a righteous person has great power as it is working.
> James 5:16b

4

The streets were now empty, and people without homes were scared and anxious. I tried to imagine what it would be like to be homeless during a pandemic. I realized how grateful I was for the heat, hot water and good food I enjoyed. I knew it was a small gesture, but I tried to carry some extra cash to give to people who were asking for it, but that could cause problems too. I gave some money to one

Bold, Bodacious and Beautiful

person, but didn't have any to give to another man standing nearby. He began yelling at me, but I truly had no cash. After that, I stopped carrying a purse, and kept cash and whatever else I needed in my pockets.

The next day, these words came to me.

Many are hurting now. You have eyes to see the homeless. They are desperate.... Carry only the essentials. Do not walk if you see no one out.... Many are sobbing in their dwellings—alone. Many who are not alone are sobbing in their hearts—wondering how they will live.... They don't have a job, a printer, the bandwidth, or even the Wi-Fi to support their jobs and children being online.... Keep in mind the stress families are feeling....

It was a good reminder as I prepared to teach my students online.

Many children are confused, lonely, bored, [and] scared.... This isn't regular school. It's school in a pandemic.... Your students are stocked with enough books. You worked hard at the end [of the term] and did what you could.... Now use what you have, and let go of going back into school.

I tried, but I couldn't quite let go of needing my laptop. I had an older laptop at home, but I knew the newer one would work much better.

Things will get crazy for a while, a week, a month, a blink of an eye—but it will feel like a long time.

261

Bold, Bodacious and Beautiful

Pray for others, but do not carry their pain. Give it to me to carry.

"Pray for others, but do not carry their pain. Give it to me to carry." This was such simple and valuable advice that stayed with me, and I have often recalled it since. The reminder that this pandemic was "a blink of an eye" in the whole scheme of life was valuable as well.

Cancel your airline tickets [to your nephew's April wedding in Arizona]....

My nephew and his fiancé ended up canceling their wedding when their venue closed a few weeks later.

....If you go to Arizona you will not return in this season. I want you in New York City.... You are meant to be here in this season....

This was not welcome news to me, but I accepted it.

The virus has cast everything into chaos: jobs, security, finances, peace of mind (which was an illusion in the first place), freedom, social gatherings, family gatherings, travel, even simple meals are all cast aside and put asunder. Health is precarious.

It was mind boggling how the world had changed in just a few weeks.

....Fight fear daily with my weapons—not yours.... Fight with me—or only stand with my armor on and

Bold, Bodacious and Beautiful

> *I will fight for you. [Ephesians 6:10-18]*
> *Remember… the angel—one angel—that vanquished*
> *185,000 men? [2 Kings 19:35] I have plenty of*
> *angels to fight for you, my child…. I also empower you*
> *to be a strong warrior…. You are not helpless. You*
> *are a great tiger, a strong warrior who wields a sword*
> *and a godly woman of me. Use this time well and*
> *with me. Don't fill it up senselessly for it will come to*
> *an end, and then the real battle will begin….*

The *real* battle? Then what was this? I also wondered what the talk about spiritual warfare meant.

The next day, this is some of what I heard.

> *…You've spent your whole life observing, hesitating,*
> *staying quiet in groups and working behind the scenes.*
> *Now is the time to step up and take center stage.*

This was true. In some ways I was being lazy, and in others I was letting fear direct my actions (or inaction), but I had little desire to be "center stage."

> Have I not commanded you? Be strong and
> courageous. Do not be frightened, and do not
> be dismayed, for the LORD your God is with
> you wherever you go.
> Joshua 1:9

5

Spring Break felt endless, and I was actually excited to start online school in a few days. That was a

Bold, Bodacious and Beautiful

first. When had I ever wanted Spring Break to end? Never. Though I was nervous about teaching online.

The words I heard that day were a challenge to me because worry was my "go to" emotion.

> *You must not worry. This season will be an adventure—like the rides [in theme parks].... Eat healthily. Eat healthy spiritual food, too. Resist things that only entertain, but don't <u>feed</u> you.*

I loved roller coasters, the combination of fear and exhilaration was thrilling. Perhaps I could experience this season the way I experienced theme park rides?

> *…Your glass will never be empty—even beyond this. Learn to trust me in the unknown, and I will always provide….*

Trusting God in the unknown was something I had dabbled in, but never fully embraced. I came to the realization that I wanted to do it now. I wanted to embrace trust, and not just blind trust in the "universe," but trust in the God of the Universe who actually seemed to be talking to me these days.

> *…Every day is a gift….*

It was true. I just hadn't realized it before.

6

On the last day of Spring Break, I believe I heard this.

Bold, Bodacious and Beautiful

> *You will reach many as you calmly and lovingly tell your story…. I have taken you into a deep and focused place, and I will take you deeper still…. Do not fear….*

  "I have taken you into a deep and focused place, and I will take you deeper still." This statement was reassuring and frightening. I did want to go deeper into my relationship with God, but I had no idea what it would take to get there.

> [1]I love the LORD, because he has heard my voice and my pleas for mercy. [2]Because he inclined his ear to me, therefore I will call on him as long as I live.
> Psalm 116:1-2

***

7

The first Monday after Spring Break was set aside for online professional development. These words came to me early that morning.

> *Be fully present in the meetings, and remember I am present with you. I am your dinner partner when sadness comes upon you…. I am already there beside you and in and around you. Call upon me and put on my armor today….*

  A few hours before the meetings were to begin, I walked across Central Park to school. I had

Bold, Bodacious and Beautiful

been given permission to enter the building to retrieve what I needed in order to teach, but I only had a half hour. My list was extensive, and my new laptop was at the top. It was good to see the security team as well as a dear lady who worked in the middle school office. Otherwise, there was no one else in the building.

When I reached the 9th floor, it was dark, and all the furniture from my classroom had been moved into the hallway. My classroom was empty, but someone had been kind enough to water my plants at the sink. I was absurdly happy that I would be able to take them home with me. One of them was covered with pink flowers, and it had been on my desk all year. I thought it would be comforting to have it on my table as I taught online.

I methodically went through my list and found almost everything I needed. I had to use my phone's flashlight to find things inside my desk since the hallway was dark. I found the books I needed, and I was able to make PDFs of them so that they could be shared with my students and colleagues. When I was finished, I had three large shopping bags filled with materials and miscellaneous items, including two plants that belonged to a friend and colleague. I hailed a cab on Park Avenue, which was almost completely deserted. The cab driver told me how difficult it was for him to make enough money to live on now that everyone was staying home. His story was more and more common. I wished I could do something substantial to help him.

Bold, Bodacious and Beautiful

After returning home, I had a day of online meetings and training, so it was a relief to have my computer.

> ...I will trust, and will not be afraid; for the LORD GOD is my strength and my song, and he has become my salvation.
> Isaiah 12:2

8

Tuesday consisted of an hour-long Zoom meeting with my students. I started with a check-in where everyone who wanted to could share about how they were feeling on a scale of 1-10. Then we would review new "digital school rules," review a homework assignment, and I would continue to read the book *Wonder* to them. We were beginning our final social studies unit on the Wampanoag and the Arrival of the Pilgrims. I had no idea how this first meeting would go, but it went well. I could tell the children were happy to see each other and me.

The rest of the day was spent on professional development sessions and work time to prepare everything from new schedules and new digital assignments to updating online class links on our class portal. We teachers still had a tremendous amount of work to accomplish before the next full day with our students.

These were the words I heard early that morning.

Bold, Bodacious and Beautiful

> *Your hard work before spring break will pay off immensely.... I will help you to sift through the work and tasks.... Rely on me, and ask me for wisdom and insight. Now go forth unafraid and <u>enjoy</u> your day....*

The words were reassuring to me, and maybe for the first time in my life, I did rely on God all day. I had to. Later, I was surprised to find that I had enjoyed my day.

> [32]You shall be careful therefore to do as the LORD your God has commanded you. You shall not turn aside to the right hand or to the left. [33]You shall walk in all the way that the LORD your God has commanded you, that you may live, and that it may go well with you, and that you may live long in the land that you shall possess.
> Deuteronomy 5:32-33

9

On the first day of April, I felt I heard many words from God. When there was a pause, I asked if there was more.

> *Yes, my dear, I do have more to say, and listen well. Every time you despair you are throwing away trust in me and who I made you to be.... You are about to enter a dark time in the world. Hold on tightly to my hand.... You are not alone. I am with you and in you —surrounding you and above you. I am your posse*

Bold, Bodacious and Beautiful

> *that walks on your right side and your left side, before you and behind you and above you…. Keep your eyes fixed on me….*

I loved the idea of God as my "posse," and I've often thought about it, especially when I am afraid. That day, I wrote in my gratefulness journal that one-and-a-half days of teaching, as well as the professional development time, had seemed like a month. Online teaching did not come naturally to me. Our new grade leader had helped me to navigate some of the technology and she also shared a game I could play with my students. I was deeply grateful. I also felt God's presence with me, especially when I was tempted to despair.

> On the following day, the words continued. *You hear my voice, but imperfectly. You are like a young child in this [hearing from God]—past the toddling stage, but not yet an adult. Stay the course…. I delight in you, my daughter. I will tell you when to share and when to keep it to yourself. Even Mary [the mother of Jesus] silently treasured my news in her heart [Luke 2:19]….*

Sometimes when I was writing down the words I was hearing from God, I would hear two similar words, and I would wonder which one to use. I was coming to the realization that it was better to receive words imperfectly as opposed to not hearing them at all. It was also all the more reason to be careful about sharing them. As I write this book, I

Bold, Bodacious and Beautiful

feel the tremendous responsibility to accurately share the information I received.

> *Stay <u>very</u> positive with your students…. Give only positive feedback at this time…. Smile. <u>Be</u> joyful. <u>Be</u> in me. They will see it even though you do not speak of me. They still see me in you.*

When my spirit faints within me, you know my way!
Psalm 142:3a

10

The first week of online school had passed, and we had all survived. My students seemed to enjoy the first few days, and I was amazed by how adept they were at navigating the technology. We were all making the best of the situation, and while I was grateful for technology that worked, I longed to read to them while they sat on the rug and held stuffed animals. I also regretted how I had taken for granted my ability to walk around the class and see so clearly and immediately their academic (and social and even emotional) progress. I missed being with them.

That weekend, I felt I heard these words.
This is a brand new day. Each day—even in this season of repetition, is a time for new adventures and blessings. Keep your eyes open to my blessings and opportunities to bless others….

With more time on my hands, I was able to spend time listening to several of my favorite pastors.

270

Bold, Bodacious and Beautiful

Their sermons were inspiring, uplifting, and life-affirming to me. I wanted to share what I was learning on social media, but I also felt uncomfortable sharing too much; I didn't want to force my beliefs onto others. As I was pondering this, these words came to me.

I will pour out my spirit on the world. Yes, post Bishop T. D. Jakes. Now.

"I planted the seeds, Lord. Now will you do the work? The heavy lifting [of bringing people into a relationship with you]?"

Yes. That's all I ask. You plant, and I grow the seeds. Or I plant, and you water the seeds. Or I plant and water the seeds, and you tend the tree. Or I plant, water and tend the tree, and you harvest the fruit. It is different in different seasons.

"What is this season?" I asked.

This season is a season of harvest.... I will show you how. You have been a seed planter—but I will make you a harvester.

I wondered what that meant, but I didn't ask. He said he would show me how, and I trusted him to do it.

Enjoy this day, Gini. Look to me. In quietness and confident trust is your strength. Don't forget it. Amen. Amen. Amen.

271

Bold, Bodacious and Beautiful

> For thus said the Lord GOD, the Holy One
> of Israel, "In returning and rest you shall be
> saved; in quietness and in trust shall be your
> strength." But you were unwilling…
> Isaiah 30:15

11

I didn't see how I was harvesting anything,
but I liked the metaphor. I continued to go on daily
walks in Central Park, and for the first time in all my
years of living on the Upper West Side, I was getting
acquainted with the northern area called the North
Woods. Over the years, I had spent most of my time
walking in the more highly populated southern
regions around the reservoir and the Great Lawn. I
had walked in the North Woods now and then, but I
almost always got lost, so I tended to avoid that part
of the park.

Now, I was discovering the wooden bridges
and the tinkling streams that teemed with birdlife. Air
traffic and vehicular traffic had almost ceased. Maybe
that was why there were more birds and small
animals, like chipmunks, than ever before. I learned to
identify a tiny Downy Woodpecker that some of the
local birdwatchers had named "Debbie." I was
transfixed by the beautiful songs of Gray Catbirds,
which I had never noticed. I also caught glimpses of
yellow-winged blackbirds with yellow or orange
swishes on their wings. And there were more
Northern Cardinals, Baltimore Orioles and Blue Jays
out and about. Though I felt a certain solitude on my

Bold, Bodacious and Beautiful

walks, I was distracted and delighted by the colorful creatures that surrounded me.

As I walked, I sometimes thought about parts of Psalm 91.

> 3 For he will deliver you from the snare of the fowler and from the deadly pestilence. 4He will cover you with his pinions, and under his wings you will find refuge; his faithfulness is a shield and buckler. 5You will not fear the terror of the night, nor the arrow that flies by day, 6nor the pestilence that stalks in darkness, nor the destruction that wastes at noonday. 7A thousand may fall at your side, ten thousand at your right hand, but it will not come near you.

These were some of the words I felt I heard in my mind.

> *You are not as fearful about the virus, but teaching and teaching well is on your mind. I will empower you to reach your students....*

I had a very strong sense that God would shield and protect me from the virus.

> *I am with you today and always. Especially in the scary, lonely times, I am by your side. Take my hand and walk with me. Be aware of my presence.... Enjoy my day with me [beside] you.*

> I am the LORD; I have called you in righteousness; I will take you by the hand and

Bold, Bodacious and Beautiful

> keep you; I will give you as a covenant for the
> people, a light for the nations...
> Isaiah 42:6

12

Passover was the following evening when I felt I heard this

> ....*See the good gifts I give you? Peace in your classroom—your virtual one—new bike tires, sunny days, heat, hot water, good food [and] my joy. Take it all and more. Take all of me. Go deeper now. The Passover is <u>pivotal</u>....*

> What did "the Passover is pivotal" mean?
> *Be joyful today. The joy of <u>me</u> is your strength.... Embrace me, and let me embrace you.*

That day, I took out my bike with the brand new tires and rode around Central Park. After a while, I stopped and sat on a high rock near the Conservatory Gardens. It had been the site of a tavern in the 1700s, a convent in the 1800s as well as a Civil War hospital and the home of one of the architects of Central Park when it was being constructed. I loved the history of the place—that I could still see an old stone wall and stairs that had once been a part of the convent. As I sat in the cool sunshine and watched a few people walk by I felt a deep sense of peace and joy. That evening I listened to a profound sermon called "Full Plates, Empty

274

Bold, Bodacious and Beautiful

Tables, Silent Servants" in a series called "Who's the Minister Here?" by Michael Todd.

> Then he said to them, "Go your way. Eat the fat and drink sweet wine and send portions to anyone who has nothing ready, for this day is holy to our Lord. And do not be grieved, for the joy of the LORD is your strength."
> Nehemiah 8:10

13

The next day, teaching went well, but I felt off, and I decided to end a meeting early. Later, I met my sister on a Zoom call, and I was surprised by how irritated I felt. It was the first time I had seen her face since her visit, and normally I would have been over the moon.

My Connect Group co-leader and I were also having some issues with a new person who was calling us at night and talking for hours at a time. We weren't really sure how to have boundaries, but still be available. I didn't have the physical or mental strength for this person, not to mention the insight for how to help her. I managed to fit in a quick bike ride, but it felt like a chore. Everything that day felt difficult.

> The next few days were a blur, but around this time I felt I heard these words. *Don't panic. I have you in this pandemic…. You won't be able to get where you want to go or see who you wish to see—but in the end you will. I will connect you all…. Rest in me. I hear your prayers…. What do you wish?*

Bold, Bodacious and Beautiful

I was scared. New York City was different now that almost everything was closed. It felt desolate and depressing. I wanted to see my friends and students. I wanted to be free to go to church and movies and Broadway shows. I wanted life to go back to how it had been just a few weeks ago.

> *Desire for the world to know me. Desire it first. I keep your family in my hands…. Pray for them….*

Of course I desired for the world to know God, but if I was being honest, it would be toward the bottom of my list of prayer requests. God began to give me a deeper desire to pray for a spiritual revival, especially in New York City.

At some point I felt worse, and a friend advised me to take Tylenol rather than Ibuprofen in case I had Covid. Unfortunately, I didn't have any Tylenol, and I couldn't find any online that would be delivered within the week. I walked to two nearby pharmacies, but they were also out of Tylenol. After that, I was too tired to keep looking, and I went home.

Later, I called my doctor. She was unavailable, so I spoke to the doctor on call who asked me about my symptoms and told me I most likely had Covid. I would need to quarantine for fourteen days. I asked how I would know if I needed to go to the hospital, and she said that if I was unable to walk five steps without having to sit down to catch my breath, I should go to the hospital. Otherwise, I should stay

Bold, Bodacious and Beautiful

away from hospitals and Urgent Care centers. I was having trouble breathing, but she said it didn't sound like it was a life threatening situation. It was a concern to me, though, and it felt terrifying to not be able to breathe normally. Another worry was not being able to go outside for the fourteen-day quarantine period. I couldn't imagine being unable to go for a walk or feel sunshine on my face for two weeks. My daily walks in the park brought me peace of mind and joy. I felt close to God when I was walking in nature, and I needed the exercise.

I had always been a person who had trouble accepting help from anyone other than very close friends or family members. A few years earlier, I had pneumonia, and I couldn't bring myself to say yes to most of the kind friends, colleagues and neighbors who offered to bring me soup, run errands or help in some other way. I didn't want to put anyone out, or at least that's what I told myself. Instead, I walked to the grocery store, picked up prescriptions and cooked for myself when I was weak and would have been much better off resting. When I recovered, my sister told me I needed to learn how to accept help from others, and I knew she was right. Why couldn't I ask for and accept gestures of kindness? Was not wanting to "put anyone out" really just a strange form of pride? Maybe I didn't want to owe anyone anything? Was I trying to prove I could do it all on my own, and I didn't need anyone? I didn't know the answers to those questions, and it bothered me.

Bold, Bodacious and Beautiful

I was thinking about that time of life as I contemplated quarantining and recovering from Covid alone. The thought of being alone and doing everything by myself overwhelmed me with fear and dread. I was worrying about how I would get some Tylenol when something extraordinary happened. One of my colleagues called because she had heard I was sick. After explaining I couldn't find Tylenol anywhere, she called one of our school administrators who lived nearby. The administrator offered to look for some and drop it off at my door if she found it.

All the old self talk came back in full force. "How will she be able to find any when I can't? She has two young children to care for while working from home, and she is much too busy. Am I being too needy? I barely even know her."

This time I felt sick enough to silence those inner voices (or at least turn down the volume) and accept the help. The administrator soon texted to let me know she had found it, and I was filled with a profound sense of relief and gratitude. When I opened the small gift bag she left outside my door, there was a can of chicken noodle soup and a bottle of Tylenol along with a kind note that I put up in my kitchen. The euphoric feeling of saying "yes" was so overwhelming that I cried. I felt so deeply blessed.

Let us then with confidence draw near to the throne of grace, that we may receive mercy and find grace to help in time of need. Hebrews 4:16

Bold, Bodacious and Beautiful

14

During the next few weeks, I spoke to four different doctors who all agreed it was not worth the risk to get tested for Covid because the city was running short of tests and the clinics were overflowing with sick people. If I didn't already have Covid, I would most likely get Covid after going to a testing site. I knew without being tested that I was sick with something I had never experienced before. It felt a bit like pneumonia, but also different. I was told repeatedly to just stay home and rest. A friend sent me a link that showed how to do breathing exercises, and I began to do them in earnest.

Having Covid was by far the strangest illness I had ever experienced. I wasn't able to breathe well while lying on my back, and I couldn't sleep during the day even when I felt exhausted. It was easier to breathe on my stomach, sort of, or sitting up with my legs out on an ottoman. My breathing would be better in the morning and then get worse again in the late afternoon, so it was difficult to report to people how I was doing. The "Covid wave" was a fitting description. It would crash upon me and then recede, and I would feel better. Then it would all happen again the next day. I was tired most of the time, and I also felt like I had brain fog. Little tasks such as posting assignments for my students and planning curriculum took about three times as long as they normally did. Tylenol took care of most of my headache, back ache and sore throat, so I took it

279

Bold, Bodacious and Beautiful

around the clock for over a week. Fortunately, I slept well, and I was able to breathe better at night. This was a gift for which I was deeply grateful. I continued to have strange rambling dreams. I also never lost my sense of taste or smell which was a blessing because as the days and weeks passed, people began to send me food: meals from restaurants, home cooked food, groceries and natural medications.

I knew people were praying for me—even people I didn't know. My sister and my friend from California began to call me every day to check in, and those calls were my lifeline. We also had a WhatsApp thread on which we communicated daily with voice messages, notes and photos. Two of my cousins, one in California and one in Hawaii, and my sister also communicated often with each other via voice messages. It was another deep blessing to grow closer to my cousins at a time when I was physically alone.

I didn't write any words I felt were from God during those first few days. I don't remember if I heard any, but I did have a sense that I was being taken care of. My biggest worry was how I would teach. Thankfully, I was able to take a day off and then we had a four-day weekend for Passover and Good Friday.

On Good Friday, I had another strange dream in which I was in a real-life board game, and I came to the "Covid" square. I was trying to figure out what to do, but I was stuck on it and I couldn't get off. It wasn't a frightening dream, and I woke up at 3:00 AM. That was when these words came to me.

Bold, Bodacious and Beautiful

> *See how many people love and care for you, Gini? You are covered in prayer. Rest in it. Rest after you [take] your Tylenol…. Enjoy the love you feel.*

I *was* enjoying the love in spite of the fear, confusion and uncertainty I felt. In fact, I was feeling an extraordinary degree of peace. People kept asking me how I was coping, and I felt it was all God's doing. Also, "opening the door" to saying "yes" to the kind gifts and support from family, friends, colleagues, students and their parents and even acquaintances was like opening a floodgate that never overwhelmed me yet continually provided everything I needed in this season.

> *I am by your side, as you know. Allow me to use you "in great and mighty ways." See what I will do. Trust me in this, Gini…. Go back to sleep, Love.*

At that moment, I did trust him and I went back to sleep.

> The apostles said to the Lord, "Increase our faith!"
> Luke 17:5

***

15

I consciously tried to spend the day with Jesus on Good Friday, as well as think about his death on the cross. [Luke 23] I also wrote down everything for

Bold, Bodacious and Beautiful

which I was grateful including a friend burning cedar for me and singing four songs per day for my healing. Another friend said my name in healing prayer at Shabbat. My Connect Group co-leader, who lived in Brooklyn, was driving into Manhattan with her husband and bringing me homemade chicken soup and bread.

My dad had sent me an overnight package of Eucalyptus oil, Throat Coat tea and an herb that supported respiratory health. The UPS store was closing when he arrived, but when he explained to the agents that he was sending the package to his sick daughter in New York City they kindly stayed late. He also sent me a thumb drive of all of our family's silent home movies when I was a young child. Later, we were able to press "play" at the same time and watch them together while talking on the phone. It was almost like being in the same room with him.

The list went on. I felt strengthened by my daily phone calls with my sister and also my friend who lived in California. That evening, I was able to make some baked squash and a ginger drink, and I felt stronger. I also watched our Good Friday church service online. Finally, one of the biggest blessings was watching the first season of *The Chosen* on YouTube that day and during the following week. All of this was just one day's worth of blessings.

The next day, the words that I felt were from God continued.

> *Yes, you are in a different place than you were a week ago—both physically and spiritually. Don't let*

Bold, Bodacious and Beautiful

> *breathing, texts or anything distract you from me…. Answer your texts all at one time and put your phone away…. Many people know, care, love you and are praying. They think you are alone, but you are not. Rest in me today. Remember what I did (and do) for you. Remember me…. Be kind and patient with people's responses. They are not perfect, nor are you.*

I was having trouble keeping up with texts, and repeating daily updates multiple times, such as why I hadn't gone for a Covid test. Or if I didn't respond right away people would worry. And most of the time, I didn't know how to respond to questions of how I was feeling because in the course of a day I generally felt all over the place. Most of how I felt depended on my energy level and my ability to breathe easily or not. But on the other hand, it was life affirming to feel such love from friends and even acquaintances and to know how much people cared. It also kept me busy, but still able to rest.

> [25]by the God of your father who will help you, by the Almighty who will bless you with blessings of heaven above, blessings of the deep that crouches beneath, blessings of the breasts and of the womb. [26]The blessings of your father are mighty beyond the blessings of my parents, up to the bounties of the everlasting hills.
> Genesis 49:25, 26a

Bold, Bodacious and Beautiful

***

16

There were two constants during that time in New York City. One was the 7:00PM thank you to first responders every evening. People would bang pots and pans, play drums and horns, clap, yell and basically make a lot of noise for a couple of minutes. The streets and sidewalks were so empty and deserted, and these few moments of noise helped me to feel that I was not alone. It reminded me that there were other people in many of those apartments, even though I couldn't see them. I couldn't wait for the 7:00PM thank you each day.

I also looked forward to listening to the governor's daily address. There was something comforting about the consistency of it. Even though we would learn how many people had died on the previous day, we would also hear a few encouraging words about being "New York tough" and it helped to buoy my spirits. Those two daily events added a rhythm and structure to my strange and lonely days.

> On the day I called, you answered me; my strength of soul you increased.
> Psalm 138:3

***

Bold, Bodacious and Beautiful

17

The day after I received the package from my dad, I felt I heard this.

> *You never would have known the outpouring of this love if you hadn't gotten sick with the Covid virus. Yes, it will mutate and cause more havoc, but you <u>will</u> get through it. Now you know how. You know what means a lot—even a can of Campbell's Soup means a lot. A small note, a mask, tea and herbal drops— because they represent love. Use it all and drink it all in—literally and figuratively…. Now you know the fear of not being able to breathe, [and] the fear of being alone. The fear of the hospital, [and] the fear of death. I will enable you to bless those going through it…. You will bless your students and so many others…. Be prepared. You have been prepared for this next season of your life. Hang on, Gini. Hang onto me and enjoy the ride….*

It doesn't make sense, but in some strange way I was actually "enjoying the ride" at times and in spite of everything. I often felt surrounded by deep peace, and I felt the love of people who were near and far. I also felt a closeness to God on a deep level that I had never experienced before. I knew he was taking care of me. It didn't mean I wasn't lonely, sick and anxious, but peace that confounded all understanding bolstered me up in the midst of it all. I even thought I could most likely teach in the mornings during the following week.

Bold, Bodacious and Beautiful

> And the peace of God, which surpasses all
> understanding, will guard your hearts and your
> minds in Christ Jesus.
> Philippians 4:7

18

A few days later, I realized it had been a year since I felt I had started hearing from God. I couldn't believe it. A whole year. I never would have dreamed that God would continue to speak to me for an entire year. The realization was overwhelming, and I was filled with a profound sense of gratitude.

> These were the words that came to me.
> *Yes, it has been about a year, and what a year it's been!... I intend for you to go deeper still. I will be your husband, mentor, guide and rock. Always look to me no matter how many people you have in [your] life. Let me carry you during this time....*

> What did it mean to let God carry me? I wasn't fully sure, but liked the idea of it.
> *Be <u>me</u> to your class, and see what I will do.*

I couldn't wait to see what God would do, but the problem for me was being "like" God to my students. Even under the best of circumstances, when I was in the classroom and feeling healthy, I was not adept at imitating God to my students.

Later, I must have asked God if I was making up the words I was hearing.

Bold, Bodacious and Beautiful

No. How many times must I say these words are ME not you?...

Many times, apparently.

Let us then with confidence draw near to the throne of grace, that we may receive mercy and find grace to help in time of need.
Hebrews 4:16

19

It was day seven of the virus, and I had a sweet time with my students that morning. It was life affirming to see their faces on the screen and hear how they all were doing. However, after teaching, posting assignments, helping out in math class and answering emails, I was utterly depleted and feeling ill again. In addition, my co-Connect Group leader and I continued to feel challenged by the new member who seemed to have needs we weren't equipped to meet. I knew I couldn't continue to teach school and lead our Connect Group in the same way I had before I became sick, and I asked for help. Fortunately, so many people stepped in to help me and cover the teaching for the rest of the week. My preceptor (learning specialist) and the school administration completely took over the teaching. Additionally, my Connect Group co-leader and I were given the support we needed to redirect the new member to a place that could give her the support she desired.

In the meantime, my co-leader also took over leading our Connect Group for the next few weeks. I

Bold, Bodacious and Beautiful

felt guilty for not being able to keep up with my responsibilities, but I also felt blessed and relieved and, to be honest, surprised. I had asked for help and help was given in abundance. One of the members of our Connect Group even ordered a delicious dinner for me that evening, and I cried as I ate it.

Later that evening, these are the words I felt I heard.

See how I provided? You asked for miracles, and I gave them to you—Wi-Fi working, a quiet moment by the window, dinner delivered to you [and] coverage for the rest of the week.... I provided for you, and I will continue to do so....

Maybe this was all a part of "letting God carry me."

20

The next day, I was free to rest. I informed my therapy group that I had Covid, and I didn't feel strong enough to even be on the Zoom call. My therapist (sounding a lot like God) suggested I just rest in their presence which I did. It was interesting to me that all the members that were part of a couple were feeling stress on their relationships, and most of the single people (including myself) were feeling alone and isolated during the quarantine. In some part of my mind, I believed if I were married I would automatically be having a fantastic time being quarantined with my husband. Being a part of a therapy group was an eye opening experience in so many ways.

Bold, Bodacious and Beautiful

The following day was day nine of Covid, and the end of the "peak" time when it was supposed to be at its worst. This is what came to me earlier that morning.

It is halfway through the month, and see how far I have carried you? I have carried you as a mother cat carries her kittens, as a mother carries her child. They [the babies] need do nothing but trust in the tender love and protection of the parent.... Let go of guilt with your Connect Group member. You did the right thing, and the right thing isn't always the thing that feels the best, but it is the action that is the best. I have [her] and she now knows where to reach out to —to someone who is better equipped to help her. It is her choice whether she does this or not....

God had carried me without my awareness of it.

You yourselves have seen what I did to the Egyptians, and how I bore you on eagles' wings and brought you to myself.
Exodus 19:4

21

That same day, I finally had a tele-appointment with my doctor. I was astounded when she told me I needed to exercise, get out and take walks. Of course, I had to wear a mask and stay six feet away from people. She also told me to stop taking Tylenol. I will never forget the moment I stepped

Bold, Bodacious and Beautiful

outside and felt the sun on my face or the joy of walking beneath a tree bursting with white blossoms as I walked the three long blocks to the park. It was pure bliss. By the time I reached the park, I was too tired to enter, so I sat on a rock and watched the pigeons and then slowly walked home. It was enough. A gift. I was surprised by how weak I had become in such a short period of time. When I returned home, I saw that my sister had sent a whole case of San Pellegrino, which I had been craving. Additionally, a friend who lived in Arizona texted that her second granddaughter had been born that day. The day was full of unexpected blessings, including two phone calls from my dad and the energy to cook a chicken dish I had seen in a video.

> Every good gift and every perfect gift is from above, coming down from the Father of lights, with whom there is no variation or shadow due to change.
> James 1:17

22

The following day, I felt I heard these words from God.

> *I love how you notice my creation and thank me for it. I delighted in your delight when you walked outside and into the sunshine yesterday. I delight in you thanking me for everything…. Delight yourself in me and in those you love. I am expanding your heart to*

Bold, Bodacious and Beautiful

love <u>all</u> [people] and me even more. Let me fill you with my deep and abiding love.

It rarely, if ever, occurred to me that God would delight in my delight and thankfulness. In some ways, I thought of God as more of a cold and sterile machine than a passionate person with emotions and feelings.

Don't be afraid of dreams and what <u>I</u> say about them…. Keep seeking wise counsel…. My words line up with my word [the Bible]. That's how you know it's me.

Beloved, do not believe every spirit, but test the spirits to see whether they are from God, for many false prophets have gone out into the world.
1 John 4:1

23

Day 11 was my best day of breathing, and the ongoing headache had lessened. I needed groceries, so after deliberating for a while, I asked a friend from my spin class if she would be able to pick them up for me, and she did. I never would have considered asking in the past, but I was venturing out into the hitherto unknown world of asking for and receiving help.

I thanked God for all of it—the growth, my improved breathing, and my neighbor who brought me fresh fruit and vegetables when I needed them. I

Bold, Bodacious and Beautiful

was even able to go on a short walk to the edge of the park and back. My toilet had stopped flushing and began dripping, and I tried thanking God for that, but it felt strange and almost fake since I didn't *feel* thankful. My California friend and her husband even prayed and took communion with the hopes that God would miraculously fix it, but I ended up having to wait five days (until after the end of my quarantine) to get it repaired. I hadn't mopped my floor once since becoming sick, and it was staying clean. Normally, my feet would be dirty just a few days after mopping, but the lack of vehicular and air traffic had caused the usual New York City dirt and soot to almost cease.

Earlier that day, these are the words I heard. *You did well to take care of yourself yesterday. Do that in the coming weeks…. Let someone shop for you.*

"I just asked [my friend from spin class]," I informed God.

Take it slowly today, too…. Keep your face turned to me…. Let me be your joy.

When memories of childhood sexual abuse began surfacing in my 30s, I became furious with God. One day, I was talking to a wise friend who encouraged me to feel my feelings. After all, God already knew my feelings, but she cautioned me to not turn my face *AWAY* from God. I didn't know that I could be angry and still keep my face turned *TO* God. I began to talk to God about my anger, and I found

Bold, Bodacious and Beautiful

that he was with me through the long process of coming to terms with it all. I had experienced the unexpected comfort of keeping my face turned to God during one difficult time of life, and it gave me the courage to do it again.

> ...you, LORD, have helped me and comforted me.
> Psalm 86:17b

24

In the typical Covid fashion, the next day wasn't great, and I spent some of it crying. I wrote in my gratefulness journal that I was feeling like a leper and also judged for not recovering quickly. I wondered if anyone would come near me after the quarantine? I didn't have the energy to lead our Connect Group, and I was feeling lonely, alone and overwhelmed by texts. However, I wrote that I felt "God's presence with me even when I feel like sh#%." I had spent the last two days reading over student work which I knew didn't aid in my recovery. But on the bright side, I was able to take a longer walk—about 10 blocks. I was also overwhelmed when a friend of my sister's, whom I had never met and who was fighting cancer herself, sent me a gift basket. The kindness of people was a constant surprise and blessing.

Early that morning, these were some of the words I felt I heard.

Bold, Bodacious and Beautiful

> *...Think about things that are pure, kind, gentle, loving and peaceful. Keep your mind focused on me. Thank you for thanking me about your broken toilet....*

God noticed that? I definitely wasn't in the habit of thanking God in *every* situation, but I thought maybe it was a habit I could cultivate. [1 Thessalonians 5:18]

> *...Seek to bless, but be aware that in the process others may be hurt.... This season is a time to show up and show love to others. Let me empower you to do this and do it well.... Don't forget to pray for your family, students and Connect Group—and your city....*

I continued to pray that God would empower me to love the people in my life.

> Above all, keep loving one another earnestly, since love covers a multitude of sins.
> 1 Peter 4:8

25

On Day 13, I was still exhausted and weepy. I thought I would be fully recovered by the end of quarantine. After all, some people felt better after only a few days or a week.

This is some of what I heard on that day.

> *...You are in the midst of intense spiritual warfare.... Rebuke anxiety often and in my name.*

Bold, Bodacious and Beautiful

> *This is warfare, Gini. The streets are empty, but the spiritual realms are not. The battle lines are drawn up. Can you feel it? Can you feel the roar that is to come?... Stand firm in me.... It's the Roaring Twenties. Prepare for battle, my love....*

"How do I prepare?" I asked.

I have prepared you with my Word [the Bible] and my presence and my words.... Warfare is scary, but not impossible and utterly possible with me by your side..... Relax in the midst of chaos.... Enjoy life as it is now. Don't look back—only forward.

God was telling me to relax in the midst of chaos and enjoy life. Was it really possible?

I was fortunate to be able to walk through Covid with a friend of mine who was also sick, and slightly ahead of me in the recovery process. We texted each other about "The Covid Wave," and it was comforting to know someone understood the frustration I was feeling.

After getting ready to teach, as well as prepare for parent conferences which I had postponed, I went for a walk in the North Woods and got lost. Normally, I would feel irritated, but this time it occurred to me that I might not have the strength to make it home before my energy ran out. Fortunately, it was a warm sunny day, and after praying for help, I found a familiar path and returned to my apartment.

That afternoon, my Connect co-leader and her husband brought me another delicious meal, a

Bold, Bodacious and Beautiful

whole tray of chicken and vegetable lasagna with white sauce and a loaf of banana bread. I couldn't believe how much food they left at my door. I opened my third floor window and waved at her as she got into her car and drove off. It was so good to see her, even if it was from a distance. My toilet was still broken and leaking, but I felt blessed, and indeed, I was blessed. It was another Covidy day that began with tears and ended with mouth-watering lasagna, a glimpse of my friend—and joy.

> [4]My heart is in anguish within me; the terrors of death have fallen upon me. [5]Fear and trembling come upon me, and horror overwhelms me. [6]And I say, "Oh, that I had wings like a dove! I would fly away and be at rest; [7]yes, I would wander far away; I would lodge in the wilderness; Selah [8]I would hurry to find a shelter from the raging wind and tempest."
> Psalm 55:4-8

26

On day 14 my body felt about the same as it had the previous week. I heard these words.

> *You have come through the 14-day incubation…. You will enjoy teaching today, and yes, that enjoyment will continue. Rest after you teach, and rest often. Be good to your body and mind. I will be good to your spirit. Stay the course. I will tell you what to say to your students. Be simple. Be direct. Be kind. Smile.*

Bold, Bodacious and Beautiful

Laugh.... Be the woman... I made you to be. Step into spiritual maturity now.

For the most part, the words were simple, but I would soon realize they were not necessarily easy to follow. I also didn't know how to "step into spiritual maturity" but I sensed that God would show me the way. Maybe he was already.

Early the next day I felt I heard these words. *Yes, your mind is racing—it is a mix of passion for what you love and the remnants of anxiety. Embrace my peace for truly restful nights. Embrace my joy so you feel the passion fully, and my love will vanquish all fear. Keep desiring the fruit of the spirit—as you desire fresh fruit and vegetables at this time....*

I had a list of the fruit of the spirit on my wall where I could see it as I taught my students on Zoom: love, joy, peace, patience, kindness, goodness, faithfulness, gentleness, and self-control. Often, when I was feeling anxious, frustrated, fearful or whatever, I would look at that list and ask for whatever I wanted instead. For instance, I would ask God to replace fear with love or frustration for peace. I hoped this was a way of nurturing the gifts and growing in spiritual maturity.

...Stop doing work when you are tired and rest, walk and relax with Godly enjoyments—The Chosen, Pilgrim's Progress [movie], Me, sermons, cooking,

Bold, Bodacious and Beautiful

> *even cleaning. Rejoice in all that goes well and thank*
> *me and seek me when things do not.*

But the fruit of the Spirit is love, joy, peace,
patience, kindness, goodness, faithfulness,
gentleness, self-control; against such things
there is no law.
Galatians 5:22-23

***

27

Later that morning, as I was reading my daily
devotional book, the words continued.

> *You are surprised that each reading is perfect—that*
> *[the] Jesus Calling devotional aligns with the words I*
> *gave you earlier this morning. Why? It is all me.*
> *When I give you words to write in a book they will be*
> *perfect for the hearers who are in the right season....*

God had a way of underscoring ideas he was
teaching me. That day the words from him were
repeated in my devotional reading. At other times, a
passage I had just read in the Bible might be
mentioned in a sermon I listened to later. It was
uncanny, but after a while I came to understand that
these "coincidences" were actually one of the ways in
which God works.

In spite of the encouraging words, that day I
felt lonely. It had been over a month since I had spent
time in the company of an actual human being.

Bold, Bodacious and Beautiful

Teaching went well, although I was concerned about one of my students who seemed to struggle with attending school via Zoom. How could I help him internalize the material we were covering? I didn't know. And on top of everything, my Wi-Fi went out numerous times throughout the day. Thankfully, it always came back on, but the disruption made for choppy teaching and discussions.

Teaching on Zoom required a great deal of mental and even physical energy. Unless I was lying back with my legs stretched out in front of me, sitting up was work. I needed to lie down twice a day for about 20 to 30 minutes. On the positive side, the toilet was finally fixed, and I was able to go on a beautiful walk in the mostly empty, rainy park. Then I came home and enjoyed the lasagna my friend had made. That pan of lasagna fed me for many days. But I missed being with people.

These were the words I heard that day.

You've been in a deep season of solitude. Embrace it, and don't waste it. Pray... Lean into the day with joy and a sense of anticipation and wonder.

These words spoke to me, and I was encouraged to "embrace and not waste" this "deep season of solitude" by praying. Author Henri Nouwen writes about the difference between loneliness and solitude, and these words from God brought to mind the way Nouwen compared loneliness to a desert and solitude to a garden. I

Bold, Bodacious and Beautiful

embraced the challenge to "lean into the day with joy and a sense of anticipation and wonder."

> For thus says the LORD, who created the heavens (he is God!), who formed the earth and made it (he established it; he did not create it empty, he formed it to be inhabited!): "I am the LORD, and there is no other." Isaiah 45:18

28

The following day, my students held up signs and drawings for me on Zoom in honor of Teacher Appreciation Day. It meant a lot, especially since one of them had organized it all. These were the words that came to me.

> *…Call to me when you are in need; tell me about your joys; share your worries with me, and allow me to carry them. You needn't carry your burdens. Like a small child trying to carry a large suitcase—that is her father's job…. Allow me to do your heavy lifting…. I love you with an everlasting love…*

These words brought to mind a story Corrie Ten Boom told in her book *The Hiding Place*. When she was a young child traveling on a train with her father, she had asked him what sexism meant. He didn't answer and was silent for a while until the train stopped. Then he asked her to carry his heavy suitcase off the train. "It is too heavy," she responded. He agreed and explained that it would be

300

Bold, Bodacious and Beautiful

irresponsible of him as a father to ask his child to carry so much weight. Like the suitcase, he explained, some knowledge was also too heavy. He asked her to allow him to carry this knowledge for her until she was older.

> ...the LORD appeared to him from far away. I have loved you with an everlasting love; therefore I have continued my faithfulness to you.
> Jeremiah 31:3

29

The next day was parent/teacher conferences, and these words came to me.

> *Rest in me today. Answer with gentleness…. Wait and listen. Watch, observe and smile. I am with you, and I have granted you much favor. Do you not see it?*

I had decided to split my parent teacher conferences between two different weeks because I did not have the stamina to facilitate twenty of them in a single day. The first half went well on Zoom, and I enjoyed speaking to the parents of my students. I had prayed that the Wi-Fi would work, and thankfully, it never went out. As I was thinking about some of our conversations, I glanced out the window and saw that Mama's Pizza across the street had reopened. I felt a surge of joy, and I hoped it was a sign that the city was getting back to normal.

Bold, Bodacious and Beautiful

My breathing, on the other hand, still wasn't back to normal, and there were long periods of time during each day when I could not seem to take a deep breath. A friend had cautioned me about the effects of a prolonged lack of oxygen on the brain, and she encouraged me to purchase a pulse oximeter. It was difficult to obtain an oximeter at that time; either they were very expensive or the delivery date was weeks away. It was another need I talked to God about.

> Trust in him at all times, O people; pour out your heart before him; God is a refuge for us. Selah
> Psalm 62:8

30

The following day was a Saturday. I was feeling lonely again, and I had trouble breathing all day. I felt like I was able to take about eighty-five percent of a deep breath. I began to see a correlation between working too long, becoming exhausted, and then not being able to think clearly or breathe well. I hadn't rested much on the previous day during the parent/teacher conferences. What if my life was going to be like this forever?

Panic set in. It was, after all, day 19 and I was still dealing with the lingering effects of Covid. How would I continue to do my job and do it well? Why wasn't my breathing getting better and my energy returning? After sharing these concerns with some people who knew me well, I asked the school

Bold, Bodacious and Beautiful

administration if I could work part time the following week. They agreed. I also called my friend who was now fully recovered from Covid, and she graciously offered to drive into the city to bring me her pulse oximeter. These are the words that came to me.

See what happens when you ask? People want to help you. See what I will do today. Enjoy my loving presence around you….

The following day, my friend brought the oximeter, and it was wonderful to see her. We chatted in the hallway for a few minutes while she stood six feet from my apartment door. I needed that visit, and when she left, I felt encouraged. The oximeter indicated that my oxygen levels were fine even though I couldn't seem to get a full breath. I was relieved.

These were the words I heard that day.

Yesterday was difficult, and you did not feel my love surrounding you…. Your sister's voice comforted you. Why not mine?

It was a good question, and I didn't know the answer.

[7]Therefore, as the Holy Spirit says, "Today, if you hear his voice, [8]do not harden your hearts…"
Hebrews 3:7-8a

Bold, Bodacious and Beautiful

31

On Monday, although I enjoyed teaching and being with my students on Zoom, I had a headache, sore throat and difficulty breathing. I cried as I walked in the park. A friend, who was a teacher, called me. The timing couldn't have been more perfect, and I felt hopeful once again. These were the words that came to me that day.

> *...Remember, this is but a moment. Do not look to the world or your governor or anything else.... Keep your mind on me. Your eyes on me....*

> This didn't feel like a moment. At all.
> *You will be in Phoenix soon enough. Rest in that knowledge.... Enjoy the simple things in life—a hot bath with [a] bath bomb [your sister sent], a cup of tea, birdsong, rain, sun. Let my joy fill you in this time.*

I believed I would be in Phoenix "soon enough" because the year was drawing to a close, and I would go for a visit. I just had no idea how long that visit would be. Two weeks? A month? Three months? Meanwhile, I continued to receive daily WhatsApp messages from my sister and my friend who lived in California, as well as almost daily gifts of books, bath bombs, masks (which were in short supply), clothes and other surprises. Each text, note and gift was a tangible expression of love that brought joy to my days. One of my colleagues sent me a huge dinner (that was actually two meals) at least once a week

Bold, Bodacious and Beautiful

during these months, and those meals blessed me more deeply than I could express.

> [35]"For I was hungry and you gave me food, I was thirsty and you gave me drink, I was a stranger and you welcomed me, [36]I was naked and you clothed me, I was sick and you visited me, I was in prison and you came to me.' [37]Then the righteous will answer him, saying, 'Lord, when did we see you hungry and feed you, or thirsty and give you drink? [38]And when did we see you a stranger and welcome you, or naked and clothe you? [39]And when did we see you sick or in prison and visit you?' [40]And the King will answer them, 'Truly, I say to you, as you did it to one of the least of these my brothers, you did it to me.'"
> Matthew 25:35-40

***

32

At this time, there were hardly any flights available, but my sister found one from New York City to Phoenix on the day after school finished. I wanted to go, but I wondered how long I would be gone and what to do with my apartment if I ended up staying for longer than a month. These were the words that came to me.

> *Allow me into each decision, and I will help you make it. See, there is a cheap flight to Arizona…. You are*

Bold, Bodacious and Beautiful

> *free to stay or go…. Which will you choose?…*
> *Consider the cost for there <u>will</u> be a cost either way….*
> *Yes, there are many possibilities open to you…. I will*
> *help you to count the cost. Yes, teaching at 5:15 AM*
> *is a cost—so is not being close to your materials—but*
> *less so as the year progresses.*

I realized that if the New York City schools stayed closed during the following year, I could possibly teach remotely from anywhere. However, a day that began at 8:15AM in New York would begin at 5:15AM in Arizona, at least for part of the year. That was a definite cost. It also didn't make sense that I could be away from my teaching materials as the year progressed. In hindsight, I have learned that as children become more facile with online learning, they are able to accomplish many tasks and activities without hard copies of assignments, books and other materials. Having said that, those materials did make learning more accessible to many of my students.

I continued to enjoy interacting with my students on Zoom. I was concerned that several of them weren't keeping up with the online assignments, though. Was I assigning too much work? Did I need to check in with them more often? Were they uninterested in the work? Were they on their screens too much? Were they depressed, bored, tired, lonely or something else? I couldn't imagine how difficult it was to be a child (and a parent) during this season.

There was also a noticeable disparity among their individual situations. Some were biking, hiking

Bold, Bodacious and Beautiful

and playing outside with their siblings and pets at their country homes in the mountains or at the beach, while others were only allowed outside their New York City apartments once or twice a week. Regardless, some flourished despite the restrictions, at least academically. All of them were excited about the upcoming states project in which they would be quizzed on the spelling, placement and capitals of each state.

33

A few days later, I felt terrible again. I had worked too much and not rested enough. Even when I was teaching part time, I still had assignments to plan and post online, emails to answer, online writing and quizzes to correct and return digitally as well as Zoom meetings to attend. The list felt endless, and the tasks took much longer when I was tired and feeling the brain fog. I was also weary of answering people's well-meaning questions and listening to their advice. Every time someone told me "take this" or "do that," I felt accused of neglecting myself; it was my fault I wasn't recovering as quickly as I should have. I knew that wasn't their intention, but I felt blamed regardless. It was frustrating to try to explain why I wasn't feeling better when I didn't know the answer myself.

These are some of the words that came to me on the last day of April.

Bold, Bodacious and Beautiful

This is a part of "staying the course," forgiving those who hurt, neglect or misinterpret you. People who judge you…. Have brief feelings, and then move on.
…Take another week of rest…. Let me take care of your students, and let the parents take care of you a bit. See what I will do. Ask and it will be given to you, knock and the door will be opened. Seek and you shall find. I will guide you in your next steps. Rest and sleep now.

[7]"Ask, and it will be given to you; seek, and you will find; knock, and it will be opened to you. [8]For everyone who asks receives, and the one who seeks finds, and to the one who knocks it will be opened…."
Matthew 7:7-8

34

On May 1st, my doctor called me early in the morning, and after discussing my ongoing symptoms she advised me to get an EKG and chest x-ray at an Urgent Care center. This was supposed to be the second day of my parent/teacher conferences, but I felt I would be able to get home in time. Fortunately, the Urgent Care was several blocks away, and it was empty early that morning. The doctor said everything looked normal, and thought I was at the "tail end" of it. I should feel better in seven to ten days with rest. I ended up canceling the second half of the conferences again, and my school gave me the following week off to rest.

Bold, Bodacious and Beautiful

The next day, day 26 of the virus, these words came to me.

> *You are coming to the end—the end of this book, the end of the year, the end of the virus and the end of teaching at [your school]. Yes, really….*

I still couldn't quite believe the last two "ends."

> *Remember how I've cared for you in your past. I brought you to Amsterdam, to Russia and Ukraine, [and finally] to New York City—all alone and with two suitcases….*

It's funny, but I could hardly believe that, even though I had lived through it.

> *…I told you before, you had two very different paths you could choose. Now you have a better idea of life in New York City, but do you have a realistic idea of life in Arizona? Or somewhere else?… You have a habit of leaving rich, full communities and "moving on" to the next thing. Those moves have been to better places, but they always came at a cost….*

The cost was making new friends and building a sense of community again and again, especially when I changed churches. Fortunately, I had been teaching at the same school for twenty years, yet even there I had watched many friends and colleagues come and go over the years.

> *I told you to rest next week. <u>Do not go back early</u>…. See what I will do….*

309

Bold, Bodacious and Beautiful

If I felt better, it felt natural to return to work, but was it the reason I wasn't getting better? I didn't know, and neither did the doctors.

…Get ready for a new era…. I will give you all the "things" you need—more than you desire. See what I did during this time?

God had given me so much. On one hand, I felt hopeful and even excited about this "new era" of which he spoke. On the other, the illness felt like my new normal, and my health would always be precarious.

> For I know the plans I have for you, declares the LORD, plans for welfare and not for evil, to give you a future and a hope.
> Jeremiah 29:11

35

That Friday night, after enjoying soup sent by a friend and the nightly 7:00PM "thank you" to first responders, I didn't quite know what to do. I had no school responsibilities, and I felt too tired to read. So I sat on a chair and listened to "A Beautiful Story" by Mia Fields while gazing out of my third floor window at the intersection of 106th Street and Amsterdam Avenue.

It was windy outside, and the white fluffy clouds were sailing by. The streets were quite dark except for a string of colored lights outside the Dive

Bold, Bodacious and Beautiful

Bar. Mama's Pizza, which would normally be open and full of customers until late in the evening, now closed early. Only the occasional lone pedestrian was out on the street. After the talk ended, I don't know how much time passed as I continued to sit there, but I eventually got up and went to bed.

> [1]O LORD, my heart is not lifted up; my eyes are not raised too high; I do not occupy myself with things too great and too marvelous for me. [2]But I have calmed and quieted my soul, like a weaned child with its mother; like a weaned child is my soul within me. [3]O Israel, hope in the LORD from this time forth and forevermore.
> Psalm 131:1-3

Bold, Bodacious and Beautiful

Bold, Bodacious and Beautiful

7

SEASON OF LINGERING
(SPRING 2020)

1

The days were a blur, and I fluctuated between feeling peaceful and grateful for the love that so many people were showing to me and feeling a sense of panic that I wasn't recovering the way I should be. At times, I was confident I was on the road to recovery and then would feel worse again.

These are some of the words I heard.

This is my day that I've given to you. Use it well. Use it wisely. Wisely doesn't necessarily mean doing the most. This week it <u>truly</u> means resting and resting well. Do it if you wish to fully recover. I have healed you already. The breathing is scary and uncomfortable, but just an "after sickness," the last remnants of the virus—like a shadow. Go on walks, rest, read [and] pray. Don't worry about next year—what you will do or where you will be....

"Lord, I don't even know how to "count the cost" with regard to moving to Phoenix," I prayed.

Think about life [and] community. Your family is busy....

I hadn't thought much about that. During my week-long visits, my sister generally spent copious

Bold, Bodacious and Beautiful

amounts of time with me, but "real life" would be different.

> *Rejoice in me and in this brand new day…. Rejoice in choices. Rejoice in those you love and who love you…. See what I will bring your way….*

2

A few days later, I recorded these words.

> *You worry about today, teaching next week, overdoing it, the summer and next year. I will provide. Now look beyond "the immediate" and into the decade and beyond it. Where do you want to live and work in the last part of your life?…*

I was entering the last part of my life, and I hadn't given it any thought.

> *Hold your possessions loosely…. Be generous with them. Generosity is my gift to you. Yes, really. Rest as long as it takes to get strong, and then hang on. Hang on as you take the ride of your life…. I am healing your lungs, Gini. Trust me. Be patient with yourself and honest with the people at [your school]. Ask and it will be given to you. Seek and you will find. Knock and the door will be opened…."*

It was difficult for me to trust God and be patient with myself, but I liked the idea of "taking the ride of my life" whatever that meant.

Later that evening, these additional words came to me.

314

Bold, Bodacious and Beautiful

You most definitely did the right thing to ask for more time off.... Rest and feel your health return—a gift from me....

This is the day that the LORD has made; let us rejoice and be glad in it.
Psalm 118:24

3

A week later, I had a virtual appointment with my doctor who encouraged me to rest for yet another week. In the meantime, my school had arranged for several people, including my preceptor who was already stretched thin, to take over my teaching responsibilities. A few of the mothers of my students organized an online sign-up sheet, and the parents ordered dinners for me. Some even brought me groceries that they left outside my door. Not only that, but some sent flowers and other gifts with the food. A few of my students came along with their parents, and I waved to them from my third floor window. I can't begin to say how wonderful it was to see the kids and their parents "in person." Dinner was delivered almost every night for the next few weeks, and there was usually food left over for lunch the next day. I was completely taken care of, and I felt so deeply blessed. How different this season would have been if I hadn't learned to say "yes" to people's love and help.

I felt like I was "turning a corner." My body and especially my breathing were improving, and I

315

Bold, Bodacious and Beautiful

hoped I would continue on this upward trajectory. I felt that God continued to tell me to rest that day. In addition, I also heard this.

> *...Discern my presence daily. Every day pray the Lord's Prayer—or a version of it. Remember all parts of prayer. Remember to magnify my name daily....*

Except for the last line, The Lord's Prayer can be found in Matthew 6:9-13.

"Our Father in heaven,
hallowed be your name.
Your kingdom come,
your will be done,
on earth as it is in heaven.
Give us this day our daily bread,
and forgive us our debts,
as we also have forgiven our debtors.
And lead us not into temptation,
but deliver us from evil."
For yours is the kingdom and the power and
the glory, forever. Amen.

I realized my prayers consisted of petitions for myself or others, but I often forgot to take the time to magnify (extol) God's name and ask for forgiveness as well as forgive others. I also rarely, if ever, thought about much less prayed for God's kingdom to come to earth.

Bold, Bodacious and Beautiful

5

I spent much of the next day grading my students' state quizzes and putting new work into their digital folders, but afterward I felt terrible again and had difficulty breathing.

On the weekend of May 9th, I took an early morning walk, and the weather was uncharacteristically cold for spring. I was surprised when I saw a great blue heron in the North Woods and sat for a while to watch it until my feet started to feel numb. I had never seen a blue heron anywhere other than Maine. Some friendly bird watchers also told me about several other beautiful birds, which I spotted on my way home. It was pure magic that so much wildlife was out in the park—a new kind of New York magic, and a definite silver lining of the Covid season.

Later, I wrote in my journal about the walk.

"Oh my gosh, Lord! Thank you for that magical walk—the nice people, the great blue heron, the black-crowned night heron and the tufted woodpecker. I feel such joy even though I overdid it and stayed out in the cold too long. Thank you!"

This is what I felt I heard in response.

It is my pleasure and joy to give you unexpected, good gifts. I delight in delighting you. Your breathing will return. Just rest [for] the rest of the day. Do no work....

7"But ask the beasts, and they will teach you; the birds of the heavens, and they will tell

Bold, Bodacious and Beautiful

you; [8]or the bushes of the earth, and they will teach you; and the fish of the sea will declare to you. [9]Who among all these does not know that the hand of the LORD has done this? [10]In his hand is the life of every living thing and the breath of all mankind."
Job 12:7-10

***

5

My school gave me a leave of absence for two weeks and hired a substitute to teach my students on Zoom. During this season, it was a monumental undertaking to give a new person access to the school's digital platform, the students' Google docs and all the online assignments. And that was only the technical aspect of my job. My learning specialist would do much of the teaching, and others on my fourth grade team would bring the substitute up to speed with the curriculum. The young woman they hired was more technologically adept than I was, and my students seemed to like her. I was finally able to mostly let go of my teaching responsibilities and fully focus on getting better.

At this point, I was checking in virtually with my doctor on a weekly basis, and she suggested I get tested for antibodies at an Urgent Care clinic, which I did. When I tested negative I couldn't believe it. How could that be? Would people think I was faking it? Did *my doctor* think I was faking it? The Urgent Care

Bold, Bodacious and Beautiful

doctor told me that some people took longer to develop antibodies and still others weren't developing them at all. That gave me some relief.

My days continued to be a roller coaster of feeling peaceful, grateful and rested to feeling tired, weak and dreary. On some days I could walk for forty-five minutes and on others I walked three blocks to Central Park, turned around and went home because my energy was spent.

These were some of the words I felt I heard.

I am the one and only God—three in one. One Spirit —no other spirit. The Holy Spirit. The same one that came down at Pentecost….

It was mind-boggling to think about the Holy Spirit that lived in me as being the same spirit that came down at Pentecost, described in chapter two of the book of Acts in the Bible.

Rest. Do not embrace fear or shame. Anxiety is gone, but it watches from afar wanting to reclaim its hold on you. Shame has no hold. None. Can you feel the difference?… Let me do the "heavy lifting;" let me lead and guide you. Let me be your all in all.

Could I feel the difference? Sometimes I could and often marveled that I was doing as well as I was under the circumstances. But at other times I felt both shame and anxiety for asking for so much time off and causing my colleagues more work. I wanted to let God do my "heavy lifting" and began to talk to him about my worries.

Bold, Bodacious and Beautiful

> Cast your burden on the LORD, and he will
> sustain you….
> Psalm 55:22a

***

6

When I thought about my future, I could not see a clear path forward, so I decided to meet for virtual prayer with a member of The Ark Ministries. He asked me to repeat a prayer, which was, "Holy Spirit, I quit." I laughed when I heard it. It felt right. Two other people prayed with me that day, including a dear friend I called my "third" mother and my sister who wanted to return to New York City to take care of me. (I talked her out of it.)

Later that day, I wrote in my journal, "God, I'm scared. I quit. I give this decision [to go to Arizona for part of the summer] to you."

This is what I felt I heard in response.

Good. This is where I want you. What if I want you to retire? Now? What if I take you to another place? Another city? What if you leave New York City? What if I ask you to stay?

I had few, if any, answers to those questions. I was afraid to leave New York City, mostly because I had lived here all of my adult life. It was home, and it was so familiar. I also didn't have a community in Arizona, even though most of my family lived there. It was scorchingly hot during the summer, and I

320

Bold, Bodacious and Beautiful

wasn't sure I could I stand the heat. I also hadn't
driven much since I was seventeen. How would I
drive, much less navigate, all the freeways that had
sprung up since I was in high school? And with what
car? How could I move across the country, especially
alone, in a pandemic and at my age? The thought of
moving felt daunting.

> *I ask you to trust me and rest and recover. Why is
> that so difficult? Why must you work when you are
> sick? Would you give your school your life? Would you
> give me your life?*

When I heard it put that way, why *did* I work
when I was sick? I felt driven by fear and shame. I
was fearful about so many things such as losing my
job or the ability to work and my students suffering in
my absence. And shame was a well-known tormentor.
You name it and I most likely felt shame about it.
Could I really trust God with my life? I generally
seemed to arrive at the same answer over and over
again, which was that I wanted to, but I didn't quite
know how.

> *The world is a scary place at times. People are
> mercurial, but I am steady. I am your rock. I am your
> resting place. I am the first and the last, the beginning
> and the end. I am that I am. I Am. I am all. All in
> all. I am the King of the Universe. Adonai. Elohim.
> El Shaddai. I am all. Everything. Embrace me. You
> said, "I quit" today. Then quit. Quit striving and
> straining and worrying and fretting. Quit planning
> and imagining the worst. Quit fixating on the future*

Bold, Bodacious and Beautiful

> *or past and missing the moment you are in. Try to take the long view. The eternal view.*

The eternal view. What exactly was it? Was the eternal view realizing that this life is really "a blink of an eye"? Was I supposed to focus on spiritual things rather than things that carry little lasting significance? Was I missing something else? And how did I hold on to this eternal perspective?

> [16]So we do not lose heart. Though our outer self is wasting away, our inner self is being renewed day by day. [17]For this light momentary affliction is preparing for us an eternal weight of glory beyond all comparison, [18]as we look not to the things that are seen but to the things that are unseen. For the things that are seen are transient, but the things that are unseen are eternal.
> 2 Corinthians 4:16-18

7

The next day, I asked God if I was just being a wuss about feeling too sick to work. Why couldn't I "buck up" and get on with it? This is what I felt I heard.

> *No, you are not being a "wuss" or lazy or weak. You are recovering. Let go of shame—this shame thinking…. Shame for "bothering" your doctor. Shame for making more work for [the school administration]. Shame for needing help. Shame for*

322

Bold, Bodacious and Beautiful

> *being sick when others are not…. Shame for asking for help. See what a blessing it's been to receive help in this season?... I have more to teach you, and you can't learn it if you are sicker and stressed. [Your colleague] is right, your lungs are healing, and you need more rest….*

These words helped me to feel more at peace with the healing process that seemed to be taking so long.

> *You will need <u>weeks</u> [to fully recover] after you feel better. Rest. Walk. Pray. Read. Listen to lots of sermons from the people you love. I will direct you. Pray for family, friends, New York City and the world. Pray. Pray. Pray.*

My feeling of peace suddenly diminished. Later that morning, I felt the words continue.

> *I will make "streams in the desert," places of refreshment in unexpected places [Isaiah 35:6]….Expand your vision of me. I will help. Learn the song and sing "Be Thou My Vision." Yes, now…Remember, this is <u>your</u> season of <u>rest</u>. <u>Practice</u> resting. Rest in me.*

I had watched a recent cartoon version of *Pilgrim's Progress,* and in the scene where Christian, the lead character, is freed from his heavy burden the song "Be Thou My Vision" played in the background. I was captivated by the beauty of it, and I replayed it several times.

Bold, Bodacious and Beautiful

Be Thou My Vision
(Poem by Dallan Forgaill, 6th or 8th century Irish
poet
Translated to English by Eleanor Hull, 1912)

Be Thou my Vision, O Lord of my Heart
Naught be all else to me, save that Thou art
Thou my best Thought, by day or by night
Waking or sleeping, Thy presence my light

Be Thou my wisdom, and Thou my true Word
I ever with Thee, and Thou with me, Lord
Thou my great Father, and I thy true son
Thou in me dwelling, and I with Thee one

Riches I heed not, nor man's empty praise
Thou mine inheritance, now and always
Thou and Thou only, first in my heart
High King of Heaven, my treasure Thou art

High King of Heaven, my victory won
May I reach Heaven's joy, O bright Heav'n's sun
Heart of my own heart, whate'er befall
Still be my Vision, O Ruler of all

Heart of my own heart, whate'er befall
Still be my Vision, O Ruler of all

The next day, the words continued.

Bold, Bodacious and Beautiful

I love "Be Thou My Vision." Many people have praised me with it over the years, and now you.

At times, I would awaken in the middle of the night and be unable to go back to sleep. My fearful thoughts of "what if" and "why can't" would run wild. One night, I tried softly singing the first stanza of the song, and I immediately felt calmer. Soon after, I fell asleep. This became a strategy for me in this season when I struggled with insomnia.

In peace I will both lie down and sleep; for you alone, O LORD, make me dwell in safety. Psalm 4:8

***

8

For the first time since the city had shut down two months earlier, I had plans for a lunch date. My friend, who had fully recovered from Covid, was driving into the city and bringing lunch. It was a warm, sunny day, and we sat on a park bench talking and eating lo mein noodles. It almost felt like a regular "pre-Covid" day.

I felt bereft after she left. I realized it might be a while before anyone who hadn't already recovered from the virus would feel comfortable coming near me. I felt starved for human companionship and began to understand what Biblical lepers must have felt. My long recovery time was weighing on me too,

Bold, Bodacious and Beautiful

and I wondered how my students were doing. Not just academically, but emotionally and socially.

Knowledgeable, caring and skilled people were taking care of my class, but my pile of responsibilities was growing. I still needed to finish the other half of my parent teacher conferences, read my students' work and write reports. Being a type A perfectionist, I had to force myself to set those responsibilities aside and rest.

That day, these were the words I felt I heard.

Today is day 40 of the virus. [Jesus spent] 40 days in the wilderness. Forty days [of rain while Noah was on the ark]. Forty days. It seems like a long time to you, but was it so very long?

"Yes. And no," I answered.

I desire you to take my hand and walk close to my side in this next season. Keep your eyes focused on me, even though there will be much to distract you…. Use this last week and a half [of not working and spend it] with me.

I liked the idea of taking God's hand and walking with him.

Do not worry about the [student] reports…. They will get done—and quite easily, too. You are welcome.

God's sense of humor always took me by surprise, and I loved it.

You must walk more and rest more. Rest your mind. Pick up your sword, as Lana said. When you feel the

Bold, Bodacious and Beautiful

> *malaise and the fog, see it for what it is—spiritual attack—and fight it. Fight it with declarations, my words, my Word [the Bible], [listening to] sermons, songs and worship [and] prayer. You have so many ways to fight it. Don't sleep in this season—spiritually speaking, that is. I will grant you deep physical rest....*

I was still enjoying listening to Lana Vawser, and she had recently spoken about "picking up our sword" of the Spirit. Now I felt I had a better sense of what it meant.

> *Enjoy your days. Delight in me and my creation. I love how you notice birdsong. Get up and walk....*

I began to fight the malaise that sometimes descended on me by doing just what God had suggested: by declaring Bible verses out loud, such as God not giving me a spirit of fear but of power, love and a sound mind. I also spent time reading the Bible, talking to God and singing. I watched church online as well as my favorite people such as T.D. Jakes, DawnChere Wilkerson, Mike Todd and others. It was enough. God was enough, and I felt encouraged each day.

> For God has not given us a spirit of fear, but of power and of love and of a sound mind.
> 2 Timothy 1:7 (New King James Version)

***

Bold, Bodacious and Beautiful

9

The prophetic class that my friends and I had participated in had come to an abrupt end when Covid struck in March. However, ten weeks later, we were all set to meet again on Zoom. I was thrilled that we would be together for our final two classes, but I missed the lunches and companionship I had enjoyed with my friends beforehand. It felt strange to see their silent faces on the screen and not be able to lean over and chat with them or walk to the subway with them after class. We texted each other during class, but it definitely wasn't the same.

This session was focused on dreams. I learned that there are three sources of dreams: 1. From God, 2. From my natural self and 3. From the demonic realm. We looked at a few places in the Bible where dreams were mentioned (Genesis 41, Daniel 2, Numbers 12:6, Acts 2:17, and Job 33:14-15) and we were encouraged to keep a dream journal. (These Bible passages can be found at the back of the book.)

My Connect Group met virtually for tea and games after our online church service, and I took a walk in the morning and another in the evening. That evening, I also watched Darren Wilson's movie called "Finger of God." My wonderful homeroom parent reached out concerning groceries and meals. It was a full day, and I felt deeply cared for by God and my community.

These were some of the words I felt I heard that day.

Bold, Bodacious and Beautiful

> *...Say yes to me, my daughter, even when you don't appear to have the gifts…. You do well to let [your co-leader] lead your Connect Group. I am empowering her in ways I intended. Some of your other members also said yes to leading. See how skilled they are? Tell them…. Is it not interesting how being sick empowered three people?... See how beautifully they do it?*

They did lead beautifully, and I was impressed. I also learned something slightly different from each one of them. One person tended to dive into the research regarding the information she was sharing, and another came up with interesting discussion questions and the third led with music. They allowed me to feel better about taking time off from leading, especially knowing that God was doing his work in their lives.

> *Enjoy your day, Gini. Rest, worship, be with your Connect Group, [and] be in the prophecy class even though it is on Zoom…. Be present.*

I *was* present, and it was a beautiful day.

I will greatly rejoice in the LORD; my soul shall exult in my God…
Isaiah 61:10a

10
A few days later, I felt I heard these words.

Bold, Bodacious and Beautiful

> *Be <u>here now</u>—not in Arizona, even in your mind. Be here now with <u>me</u>.*

These words were what I needed to hear because I was still thinking about going to Arizona in the summer. How long would I be there? A few weeks? A month? All summer? What would I do with my apartment? I had almost a month before school ended, and I needed to be fully present.

I finally had an in-person doctor's appointment with my doctor. I hadn't been anywhere other than the park and Urgent Care since getting sick two months earlier, and it felt strange to be going somewhere. Anywhere. I hadn't worn anything other than jeans or leggings and sneakers or used mascara in all that time. (I was extremely grateful for the haircut I had gotten the week before my sister's visit.)

These were some of the words that came to me.

> *I will give your doctor uncommon wisdom and insight—as you asked. Rest in me. I will see you safely there and back. Do not worry about the taxi…. I wish [for] you to have the comfort of your doctor's care in person.*

It was good to see my doctor, but she didn't find any reasons why several of the Covid symptoms suddenly appeared whenever I became tired, and they all disappeared just as quickly after I rested for twenty or thirty minutes. For instance, I had trouble breathing, headaches, a "pain behind the eyes" sick

Bold, Bodacious and Beautiful

feeling, brain fog and a sore throat if I didn't rest twice per day.

However, she suggested I push myself on my walks and aim to take two per day. She even suggested that I walk home from her office through the park. I hadn't walked that far since before getting sick, but she said to rest on a park bench if I got tired.

It was a beautiful day, and the joy of spring in New York City was tempered by a slight feeling of gloom as I walked up a nearly empty Fifth Avenue and past the deserted Metropolitan Museum of Art. Typically, hundreds of people would be sitting on the stairs, buying hot dogs, getting in and out of taxis and buses and browsing through the prints and other art being sold. The fountains would be bubbling, and I would hear multiple languages being spoken. Today, one lone person sat on the steps.

Central Park was more populated, and I felt cheered as I walked in the sunshine along its familiar paths. Gardeners were out in force cutting the grass, and parents walked their sleeping infants in strollers. I was able to walk for more than an hour all the way home surrounded by the smells of blooming flowers and cut grass. It was heaven.

> ...the tongue of the wise brings healing.
> Proverbs 12:18

Bold, Bodacious and Beautiful

11

A few days later, I took two hour-long walks, and I felt God say,

See how much stronger you are?... Enjoy these days…. Enjoy every moment, my love.

The next day I wrote in my journal, "I feel lost and anxious, Lord. Should I stay [in New York City] or go? Where should I be?...."

This is what I felt I heard….

The future is very uncertain to you, but not to me. Trust me with what's to come, and I will guide you. Listen to my still small voice….

I began watching a miracles and healing conference on Zoom that was hosted by IAHM, a healing ministry based in Switzerland. Many people spoke about God's miraculous power healing them, but one story stood out to me. It was about two sisters, both of whom were unable to walk, and they spent most of their time in wheelchairs. When someone prayed for healing for each of them, one girl got up and was able to stand. Eventually she was able to take a step, and later she was able to walk. It happened over time. When asked why she was able to walk, she answered, "You need to stand up on the inside before standing on the outside." It was such a simple, yet profound and thought provoking answer. I wondered if you need to <u>see</u> yourself as healed before you are actually healed? Or perhaps sometimes you

Bold, Bodacious and Beautiful

need to be healed on the inside before physical healing occurs? It was a lot of food for thought.

Later that day, I was able to vacuum and dust my apartment. It had been five or six weeks since I had cleaned, and my place, especially the floors, had stayed incredibly clean during that time.

The next day, I felt sick, and I even wondered if I had Covid again. This is what I felt I heard.

You have forgotten what I said. How easily you forget my love and promises to you. Remind yourself of them often….

It was true. I wasn't in the habit of reminding myself of God's promises, but I wanted to be.

3Blessed be the God and Father of our Lord Jesus Christ, the Father of mercies and God of all comfort, 4who comforts us in all our affliction, so that we may be able to comfort those who are in any affliction, with the comfort with which we ourselves are comforted by God.
2 Corinthians 1:3, 4

***

12

On May 24th, these words came to me.

"Be Thou My Vision" was written at a time of great darkness—when there was no vision. It was and is a plea for clear sight, direction and insight. A plea for

333

Bold, Bodacious and Beautiful

> *stamina, courage and love. It was and is a prayer for hope, a prayer to go on and not give up. It is your prayer in this season… I have heard it, and I will answer.*

"Be Thou My Vision" *was* my ongoing prayer, and I hadn't even realized it.

> *Go to Arizona for a season—maybe a longer season than you think. I will bring someone to stay in your apartment, and it will be a great gift to them. And to you. You will rest easy knowing they are there.*

A longer season? What did that mean? Longer than the summer? How could I impose on my sister and her husband's hospitality for even a month, much less longer?

> *Your time with your family will be a blessing beyond belief. Bring some fall clothes and maybe even a coat. Bring your laptops—both of them and all the cords, etc. Bring [the book to read to your class at the beginning of the year]. Bring your brown hiking boots; you can use them in Arizona, and also when you return, if it is cold. You won't forget New York City. You will come back, just not when you think.*

My heart was pounding. Was it fear? Anticipation? Anxiety? Relief? Maybe it was a combination of all of those emotions.

> *Bring:*
> - bathing suits
> - hiking boots

334

Bold, Bodacious and Beautiful

- sweatshirts
- leggings– all of them
- jeans
- t-shirts
- laptops, [and the book to read to my students]
- sneakers, flip-flops, Tevas
- your black dress– [for your nephew's] wedding
- coat– down coat
- Bible study books and Catherine Martin's books

> *I will give you great joy and continued rest in this season. Go after school ends if you wish—a one-way ticket. Pray about all of this with [someone from] The Ark. You will always be split. Part of your heart lies here and part in Arizona. Embrace Arizona for now, and get close to your family. Meet with your nephews and their partners. Embrace them all, and sow into them. Bring each of them a book…. [Your sister] will have the things you need. She longs to share her clothes with you.*

I began to think about books that I could bring for each of my nephews and their partners.

> *You will do the professional development in Phoenix, and it will all work out. You will rest, swim, hike, nap and play with baby dogs and people.*

Bold, Bodacious and Beautiful

God was answering my questions, even before
I had a chance to be fully cognizant of them.

> *Your body is developing antibodies…. Continue to*
> *walk and nap. I will be with you in the bus, taxi and*
> *plane. You can do all this…. You will see how each*
> *detail falls into place. I am a God of "the big picture"*
> *and small details. "God's got this" as [a leader of*
> *The Ark] likes to say….*

What if my phone died? It didn't, but I did
end up getting a new one, and I was able to activate it
without any help from the phone company which felt
like a miracle. I ended up paying my rent and other
bills online which was easy, and I had my mail
forwarded through August.

> *Enjoy the day and the sunshine, my daughter. Don't*
> *give way to worry. Worry has no place in your life.*
> *Enjoy reading the work of your students. I will give*
> *you eyes to see—truly see—how they are doing. I will*
> *also give you narratives for their reports.*

I looked at the list of items I believed God
had told me to bring. Most of them were for the fall
or winter, and it would be over one-hundred degrees
for months in Arizona. My hiking boots were also
snow boots. When would I need *them*? The list made
very little sense to me. I had bought the black dress
for my nephew's spring wedding that was now
rescheduled to October. Would I be in Arizona for
that long? October was still relatively warm, so when
would I need the down coat? Also, I had three weeks

Bold, Bodacious and Beautiful

to find someone to stay in my apartment, but the few people I asked were not interested, at least for the price of my rent. Part of me trusted God and the words that I felt were from him, but another part of me did not.

> Seek the LORD and his strength; seek his presence continually!
> 1 Chronicles 16:11

***

13

Our last prophetic class met on Memorial Day weekend via Zoom. Normally, a class would never be held on that weekend because so many people would be out of town, but this year everyone was staying at home. During the final part of the session, we broke into small groups and spoke words of encouragement or "prophesied" over each other. This meant someone volunteered to be the "receiver." The rest of the group shared words, scripture or visual images they felt were from God regarding that person. It was challenging to be on the receiving end as well as the "giving" end of this exercise. When it was my turn, many encouraging things were said, and someone spoke this Bible passage over me:

> Don't be pulled in different directions or worried about a thing. Be saturated in prayer throughout each day, offering your faith-filled

Bold, Bodacious and Beautiful

requests before God with overflowing
gratitude. Tell him every detail of your life,
then God's wonderful peace that transcends
human understanding, will guard your heart
and mind through Jesus Christ.
Philippians 4:6, 7 (The Passion Translation)

How perfect was that verse? I thought to myself.
Later, these words came to me.
See how many gifts you've been given in this season?
The prophecies, the food and gifts, calls and texts,
cards and emails?... So much love….

It was true. I had received more love in this
solitary season than I had in my entire lifetime. I
wondered if the love was there all along, but I had
not been able to see it or accept it.

Go easy this week. Stop and rest often…. You are
getting reacquainted with your students [by reading
their work]: the ones who openly love and express, the
ones that hide, and the ones who are bored and lost.
Love and accept them all….

Loving my students was not difficult to do. I
missed them and felt cheated that I was not able to
spend these final weeks with them. This group of
students was so completely loveable.

You shall go away, but I will bring you back, and you
will be happy to be back—even to the chaos. Get up
early in Arizona, and stay connected with your New

338

Bold, Bodacious and Beautiful

> *York people at this time. Yes—even [your therapy] group. You will need them, and <u>they will need you</u>.*

I had been contemplating ending therapy, but now I felt I would most likely need the support of my group members, especially if I ended up staying in Arizona for a while.

> *Remember, this is your week of rest. If you rest well you will actually accomplish more.*

And he said, "My presence will go with you, and I will give you rest."
Exodus 33:14

14

On Memorial Day, I met virtually with a member of The Ark for prayer, specifically for direction regarding my trip to Arizona. The person I prayed with asked God to show me three confirmations that I should go to Arizona. This idea of asking for confirmation resonated with me. I also read my students' work and posted Progress Notices (notes to parents) for them all. Then I got a sore throat and rested.

I didn't listen to the news, but the following day I learned that George Floyd had been killed. I was disgusted and filled with dread and anger when I saw the film footage, as were many other people. Multiple protests broke out throughout the city each day after that.

Bold, Bodacious and Beautiful

During the final week of May, a palpable feeling of unrest permeated New York City. The week passed quickly as I continued to catch up on student work, while taking the time to walk and rest.

These are some of the words that I felt came to me during that week.

You've hidden in the shadows away from the limelight…. Be a light for the nations…. Shine my light on and for others…. It only takes one.

A light for the nations? What did that mean? I still don't know the answer to that question as I write this book.

You prayed for your city, and I have heard….

I believed God heard my prayers, but I still felt gratified and slightly surprised to hear it.

…Begin the book that was written by your mom's friend…. She is excited to have you in her class. It could be a focus for your summer if you so wish it. Do you?

"Yes, Lord!" I wrote.

Good. I desire it for you, too…. See how powerful these times are? I speak clearly to you and guide you. Do not resist these times or attempt to sleep through them…. Use your time in Phoenix to assess the time in Phoenix. Get a feel for how it would feel to live there. This is another gift to you—another Selah moment, as it were…. Yesterday you had two confirmations—your [therapy] group and your cousins

Bold, Bodacious and Beautiful

all said, Go to Arizona. Remember when [two of your colleagues] said the same?...

I had my three confirmations within a day. I was also excited to begin a summer Bible study via Zoom called *A Woman's Walk in Grace: God's Pathway to Spiritual Growth* with Catherine Martin. The study overlapped with teaching for a few weeks, but my gut told me that I would need it as a spiritual anchor while I was in Phoenix. I did. Over the following years, the studies grew into a vibrant online community for which I was deeply grateful.

[20]Now to him who is able to do far more abundantly than all that we ask or think, according to the power at work within us... Ephesians 3:20

15

The words I heard continued that week. *Yes, your sister's and your relationship will be strengthened. When was the last time you spent more than two weeks together? Your sister has come through a difficult time, too. Even though she herself wasn't sick, she had to go through it all with you—your tears and labored breathing and fear. She has been with you every step of the way. Every step. She may need occasional space with her family and friends. Offer it to her, and give it to her without feeling left out or hurt.*

Bold, Bodacious and Beautiful

I hadn't thought much about the effect my ongoing sickness had and was continuing to have on my sister, and I felt a stab of guilt for having been so focused on myself and my situation. Of course she would need time with her friends without me.

> *Be open to joy in the midst of chaos and confusion. This will be a long and twisting season—not necessarily of Covid, but of chaos….*

I didn't like the sound of that.

> *Do not fear the unknown or the known…. You will see what this means in time. Time is a funny thing. We often want to rush it or slow it down. Just be still and know that I am God [Psalm 46:10].... Enjoy time: time with family, time with people, time with love —surrounded by love…. Don't be afraid to ask for time. Use it, and pursue them.*

Since receiving these words from God, my understanding of time has changed as I continue to spend time with him. For instance, as I write I feel compelled to work on this book even though I had a very busy day, and I am tired. I asked God to expand the hour that I decided to dedicate to the book, and I feel he did. I accomplished much in a very short amount of time. This has happened quite often, especially as I settle into a new home, city and job.

Later that same day, I felt these words come to me.

> *Yes, you may purchase a one-way ticket to Phoenix. Do you trust me?*

Bold, Bodacious and Beautiful

"Yes, but I want to trust you more," I responded. Nonetheless, I purchased a one way ticket to Arizona, and I would fly out on the day after school ended.

> *Trust me, my daughter. Use these last two weeks well. I know you want [a certain person] to stay at your place, but perhaps I have someone else…. Pray for creative solutions, and see what I your Lord will do. Amen.*

My times are in your hand…
Psalm 31:15a

***

16

On the last Friday of May, I finally conducted the second half of my parent teacher conferences, and these were the words I felt I heard.

> *Today smile, answer with a soft word, speak kindness and love. This is a difficult season…. You do not know the personal and financial difficulties families are going through….*

It was wonderful to see the parents and thank them for their love and outpouring of their support. I looked forward to seeing my students on Monday for the first time in several weeks. The substitute teacher would continue to stay on, which was a godsend. She and my preceptor had already set up a chart that

Bold, Bodacious and Beautiful

meticulously tracked each student's progress on every step of the final Pilgrim research project. Their continued assistance enabled me to catch up on student placement for the following year, report writing and the list of additional tasks to wrap up the year.

I was leaving in two weeks, and no one I had spoken to was interested in subletting my apartment, so I prayed asking God if I should advertise. Many people seemed to be leaving the city, and more than half of the apartments in my own building were now empty. This is what I felt was the response.

....You have an idea of what you should do, and I have another. Take my hand and let me lead you....

I wasn't sure I could fully trust God's idea of what I should do. Didn't I need to wrap up everything *now?*

...Do you really want to return before the end of the summer? Yes, you will most likely choose to stay longer. Be aware of this as you pack, dear one. Don't pack too many clothes. Your sister has them all.... Yes, bring your down coat. Get it out now so you don't forget.... What do you have that you can use for school [next year]?... Bring them for peace of mind.

The thought of packing for next year terrified me. What if something went wrong in my apartment? How would I know how to teach from so far away? When would I be returning to New York City? What if my sister and her husband got sick of me staying

344

Bold, Bodacious and Beautiful

with them? Where would I go? My list of worries was long.

> [31]Therefore do not be anxious, saying, 'What shall we eat?' or 'What shall we drink?' or 'What shall we wear?' [32]For the Gentiles seek after all these things, and your heavenly Father knows that you need them all. [33]But seek first the kingdom of God and his righteousness, and all these things will be added to you.
> Matthew 6:31-33

***

17

The last day of May was Pentecost in the liturgical church calendar. In the yearly church celebrations, which are also called feasts, Jesus' death is observed on Good Friday, his resurrection is celebrated on Easter and his ascension into heaven is commemorated on Ascension Day. Pentecost is celebrated fifty days later as the time when the Spirit of Jesus, also called The Holy Spirit, descended upon the disciples and members of the early church with the sound of a mighty rushing wind. Small tongues of fire appeared over them, and they were supernaturally able to speak in other languages, or tongues. People from different countries who were visiting Jerusalem heard what was happening and rushed to the scene. They were surprised to hear Jewish people speaking to them in their native

Bold, Bodacious and Beautiful

languages. The story can be found in the Bible in Acts chapter 2 as well as at the back of this book.

On this day, I was writing my reports in one application and pasting them into another when they suddenly disappeared. I couldn't figure out how to get them back. I could feel myself begin to sweat and panic, and I prayed that God would help me to figure out where they were. A bit later I recovered them, and I felt incredibly relieved and grateful.

These are the words I felt I heard early that morning of Pentecost.

> *I have been with you during the season of loneliness— but you were <u>not</u> alone, through the season of sickness —but you did not go to the hospital as you asked [not to, and] through the season of fear—but I was your peace and protection.*

It was true. I had been terrified of going to the hospital, and I never had to. I hadn't realized it or thanked God for that blessing, but I did now. I had felt his peace and protection, and I thanked him for that, too.

> *Now you stand—we stand—at the threshold of the new season…. You [imagine] it one way, but it will not be that way. Just like this last season was both longer, lonelier and sweeter than you ever imagined, so the new season will be different…. Be open to doing things you've never done before. Be the strong resilient woman I've made you to be….*

Bold, Bodacious and Beautiful

As I read these words now, images of driving and taking care of a car, navigating a city that has changed in many ways since the 1970s, moving across the country and beginning a new job in my late 50s all come to mind. The next season was like the previous one in some ways, both sweeter and more joyful and more terrifying than I could have imagined.

> *Do not lose touch with your New York City connections.... Do you not realize what a gift that is?*

Sometimes it is difficult to realize what you have without the gift of hindsight. Now I can see what a deep and lasting gift my many Zoom calls with friends and my therapy group were, but at the time, the Zoom calls were exhausting. I was surprised how quickly I became bored and tired while working on my computer for hours on end. Being with friends on Zoom calls began to feel like work, yet at the same time it was my only connection with those I loved.

> *Let your substitute [teacher] do the heavy lifting. Work on your reports each day and <u>rest</u>. <u>Rest</u>. <u>Rest</u>. Walk in the park, too, and say your goodbyes to it. It has been a friend of sorts to you: a daily adventure [and] a source of unexpected gifts and surprises. Say goodbye for now.*

18

Central Park had been my place of joy and rest and exercise for many years, but walking by myself through it day after day during this season had been both a blessing and a source of pain. Now that

Bold, Bodacious and Beautiful

the weather was warmer, families and groups of people were enjoying being together in the sunshine. Seeing so many people together intensified my loneliness. Where were my friends? Why did they all seem to live so far away? At this time, New Yorkers avoided subways and buses and other forms of public transportation if they could. Why hadn't I cultivated and sustained more friendships in my neighborhood?

> *Turn your eyes and heart to your family, to heat and sunshine, to frustration, at times, and uncertainty, to Phoenix and old friends. Turn your heart to me. But keep your Connect [Group] and [therapy] group and [online church] on Sundays….*

Later, all of these groups helped me feel connected to my home and community during the months in Arizona.

> *Now [for] the last things: ending the school year, reports, packing and a tenant in your apartment. Seek out prayer with The Ark, and see what I will do.*

I decided I would pray with someone from the Ark, and later that morning, I felt the words continue.

> *Do not fear that you feel ill…. Rebuke worry in the name of Jesus Christ. Rebuke it and rest today and see what I will do. Keep your eyes on me and only me, my daughter. Not your plans and not your list or anyone else's list.*

Bold, Bodacious and Beautiful

My two weeks of rest had come to an end, and while I was excited to see my students, I was trepidatious about tackling the pile of work that was awaiting me.

> [6]So we are always of good courage. We know that while we are at home in the body we are away from the Lord, [7]for we walk by faith, not by sight.
> 2 Corinthians 5:6,7

***

19

The first day of teaching was filled with the joy of seeing my sweet students again on Zoom. I also met with the head of the middle school, wrote three reports and [virtually] prayed with someone from The Ark about my upcoming trip. The person I prayed with said he heard three words when he prayed for me: divine, reconciliation and stretched (in a good way). I didn't really want to be stretched (in any way) in Arizona, but I liked the first two words. I didn't feel well that day, and I rested several times.

At 3:00 AM the next morning, I felt I heard these words.

> *Yes, I have carried you through a season that felt long. It was long, and it was the blink of an eye…. You've asked what I had for you in this season. You know some of it, but it will only be years from now when*

Bold, Bodacious and Beautiful

you see the full fruit of the season. You will understand in time. Trust me, Gini....

I still wonder what "the full fruit of the season" is, but I have a sense that I will know in time. Later that morning, I felt the words continue.

"Yes, the world is unraveling around the edges. Indeed, at times, it is torn to shreds, but I hold you in the palm of my hand. I am allowing you to escape some travail, but you always trade it for something else— maybe a lighter burden. Only Paradise—Heaven—is free from pain.

It did feel like the world was unraveling, at least the world I was experiencing. New York was shrouded in fear, and it felt strange to walk around my city that had always felt so vibrant and exciting, but now felt empty, lonely and shut down, except for the daily marches.

Hold my hand as we walk through the day together.... Pray for [your sister's friend who has cancer] and for Heidi Baker [a well-known missionary in Mozambique]....

The angel of the LORD encamps around those who fear him, and delivers them. Psalm 34:7

***

Bold, Bodacious and Beautiful

18

The next day, my students and I talked about the racial unrest in the city. I happened to be reading Mark 4:26-32 that morning, and I used the metaphor of seeds in our discussion. I could plant an oak seed that would grow into a mighty tree that would be a haven for birds and animals, or I could plant a poison ivy seed that would cause pain to people who touch it. If I plant seeds of hate and violence, that is what will grow. But if I plant seeds of love and kindness, then kindness and love will grow. Many of my students expressed what they were feeling, and their voices echoed the divided views of their parents and, indeed, the country.

In our Connect Group we were also divided on our views of the police versus the protestors. One member's brother was a policeman and another member's people had been hurt by the police. Everyone seemed to have passionate viewpoints, including me, and I worried that our small group would fracture into an even smaller group. I had to rest multiple times during that day, but I felt well, overall.

These were the words that came to me early that morning at 3:00 AM.

> *Yes. Yes. Yes. Keep praying for my spirit to come down on New York City. Keep praying. Keep praying. Keep praying. Come Holy Spirit, come. Come upon this city. Pour out on the city. Fill the empty hurting places in this city. Heal the hurt, sickness and anger. Heal the divide between man and God, between white*

Bold, Bodacious and Beautiful

> *[people] and [people of] color, between poor and rich, between educated and uneducated, between blue-collar and white-collar, between old and young, between male and female, between Godly and ungodly, between Democrat and Republican, between all people, animals, the earth and heaven. Heal it all. Fill them all. Cover them all. Uphold it all. Come Holy Spirit, come. Come. Come. Amen. Amen. Amen.*

I wasn't sure if these words were my words or words from God, but I sensed they were both.

Later, these were additional words I felt I heard from God.

> *Step over and through offense. Lay it at the door and come to me. Come together. Pray for the healing of your country. Your country that was founded on fine principles, but not on love—my love—for all people, everyone.*

And walk in love, as Christ loved us and gave himself up for us, a fragrant offering and sacrifice to God.
Ephesians 5:2

***

20

A few days later, this is some of what I felt I heard.

> *Chaos has begun to reign, and this is only the beginning. Do not fear the chaos. It is a smokescreen. A diversion. You see the chaos—but only see me…*

Bold, Bodacious and Beautiful

8Then shall your light break forth like the dawn, and your healing shall spring up speedily; your righteousness shall go before you; the glory of the LORD shall be your rear guard. 9Then you shall call, and the LORD will answer; you shall cry, and he will say, "Here I am." If you take away the yoke from your midst, the pointing of the finger, and speaking wickedness, 10if you pour yourself out for the hungry and satisfy the desire of the afflicted, then shall your light rise in the darkness and your gloom be as the noonday. 11And the LORD will guide you continually and satisfy your desire in scorched places and make your bones strong; and you shall be like a watered garden, like a spring of water, whose waters do not fail.
Isaiah 58:8-11

***

21

My church was part of a group of local churches who were sponsoring a peaceful protest in Harlem called the "March For Souls and Bodies." I wanted to be a part of it, but I also knew my physical limitations.

These are some of the words I heard the day before and the day of the march.

Go to the march if you feel well.... Consider the cost —carefully.... Go to the beginning [the rally], and

Bold, Bodacious and Beautiful

> *then walk home. You will be tempted to march,*
> *though. Spend lots of the day in rest and [in]*
> *preparation for your trip....*

When I climbed on the city bus that would take me to the rallying point in Harlem, it was the first time I had been on public transportation in a long time. The available seats were all taken, and several people were standing in the aisles. It felt strange to be in such close proximity to people after having diligently maintained a six-foot distance.

It was a sunny, hot and humid day. When I arrived, I met up with my Connect Group co-leader along with her husband and daughter. I can't express the joy I felt when I saw her in person. Everyone had been asked to wear a mask, and as far as I could see, the crowd had complied.

After the rally, I was tempted to march for a while, so I did. As the large crowd moved down the blocked off streets, people looked out of their windows and many waved at us. We stopped at two different points where church leaders spoke and we even sang a song. It felt exhilarating. Then all of the sudden I knew I had reached my physical limit and had to go home immediately. Thankfully, a cab came along a side street, and it felt like a miracle. When I got home, I was sticky and sweaty and completely spent, but also very grateful to have been able to participate in a march with my friend and her family before leaving New York City.

Bold, Bodacious and Beautiful

> He has told you, O man, what is good; and
> what does the LORD require of you but to
> do justice, and to love kindness, and to walk
> humbly with your God?
> Micah 6:8

22

It was the Sunday before my last week of school, and my final week in New York City for I didn't know how long. During Zoom church, my pastor interviewed Dr. Anita Phillips. She spoke with wisdom and forthrightness. Later, I looked her up and listened to "Body Language: A Conversation on Race with Christine Caine and Dr. Anita Phillips." The entire conversation resonated with me, especially when she described a "trauma informed approach." Dr. Phillips stated, "Black Americans as a group have been traumatized in a specific, systematic way." A trauma informed response for white people would include: 1. Asking what happened to them, 2. Trusting and empowering the voice of the wounded, 3. Creating safe spaces and relationships and, 4. Practicing cultural humility. She went on to add that action was the love language of Black folks. There was much more to this conversation, and it gave me a lot of food for thought.

As I thought back on past heated conversations with my friends and colleagues of color I recalled feeling extremely anxious and uncomfortable when I was faced with their anger. I realized I would have to be able to sit with the

Bold, Bodacious and Beautiful

discomfort I felt before I even came close to creating safe spaces, much less cultivate relationships. I thought I practiced cultural humility, but I had no idea if that was true or if I was deluding myself, and I was too afraid to ask.

Along with being worried about the state of my city and country, I had other smaller problems to contend with. Namely, I still had not found anyone to stay in my apartment, and I wondered why God had said he would provide someone when it looked like it wouldn't happen. I also fretted that I had not been present enough for my students since getting sick. I loved my class, and I felt the loss of not having spent the final weeks of spring with them.

Then there was the mountain of work that awaited me. I had finished my report drafts as well as notes on each student. My first week back had been a good one, and I had rested at least twice each day. I was grateful to the administration for their ongoing support and for keeping the sub on. I was also immensely thankful for the tireless work of my preceptor. Additionally, the parents of my students continued to send daily meals and groceries which was an ongoing blessing.

Thankfully, the Covid numbers and deaths were declining in New York, but they were rising in Arizona. *I'm traveling from one hotbed to another,* I thought to myself. These were the words that came to me that day.

> *You have been lavishly loved in this season even though you have been physically alone…. Feel all the love I*

Bold, Bodacious and Beautiful

send your way. Take it in. I will give you blessed and anointed ideas for next week's ending. It will be enough. It will be enough. Be my love this week, this summer, this decade....

A new commandment I give to you, that you love one another: just as I have loved you, you also are to love one another.
John 13:34

***

23

The following Monday, morning classes were canceled so we could continue our class discussion regarding the events that were taking place in the city. We talked about the power of protest: Why do people protest and how can it affect change? We also looked at several young people who had made a powerful impact on their communities and the world, including Kelvin Doe, Marley Dias, Emma Gonzales and Malala Yousafzai.

That morning, these are some of the words I felt I heard.

Do not fear. See how "un-fearful" you have become? See how the march helped?

And the words continued the next morning at 2:25 AM.

It was wise of you to turn on your light and write my words. Yes, a part of you still wonders if they are __my__

Bold, Bodacious and Beautiful

words. They are. Do not listen to the whispers of the evil one. Maybe you don't really wonder. Maybe you are learning to discern the evil whispers from your own inner voice. You have confused them for a long time, but learn to discern [between] the two.

It was true. I was learning to discern between the voice of the evil one and my own voice. I had always thought they were my voice, but now I was beginning to detect the negative and condemning thoughts that came *to* me. I had always accepted them as my own, but I was beginning to reject them and counter them with the promises of God that I found in the Bible. For instance, when I was fearful I often countered (and still do) the fear with two verses.

For God has not given us a spirit of fear, but of power and of love and of a sound mind. 2 Timothy 1:7 (New King James Version)

I can do all things through Christ who strengthens me. Philippians 4:13 (New King James Version)

***

24

That final week of school was a blur. One family sent me a huge dinner from their favorite Indian restaurant. It was enough delicious food for an entire family, and I was able to share it with my neighbor.

Bold, Bodacious and Beautiful

My friend and colleague who had sent me a meal from 5 Napkin Burger every week since I became sick, sent me my last turkey burger with Swiss cheese along with sweet potato fries and a large green salad. She told me that the staff at 5 Napkin Burger often asked about me when she called in her orders. They also asked if we would come in when all of this was over. I can't begin to express how the kindness of these and so many other people blessed me. My heart (and my stomach) were full.

I took all of my plants down to the lobby and hoped people would take them. They had been the only living things in my apartment for all these weeks, and they had brought me joy as I worked and recovered. I felt a pang of sadness, but thankfully, a few of my neighbors did take some of the plants.

The next day these were some of the words I heard very early in the morning.

> *You did well to research Christopher Emdin… [who would be our keynote speaker during the two weeks of professional development after school ended]…. Continue being open….Be gentle. Be patient. Don't try to have all the answers. Breathe and learn.*

Later that morning, they continued.
> *I will see you safely to and from Arizona. Cherish each moment there—even the ones that are difficult or unexpected. Find joy every day.*

I was learning that I could choose joy much of the time, and joy often arrived hand in hand with

Bold, Bodacious and Beautiful

gratefulness. I could choose to be grateful for small things: a hot bath, sunshine, spring flowers, a turkey burger with Swiss, a text from a friend. There were so many things to be grateful for, and I experienced deep joy in the midst of loneliness, frustration and exhaustion.

> And the ransomed of the LORD shall return and come to Zion with singing; everlasting joy shall be upon their heads; they shall obtain gladness and joy, and sorrow and sighing shall flee away.
> Isaiah 51:11

> With two more days left in New York City, I felt I heard these words at 2:00 AM.
> *Stay the course. Laugh. Love. Cry. Stay in me.... Speak your truth—but focus on mine. My truth. My words. Put my words in you. Seek out other like-minded people—and those who don't know me. You will make connections.*

I realized my truth was flawed, opinionated and narrow, but God's truth was perfect, inclusive and expansive. I desired his truth to be my truth.

> *Get excited about your trip. I am giving you the gift of joy, of family, of companionship and love, of relaxation and sun and water. Your sister is creating a vacation resort-like time and space for you....*

Bold, Bodacious and Beautiful

I felt such a mix of emotions: complete excitement and relief to finally be in Arizona with my family, worry about my apartment that still had no tenant, and sorrow to be leaving my city and friends. However, I hadn't really seen most of my friends in months, so it made leaving somewhat easier. And underneath all of that was a deep sense of fear. Fear for my city and the people who lived there. What would become of it and them? I also felt fear for myself and my future. How long would I be gone and would I come back? Then there was the fear for the world. What would be the long-term effects on all of us, and especially the children, at the end of the Covid pandemic?

[10]"For the mountains may depart and the hills be removed, but my steadfast love shall not depart from you, and my covenant of peace shall not be removed," says the LORD, who has compassion on you. [11]"O afflicted one, storm-tossed and not comforted, behold, I will set your stones in antimony, and lay your foundations with sapphires."
Isaiah 54:10-11

***

26

On the last day of school, a friend sent me three small chocolate croissants. It was such a kind gesture, and I felt joy as I ate them. However, saying goodbye to my students and their parents over Zoom was

Bold, Bodacious and Beautiful

surreal. I felt a deep sense of regret when I thought about the time I had missed with them. It had been three months since I had seen them in person.

These are the words that I felt came to me that day.

> *Smile. Rejoice! The year is done. Listen, and I will give you inspired ideas for the fall….*

I couldn't believe it. The year was finished. It had seemed like a lifetime in some ways and a brief wisp of smoke in others. I couldn't begin to fathom what the summer would be like, much less the coming fall. But for now, I set my sights on summer with my sister and the rest of my family.

And later, at 10:20 PM, I felt I heard these additional words.

> *...This trip is ordained by me, and it is my will [that] you go to Arizona now. You will see why in time. Indeed, there are many reasons. Many. Enjoy every moment of being out and about tomorrow [at the airport]. It's been a long time. Enjoy it all, even the plane ride. I ride with you.*

I had forgotten how to put on mascara, much less how to navigate a trip across the country. What would the airport be like? The flight?

> *See how you were blessed, healed and ministered to this evening? [You watched] Dr. Anita Phillips, Vous Conference and Mike Todd [online]—not to mention a delicious Greek dinner with plenty to spare [for tomorrow's trip]. Enjoy your rest now and your*

362

Bold, Bodacious and Beautiful

morning with me. Many are thinking of you and praying for you.

I hadn't considered that many people were praying for me, and the thought comforted me.

See how [your colleagues] called [out] to you after the [final faculty Zoom] meeting? See how well others love you? Now, you do the same.

At the end of our final staff meeting, before I logged off, several of my friends and colleagues shouted a hello to me. I was surprised and deeply blessed by the love I felt from them, and I desired to do the same for others. I hoped I would be able to show love to others in the same ways in which I had been loved.

> In this is love, not that we have loved God but that he loved us and sent his Son to be the propitiation for our sins.
> 1 John 4:10

27

I was packed and ready to leave. I hadn't found anyone who was willing or able to stay in my apartment and pay my rent. Although I was disappointed, I hadn't given up hope.

I felt I heard these words at 5:00 AM the next morning

Bold, Bodacious and Beautiful

...You think you are slipping out of the city unnoticed, but see the texts you got from your friends? They all care deeply for and about you....

Each text blessed me more than I could say, and once again I felt surprised.

Now move into the next level of your life. Hang on, Gini, the ride is going to be rough at times, fast and breathless, scary at times and restful at times....

The words thrilled and terrified me.

Open your heart up to love and laughter and joy. You have been in a solitary season—but no longer.... Your time with me will be just as sweet [in Arizona], my love. Let my love fill your heart.... Close your apartment, and say goodbye to New York City.

Finally, brothers [and sisters], rejoice. Aim for restoration, comfort one another, agree with one another, live in peace; and the God of love and peace will be with you.
2 Corinthians 13:11

***

28

Later, at 8:00 AM, these are the final words I felt I heard before leaving for the airport.

Yes, let my joy fill you. My joy is your strength. You have been weak, partly because you haven't been full of joy! There has been deep sadness, loneliness, fear

Bold, Bodacious and Beautiful

> *and yet <u>peace</u> in this season with moments of joy. But this next season will be <u>full</u> of joy…. Enjoy your day, every moment of it. Amen. Amen. Amen.*

As I stared out the window of the taxi at the North end of Central Park and the people who were going about their days, I remember thinking to myself that almost everyone was wearing a mask. (I didn't realize I was going to a place where almost no one wore a mask.) I also had no idea that this was the first step in a year-long moving process. At that moment, I was focused on getting to JFK Airport and wondering if my suitcase would be too heavy. (It was.) I enjoyed wandering around the shops at JFK—it felt like a holiday. I hadn't been in a shop for months. The airport was much more crowded than I had anticipated. It felt so surreal, and I had no idea how much my life was about change.

It wasn't until much later that I realized how much I had learned during that season of solitude. I had learned to be content with being physically alone while discovering I was not spiritually alone. I experienced the difference between loneliness and solitude. Solitude is a gift while loneliness felt like a knife to the heart, but God's presence walked with me through both. I now know God is enough. Truly enough. God is faithful. He is my provider, my peace, my joy and strength and my companion. He sticks closer than a brother. He is also my friend, father and spouse while at the same time being the God of the Universe as well as the God of time. The God of my

Bold, Bodacious and Beautiful

times. The realization that love is something I do first and then perhaps the feelings will come, also took root in me. Throughout those early days of Covid, I experienced the joy and relief of saying yes to gifts that were offered by my friends and colleagues as well as people I barely knew, and it felt wonderful. I felt wonderfully, blissfully blessed. Additionally, it dawned on me that I was not the "old dinosaur" I thought I was, and I was fully capable of learning the technology and everything else I needed to know in order to teach remotely. I have a feeling as the years go by, I will discover more lessons and ways of seeing God that I was completely unaware of learning at the time, but were nonetheless internalized. But for now this is what I know.

> [10]He found him in a desert land, and in the howling waste of the wilderness; he encircled him, he cared for him, he kept him as the apple of his eye. [11]Like an eagle that stirs up its nest, that flutters over its young, spreading out its wings, catching them, bearing them on its pinions, [12]the LORD alone guided him, no foreign god was with him.
> Deuteronomy 32:10-12

EPILOGUE

I never would have dreamed that I would end up spending nine months in Arizona, but that is what happened. In September, my neighbor's boyfriend needed a place to live, so he moved into my apartment for several months. It was both a blessing and a weight off my mind knowing that someone was taking care of my home, especially when wiring had to be replaced, the Wi-Fi updated and the toilet fixed (again). In spite of the repairs, he seemed to enjoy it.

In the fall, I met my new class of fourth graders on Zoom, and together we became "Noble House." Early each morning, I walked out into the pitch-black backyard and into my sister's casita where I taught. I often stopped to take a moment to look up at the stars and the moon (if it was visible) and they would remind me of God's magnificent providence in this strange season. I hoped my students and I would be able to make sense out of this new way of teaching and learning, and that the technology would work. I often felt like I was stepping off a cliff into the unknown, and in many ways, I was. But somehow, God always made a way. I was also deeply blessed and buoyed along by the generosity of my fourth grade team, my fabulous IT colleague who brought complicated ideas to life, and so many other wonderful colleagues. The generosity, kindness and

Bold, Bodacious and Beautiful

companionship of my sister and brother in law were gifts beyond measure. Their home was an oasis during those months, and I treasure the memories of walking the dogs in the desert, drinking turmeric lattes at Well Coffee, and Christmas shopping at Costco with my sister for the entire family.

That winter, the school offered a buyout to all the veteran teachers, and it seemed to be a wide open door through which I stepped. The voluntary separation would take place the following year, and I would move to Arizona permanently, whatever "permanently" meant.

Incidentally, I wore my black dress to my nephew and soon-to-be niece's wedding that took place in the desert on a lovely warm October evening. I also enjoyed the warmth of my down coat and hiking boots several times, and I was especially glad to have them when we took a weekend trip to the Grand Canyon in February. Who would have known? Well, God did.

In April, the faculty was expected to return to New York City and the school building to conduct hybrid teaching for the final trimester. A fair number of teachers had been doing that all along, but due to the lingering Covid symptoms I experienced on a daily basis whenever I became tired, I had been given the option to teach remotely for the second trimester.

During that third trimester, my students were split between two classrooms with some students remaining online. Even with the support of two wonderful learning supervisors, I can safely say it was

Bold, Bodacious and Beautiful

the greatest challenge of my teaching career thus far, but also a blessing. I was thrilled to finally meet my sweet students in person. In many ways, April felt like September as I greeted the children who eagerly walked into both classrooms.

During those three months, I was finally able to see my Connect Group friends in person when we met for picnics in the park, as well as other dear friends as we enjoyed catching up over meals in the new outdoor enclosures that had appeared on the streets and sidewalks outside of restaurants while I was away. I also enjoyed the green lushness of Central Park on my walks to and from school, especially after my months in the desert, although I didn't see as much wildlife as I had during the previous spring.

I was able to spend time with the volunteers from The Ark Healing Rooms, and I dipped my "spiritual toe" into the waters of healing prayer. Another great blessing and privilege.

It was a busy, stressful, strange, and in many ways, wonderful way to say goodbye to my friends and to the city that I had called home for thirty-six years. I keenly felt the mix of mourning all the "lasts" while the excitement of a new chapter of my life bubbled up inside of me.

God continued to speak to me early each morning, and I had the sense he would speak as much as I made time to listen. I could never have gotten through planning a move across the country, the packing and heart-stabbing goodbyes without the deep sense that God was with me and guiding each step I took. I'm grateful to say I still feel that I hear from God, and as I write this book, I am beginning my eleventh journal of words I hear in the early mornings.

Writing this book was terrifying and more time consuming than I ever imagined, but I was grateful to have the opportunity to take a year off of teaching to do it. I cannot begin to express my gratitude to my sister and brother in law for their hospitality. And of course, I owe everything to God who took me by the hand and guided me through choosing which words to share as well as helping me to tell my story.

During my final three months in New York City, I gave away almost all of my furniture, and when I closed the lock on my U-box container, it felt strange to see what remained of my worldly possessions disappear down 106th Street en route to Arizona. I prayed I would see it all again, and I did.

> And let the beauty of the LORD our God be upon us, And establish the work of our hands for us; Yes, establish the work of our hands. Psalm 90:17 (New King James Version)

***

If you would like to live your life with Jesus and invite him into your life, you can pray a simple prayer along the lines of this one:

Bold, Bodacious and Beautiful

Lord Jesus, I need you. Thank you for dying on the cross for me. I believe you lived, you died and you rose again just for me. Forgive my sin of unbelief that caused me to be separated from you. I don't want to be separated from you. I repent from my old way of living. Today I give you my life. Make me the person you want me to be. I'm yours. Amen.

Congratulations on making the best decision of your life! I encourage you to begin to read the Bible every day. The book of John is a good place to begin. Talk to God daily, and remember he already knows you and loves you. Also, find a Bible believing church, and get to know some other believers who will encourage you in your new life in Christ. He loves you so much.

***

> Behold, I stand at the door and knock. If anyone hears my voice and opens the door, I will come in to him and eat with him, and he with me.
> Revelation 3:20

> [8]Though you have not seen him, you love him. Though you do not now see him, you believe in him and rejoice with joy that is inexpressible and filled with glory, [9]obtaining the outcome of your faith, the salvation of your souls.

Bold, Bodacious and Beautiful

1 Peter 1:8, 9

¹Let not your hearts be troubled. Believe in God; believe also in me. ²In my Father's house are many rooms. If it were not so, would I have told you that I go to prepare a place for you? ³And if I go and prepare a place for you, I will come again and will take you to myself, that where I am you may be also.
John 14:1-3

³Blessed be the God and Father of our Lord Jesus Christ! According to his great mercy, he has caused us to be born again to a living hope through the resurrection of Jesus Christ from the dead, ⁴to an inheritance that is imperishable, undefiled, and unfading, kept in heaven for you…
1 Peter 1:3-4

Bold, Bodacious and Beautiful

SCRIPTURE REFERENCES

(All passages are in the English Standard Version, unless otherwise specified.)

Introduction

1 Corinthians 14:1-4
Pursue love, and earnestly desire the spiritual gifts, especially that you may prophesy. 2For one who speaks in a tongue speaks not to men but to God; for no one understands him, but he utters mysteries in the Spirit. 3On the other hand, the one who prophesies speaks to people for their upbuilding and encouragement and consolation. 4The one who speaks in a tongue builds up himself, but the one who prophesies builds up the church.

John 1:14
And the Word became flesh and dwelt among us, and we have seen his glory, glory as of the only Son from the Father, full of grace and truth.

Luke 23

1Then the whole company of them arose and brought him before Pilate. 2And they began to accuse him, saying, "We found this man misleading our nation and forbidding us to give tribute to Caesar, and saying that he himself is Christ, a king." 3And Pilate

Bold, Bodacious and Beautiful

asked him, "Are you the King of the Jews?" And he answered him, "You have said so." 4Then Pilate said to the chief priests and the crowds, "I find no guilt in this man." 5But they were urgent, saying, "He stirs up the people, teaching throughout all Judea, from Galilee even to this place."

6When Pilate heard this, he asked whether the man was a Galilean. 7And when he learned that he belonged to Herod's jurisdiction, he sent him over to Herod, who was himself in Jerusalem at that time. 8When Herod saw Jesus, he was very glad, for he had long desired to see him, because he had heard about him, and he was hoping to see some sign done by him. 9So he questioned him at some length, but he made no answer. 10The chief priests and the scribes stood by, vehemently accusing him. 11And Herod with his soldiers treated him with contempt and mocked him. Then, arraying him in splendid clothing, he sent him back to Pilate. 12And Herod and Pilate became friends with each other that very day, for before this they had been at enmity with each other.

13Pilate then called together the chief priests and the rulers and the people, 14and said to them, "You brought me this man as one who was misleading the people. And after examining him before you, behold, I did not find this man guilty of any of your charges against him. 15Neither did Herod, for he sent him back to us. Look, nothing deserving death has been done by him. 16I will therefore punish and release him."

Bold, Bodacious and Beautiful

18But they all cried out together, "Away with this man, and release to us Barabbas"— 19a man who had been thrown into prison for an insurrection started in the city and for murder. 20Pilate addressed them once more, desiring to release Jesus, 21but they kept shouting, "Crucify, crucify him!" 22A third time he said to them, "Why? What evil has he done? I have found in him no guilt deserving death. I will therefore punish and release him." 23But they were urgent, demanding with loud cries that he should be crucified. And their voices prevailed. 24So Pilate decided that their demand should be granted. 25He released the man who had been thrown into prison for insurrection and murder, for whom they asked, but he delivered Jesus over to their will.

26And as they led him away, they seized one Simon of Cyrene, who was coming in from the country, and laid on him the cross, to carry it behind Jesus. 27And there followed him a great multitude of the people and of women who were mourning and lamenting for him. 28But turning to them Jesus said, "Daughters of Jerusalem, do not weep for me, but weep for yourselves and for your children. 29For behold, the days are coming when they will say, 'Blessed are the barren and the wombs that never bore and the breasts that never nursed!' 30Then they will begin to say to the mountains, 'Fall on us,' and to the hills, 'Cover us.' 31For if they do these things when the wood is green, what will happen when it is dry?"

Bold, Bodacious and Beautiful

32Two others, who were criminals, were led away to be put to death with him. 33And when they came to the place that is called The Skull, there they crucified him, and the criminals, one on his right and one on his left. 34And Jesus said, "Father, forgive them, for they know not what they do." And they cast lots to divide his garments. 35And the people stood by, watching, but the rulers scoffed at him, saying, "He saved others; let him save himself, if he is the Christ of God, his Chosen One!" 36The soldiers also mocked him, coming up and offering him sour wine 37and saying, "If you are the King of the Jews, save yourself!" 38There was also an inscription over him, "This is the King of the Jews."

39One of the criminals who were hanged railed at him, saying, "Are you not the Christ? Save yourself and us!" 40But the other rebuked him, saying, "Do you not fear God, since you are under the same sentence of condemnation? 41And we indeed justly, for we are receiving the due reward of our deeds; but this man has done nothing wrong." 42And he said, "Jesus, remember me when you come into your kingdom." 43And he said to him, "Truly, I say to you, today you will be with me in paradise."

44It was now about the sixth hour, and there was darkness over the whole land until the ninth hour, 45while the sun's light failed. And the curtain of the temple was torn in two. 46Then Jesus, calling out with a loud voice, said, "Father, into your hands I commit my spirit!" And having said this he breathed his last.

376

Bold, Bodacious and Beautiful

47Now when the centurion saw what had taken place, he praised God, saying, "Certainly this man was innocent!" 48And all the crowds that had assembled for this spectacle, when they saw what had taken place, returned home beating their breasts. 49And all his acquaintances and the women who had followed him from Galilee stood at a distance watching these things.

50Now there was a man named Joseph, from the Jewish town of Arimathea. He was a member of the council, a good and righteous man, 51who had not consented to their decision and action; and he was looking for the kingdom of God. 52This man went to Pilate and asked for the body of Jesus. 53Then he took it down and wrapped it in a linen shroud and laid him in a tomb cut in stone, where no one had ever yet been laid. 54It was the day of Preparation, and the Sabbath was beginning. 55The women who had come with him from Galilee followed and saw the tomb and how his body was laid. 56Then they returned and prepared spices and ointments.

On the Sabbath they rested according to the commandment.

Luke 24

1But on the first day of the week, at early dawn, they went to the tomb, taking the spices they had prepared. 2And they found the stone rolled away from the tomb, 3but when they went in they did not find the body of the Lord Jesus. 4While they were perplexed about this, behold, two men stood by them in dazzling apparel. 5And as they were frightened and bowed their faces to the ground, the men said to them, "Why do you seek the living among the dead? 6He is not here, but has risen. Remember how he told you, while he was still in Galilee, 7that the Son of Man must be delivered into the hands of sinful men and be crucified and on the third day rise." 8And they remembered his words, 9and returning from the tomb they told all these things to the eleven and to all the rest. 10Now it was Mary Magdalene and Joanna and Mary the mother of James and the other women with them who told these things to the apostles, 11but these words seemed to them an idle tale, and they did not believe them. 12But Peter rose and ran to the tomb; stooping and looking in, he saw the linen cloths by themselves; and he went home marveling at what had happened.

13That very day two of them were going to a village named Emmaus, about seven miles*a* from Jerusalem, 14and they were talking with each other about all these things that had happened. 15While they were talking and discussing together, Jesus himself drew near and went with them. 16But their eyes were kept from recognizing him. 17And he said to them, "What is this conversation that you are holding with each other as you walk?" And they stood still, looking sad. 18Then one of them, named Cleopas, answered

Bold, Bodacious and Beautiful

him, "Are you the only visitor to Jerusalem who does not know the things that have happened there in these days?" 19And he said to them, "What things?" And they said to him, "Concerning Jesus of Nazareth, a man who was a prophet mighty in deed and word before God and all the people, 20and how our chief priests and rulers delivered him up to be condemned to death, and crucified him. 21But we had hoped that he was the one to redeem Israel. Yes, and besides all this, it is now the third day since these things happened. 22Moreover, some women of our company amazed us. They were at the tomb early in the morning, 23and when they did not find his body, they came back saying that they had even seen a vision of angels, who said that he was alive. 24Some of those who were with us went to the tomb and found it just as the women had said, but him they did not see." 25And he said to them, "O foolish ones, and slow of heart to believe all that the prophets have spoken! 26Was it not necessary that the Christ should suffer these things and enter into his glory?" 27And beginning with Moses and all the Prophets, he interpreted to them in all the Scriptures the things concerning himself.

28So they drew near to the village to which they were going. He acted as if he were going farther, 29but they urged him strongly, saying, "Stay with us, for it is toward evening and the day is now far spent." So he went in to stay with them. 30When he was at table with them, he took the bread and blessed and

Bold, Bodacious and Beautiful

broke it and gave it to them. 31And their eyes were opened, and they recognized him. And he vanished from their sight. 32They said to each other, "Did not our hearts burn within us while he talked to us on the road, while he opened to us the Scriptures?" 33And they rose that same hour and returned to Jerusalem. And they found the eleven and those who were with them gathered together, 34saying, "The Lord has risen indeed, and has appeared to Simon!" 35Then they told what had happened on the road, and how he was known to them in the breaking of the bread.

36As they were talking about these things, Jesus himself stood among them, and said to them, "Peace to you!" 37But they were startled and frightened and thought they saw a spirit. 38And he said to them, "Why are you troubled, and why do doubts arise in your hearts? 39See my hands and my feet, that it is I myself. Touch me, and see. For a spirit does not have flesh and bones as you see that I have." 40And when he had said this, he showed them his hands and his feet. 41And while they still disbelieved for joy and were marveling, he said to them, "Have you anything here to eat?" 42They gave him a piece of broiled fish,*b* 43and he took it and ate before them.

44Then he said to them, "These are my words that I spoke to you while I was still with you, that everything written about me in the Law of Moses and the Prophets and the Psalms must be fulfilled." 45Then he opened their minds to understand the Scriptures, 46and said to them, "Thus it is written, that

380

Bold, Bodacious and Beautiful

the Christ should suffer and on the third day rise from the dead, 47and that repentance for the forgiveness of sins should be proclaimed in his name to all nations, beginning from Jerusalem. 48You are witnesses of these things. 49And behold, I am sending the promise of my Father upon you. But stay in the city until you are clothed with power from on high."

50And he led them out as far as Bethany, and lifting up his hands he blessed them. 51While he blessed them, he parted from them and was carried up into heaven. 52And they worshiped him and returned to Jerusalem with great joy, 53and were continually in the temple blessing God.

Mark 16:19
So then the Lord Jesus, after he had spoken to them, was taken up into heaven and sat down at the right hand of God.

Colossians 3:1
If then you have been raised with Christ, seek the things that are above, where Christ is, seated at the right hand of God.

Acts 2:1-41

1When the day of Pentecost arrived, they were all together in one place. 2And suddenly there came from heaven a sound like a mighty rushing wind, and it filled the entire house where they were sitting. 3And

Bold, Bodacious and Beautiful

divided tongues as of fire appeared to them and rested on each one of them. 4And they were all filled with the Holy Spirit and began to speak in other tongues as the Spirit gave them utterance.

5Now there were dwelling in Jerusalem Jews, devout men from every nation under heaven. 6And at this sound the multitude came together, and they were bewildered, because each one was hearing them speak in his own language. 7And they were amazed and astonished, saying, "Are not all these who are speaking Galileans? 8And how is it that we hear, each of us in his own native language? 9Parthians and Medes and Elamites and residents of Mesopotamia, Judea and Cappadocia, Pontus and Asia, 10Phrygia and Pamphylia, Egypt and the parts of Libya belonging to Cyrene, and visitors from Rome, 11both Jews and proselytes, Cretans and Arabians—we hear them telling in our own tongues the mighty works of God." 12And all were amazed and perplexed, saying to one another, "What does this mean?" 13But others mocking said, "They are filled with new wine."

14But Peter, standing with the eleven, lifted up his voice and addressed them: "Men of Judea and all who dwell in Jerusalem, let this be known to you, and give ear to my words. 15For these people are not drunk, as you suppose, since it is only the third hour of the day.*b* 16But this is what was uttered through the prophet Joel:

17"'And in the last days it shall be, God declares,

382

Bold, Bodacious and Beautiful

that I will pour out my Spirit on all flesh,

and your sons and your daughters shall prophesy,

and your young men shall see visions,

and your old men shall dream dreams;

18even on my male servants and female servants

in those days I will pour out my Spirit, and they shall prophesy.

19And I will show wonders in the heavens above

and signs on the earth below,

blood, and fire, and vapor of smoke;

20the sun shall be turned to darkness

and the moon to blood,

before the day of the Lord comes, the great and magnificent day.

21And it shall come to pass that everyone who calls upon the name of the Lord shall be saved.'

22"Men of Israel, hear these words: Jesus of Nazareth, a man attested to you by God with mighty works and wonders and signs that God did through

Bold, Bodacious and Beautiful

him in your midst, as you yourselves know— 23this Jesus, delivered up according to the definite plan and foreknowledge of God, you crucified and killed by the hands of lawless men. 24God raised him up, loosing the pangs of death, because it was not possible for him to be held by it. 25For David says concerning him,

> "'I saw the Lord always before me,
>
> for he is at my right hand that I may not be shaken;
>
> 26therefore my heart was glad, and my tongue rejoiced;
>
> my flesh also will dwell in hope.
>
> 27For you will not abandon my soul to Hades,
>
> or let your Holy One see corruption.
>
> 28You have made known to me the paths of life;
>
> you will make me full of gladness with your presence.'

29"Brothers, I may say to you with confidence about the patriarch David that he both died and was buried, and his tomb is with us to this day. 30Being therefore a prophet, and knowing that God had sworn with an oath to him that he would set one of his descendants on his throne, 31he foresaw and spoke

Bold, Bodacious and Beautiful

about the resurrection of the Christ, that he was not abandoned to Hades, nor did his flesh see corruption. 32This Jesus God raised up, and of that we all are witnesses. 33Being therefore exalted at the right hand of God, and having received from the Father the promise of the Holy Spirit, he has poured out this that you yourselves are seeing and hearing. 34For David did not ascend into the heavens, but he himself says,

"'The Lord said to my Lord,

"Sit at my right hand,

35until I make your enemies your footstool.'"

36Let all the house of Israel therefore know for certain that God has made him both Lord and Christ, this Jesus whom you crucified."

37Now when they heard this they were cut to the heart, and said to Peter and the rest of the apostles, "Brothers, what shall we do?" 38And Peter said to them, "Repent and be baptized every one of you in the name of Jesus Christ for the forgiveness of your sins, and you will receive the gift of the Holy Spirit. 39For the promise is for you and for your children and for all who are far off, everyone whom the Lord our God calls to himself." 40And with many other words he bore witness and continued to exhort them, saying, "Save yourselves from this crooked generation." 41So

Bold, Bodacious and Beautiful

those who received his word were baptized, and there were added that day about three thousand souls.

John 14:16-17
"[16]And I will ask the Father, and he will give you another Helper, to be with you forever, [17]even the Spirit of truth, whom the world cannot receive, because it neither sees him nor knows him. You know him, for he dwells with you and will be in you."

Chapter 1: Season of Waiting (Winter and Spring 2019)

Matthew 22:37-39
[37]And he said to him, "You shall love the Lord your God with all your heart and with all your soul and with all your mind. [38]This is the great and first commandment. [39]And a second is like it: You shall love your neighbor as yourself.

Chapter 2: Season of Wondering (Spring and Summer 2019)

Psalm 91:4
He will cover you with his pinions,
and under his wings you will find refuge;
his faithfulness is a shield and buckler.

Isaiah 43:2

Bold, Bodacious and Beautiful

When you pass through the waters, I will be with you;
and through the rivers, they shall not overwhelm you;
when you walk through fire you shall not be burned,
and the flame shall not consume you.

Psalm 91:2
I will say to the LORD, "My refuge and my fortress,
my God, in whom I trust."

Psalm 118:14
The LORD is my strength and my song;
he has become my salvation.

Isaiah 40:31
…but they who wait for the LORD shall renew their
strength;
they shall mount up with wings like eagles;
they shall run and not be weary;
they shall walk and not faint.

Isaiah 40:28
Have you not known? Have you not heard?
The LORD is the everlasting God,
the Creator of the ends of the earth.

John 4:13, 14
[13]Jesus said to her, "Everyone who drinks of this
water will be thirsty again, [14]but whoever drinks of
the water that I will give him will never be thirsty
again. The water that I will give him will become in
him a spring of water welling up to eternal life."

Bold, Bodacious and Beautiful

Ephesians 6:10-18

10Finally, be strong in the Lord and in the strength of his might. 11Put on the whole armor of God, that you may be able to stand against the schemes of the devil. 12For we do not wrestle against flesh and blood, but against the rulers, against the authorities, against the cosmic powers over this present darkness, against the spiritual forces of evil in the heavenly places. 13Therefore take up the whole armor of God, that you may be able to withstand in the evil day, and having done all, to stand firm. 14Stand therefore, having fastened on the belt of truth, and having put on the breastplate of righteousness, 15and, as shoes for your feet, having put on the readiness given by the gospel of peace. 16In all circumstances take up the shield of faith, with which you can extinguish all the flaming darts of the evil one; 17and take the helmet of salvation, and the sword of the Spirit, which is the word of God, 18praying at all times in the Spirit, with all prayer and supplication. To that end, keep alert with all perseverance, making supplication for all the saints…

Psalm 86:15

But you, O Lord, are a God merciful and gracious, slow to anger and abounding in steadfast love and faithfulness.

Matthew 11:30

For my yoke is easy, and my burden is light.

Bold, Bodacious and Beautiful

John 17:16
They are not of the world, just as I am not of the world.

Genesis 1:12
The earth brought forth vegetation, plants yielding seed according to their own kinds, and trees bearing fruit in which is their seed, each according to its kind. And God saw that it was good.

Psalm 139:14
I praise you, for I am fearfully and wonderfully made. Wonderful are your works;
my soul knows it very well.

Matthew 5:14
You are the light of the world. A city set on a hill cannot be hidden.

Revelation 21:6
And he said to me, "It is done! I am the Alpha and the Omega, the beginning and the end. To the thirsty I will give from the spring of the water of life without payment…"

Matthew 5:13
You are the salt of the earth, but if salt has lost its taste, how shall its saltiness be restored? It is no longer good for anything except to be thrown out and trampled under people's feet.

Bold, Bodacious and Beautiful

John 1:14
And the Word became flesh and dwelt among us, and we have seen his glory, glory as of the only Son from the Father, full of grace and truth.

Hebrews 4:12
For the word of God is living and active, sharper than any two-edged sword, piercing to the division of soul and of spirit, of joints and of marrow, and discerning the thoughts and intentions of the heart.

John 6:55
For my flesh is true food, and my blood is true drink.

John 21:17
He said to him the third time, "Simon, son of John, do you love me?" Peter was grieved because he said to him the third time, "Do you love me?" and he said to him, "Lord, you know everything; you know that I love you." Jesus said to him, "Feed my sheep…"

Ephesians 6:17
…and take the helmet of salvation, and the sword of the Spirit, which is the word of God,…

Bold, Bodacious and Beautiful

Chapter 3: Season of Strife (Fall 2019)

Galatians 5:22, 23
22But the fruit of the Spirit is love, joy, peace,
patience, kindness, goodness, faithfulness,
23gentleness, self-control; against such things there is
no law.

Proverbs 27:17
Iron sharpens iron,
and one man sharpens another.

Genesis 22: 1-19

1After these things God tested Abraham and said
to him, "Abraham!" And he said, "Here I am." 2He
said, "Take your son, your only son Isaac, whom you
love, and go to the land of Moriah, and offer him
there as a burnt offering on one of the mountains of
which I shall tell you." 3So Abraham rose early in the
morning, saddled his donkey, and took two of his
young men with him, and his son Isaac. And he cut
the wood for the burnt offering and arose and went
to the place of which God had told him. 4On the
third day Abraham lifted up his eyes and saw the
place from afar. 5Then Abraham said to his young
men, "Stay here with the donkey; I and the boy will
go over there and worship and come again to you."
6And Abraham took the wood of the burnt offering
and laid it on Isaac his son. And he took in his hand
the fire and the knife. So they went both of them

Bold, Bodacious and Beautiful

together. [7]And Isaac said to his father Abraham, "My father!" And he said, "Here I am, my son." He said, "Behold, the fire and the wood, but where is the lamb for a burnt offering?" [8]Abraham said, "God will provide for himself the lamb for a burnt offering, my son." So they went both of them together.

[9]When they came to the place of which God had told him, Abraham built the altar there and laid the wood in order and bound Isaac his son and laid him on the altar, on top of the wood. [10]Then Abraham reached out his hand and took the knife to slaughter his son. [11]But the angel of the LORD called to him from heaven and said, "Abraham, Abraham!" And he said, "Here I am." [12]He said, "Do not lay your hand on the boy or do anything to him, for now I know that you fear God, seeing you have not withheld your son, your only son, from me." [13]And Abraham lifted up his eyes and looked, and behold, behind him was a ram, caught in a thicket by his horns. And Abraham went and took the ram and offered it up as a burnt offering instead of his son. [14]So Abraham called the name of that place, "The LORD will provide"; as it is said to this day, "On the mount of the LORD it shall be provided."

[15]And the angel of the LORD called to Abraham a second time from heaven [16]and said, "By myself I have sworn, declares the LORD, because you have done this and have not withheld your son, your only son, [17]I will surely bless you, and I will surely multiply your offspring as the stars of heaven and as the sand

Bold, Bodacious and Beautiful

that is on the seashore. And your offspring shall possess the gate of his enemies, [18]and in your offspring shall all the nations of the earth be blessed, because you have obeyed my voice." [19]So Abraham returned to his young men, and they arose and went together to Beersheba. And Abraham lived at Beersheba.

1 Samuel 3:10
And the LORD came and stood, calling as at other times, "Samuel! Samuel!" And Samuel said, "Speak, for your servant hears."

Revelation 3:15, 16
[15]I know your works: you are neither cold nor hot. Would that you were either cold or hot! [16]So, because you are lukewarm, and neither hot nor cold, I will spit you out of my mouth.

Matthew 11:30
"For my yoke is easy, and my burden is light."

2 Corinthians 10:5
We destroy arguments and every lofty opinion raised against the knowledge of God, and take every thought captive to obey Christ…

Revelation 1:8

Bold, Bodacious and Beautiful

"I am the Alpha and the Omega," says the Lord God, "who is and who was and who is to come, the Almighty."

John 8:12
Again Jesus spoke to them, saying, "I am the light of the world. Whoever follows me will not walk in darkness, but will have the light of life."

Psalm 121:1
I lift up my eyes to the hills. Where does my help come from?

Chapter 4: Season of Surrender (Fall and Winter 2019)

Psalm 23: 1-3 (The Passion Translation)
¹Yahweh is my best friend and my shepherd.
I always have more than enough.
²He offers a resting place for me in his luxurious love.
His tracks take me to an oasis of peace near *the quiet brook of bliss.*
³That's where he restores and revives my life.
He opens before me the right path
and leads me along in his footsteps of righteousness
so that I can bring honor to his name.

Ezekiel 36:26

Bold, Bodacious and Beautiful

And I will give you a new heart, and a new spirit I will put within you. And I will remove the heart of stone from your flesh and give you a heart of flesh.

Ecclesiastes 3:11
He has made everything beautiful in its time. Also, he has put eternity into man's heart, yet so that he cannot find out what God has done from the beginning to the end.

Philippians 4:6
…do not be anxious about anything, but in everything by prayer and supplication with thanksgiving let your requests be made known to God.

Matthew 7:7-8
7"Ask, and it will be given to you; seek, and you will find; knock, and it will be opened to you. 8For everyone who asks receives, and the one who seeks finds, and to the one who knocks it will be opened.

Psalm 46:10
Be still, and know that I am God.
I will be exalted among the nations,
I will be exalted in the earth!

Psalm 61:4
Let me dwell in your tent forever!
Let me take refuge under the shelter of your wings!
Selah

Bold, Bodacious and Beautiful

Psalm 91:4
He will cover you with his pinions,
and under his wings you will find refuge;
his faithfulness is a shield and buckler.

Jeremiah 17: 7, 8
7Blessed is the man who trusts in the LORD,
whose trust is the LORD.
8He is like a tree planted by water,
that sends out its roots by the stream,
and does not fear when heat comes,
for its leaves remain green,
and is not anxious in the year of drought,
for it does not cease to bear fruit.

Psalm 31:3
For you are my rock and my fortress;
and for your name's sake you lead me and guide me…

1 Thessalonians 5:16-18
16Rejoice always, 17pray without ceasing, 18give thanks
in all circumstances; for this is the will of God in
Christ Jesus for you.

1Chronicles 29:13
And now we thank you, our God, and praise your
glorious name.

Ephesians 5:20

Bold, Bodacious and Beautiful

…giving thanks always and for everything to God the Father in the name of our Lord Jesus Christ…

Psalm 73:23-26

[23]Nevertheless, I am continually with you; you hold my right hand. [24]You guide me with your counsel, and afterward you will receive me to glory. [25]Whom have I in heaven but you? And there is nothing on earth that I desire besides you. [26]My flesh and my heart may fail, but God is the strength of my heart and my portion forever.

1 Thessalonians 5:18 (repeated)
…give thanks in all circumstances; for this is the will of God in Christ Jesus for you.

1 Thessalonians 5:11
Therefore encourage one another and build one another up, just as you are doing.

Genesis 22:13-14 (repeated)
[13]Then Abraham raised his eyes and looked, and behold, behind *him* a ram caught in the thicket by his horns; and Abraham went and took the ram and offered him up for a burnt offering in the place of his son. [14]Abraham called the name of that place "The LORD Will Provide," as it is said to this day, "In the mount of the LORD it will be provided."

Revelation 22:13

Bold, Bodacious and Beautiful

"I am the Alpha and the Omega, the first and the last, the beginning and the end."

Isaiah 9:6
For to us a child is born, to us a son is given; and the government shall be upon his shoulder, and his name shall be called Wonderful Counselor, Mighty God, Everlasting Father, Prince of Peace.

Exodus 3:14
God said to Moses, "I AM WHO I AM." And he said, "Say this to the people of Israel: I AM has sent me to you."

Exodus 15:26
"If you will diligently listen to the voice of the LORD your God, and do that which is right in his eyes, and give ear to his commandments and keep all his statutes, I will put none of the diseases on you that I put on the Egyptians, for I am the LORD, your healer."

Psalm 23:1
The LORD is my shepherd; I shall not want.

John 14:2-3
"[2]In my Father's house are many rooms. If it were not so, would I have told you that I go to prepare a place for you? [3]And if I go and prepare a place for you, I will come again and will take you to myself, that where I am you may be also."

Bold, Bodacious and Beautiful

Matthew 7:7
"Ask, and it will be given to you; seek, and you will find; knock, and it will be opened to you."

Matthew 6:21
"For where your treasure is, there your heart will be also."

Psalm 62:8
Trust in him at all times, O people; pour out your heart before him; God is a refuge for us. Selah

Luke 2:11-14

[11] "For unto you is born this day in the city of David a Savior, who is Christ the Lord. [12]And this will be a sign for you: you will find a baby wrapped in swaddling cloths and lying in a manger." [13]And suddenly there was with the angel a multitude of the heavenly host praising God and saying, [14]"Glory to God in the highest, and on earth peace among those with whom he is pleased!"

Philippians 4:13
I can do all things through him who strengthens me.

Proverbs 27:17 (Repeated)
Iron sharpens iron, and one man sharpens another.

Bold, Bodacious and Beautiful

Mark 1:4
John appeared, baptizing in the wilderness and proclaiming a baptism of repentance for the forgiveness of sins.

Exodus 3:1-5

[1]Meanwhile, Moses was shepherding the flock of his father-in-law Jethro, the priest of Midian. He led the flock to the far side of the wilderness and came to Horeb, the mountain of God. [2]There the angel of the LORD appeared to him in a blazing fire from within a bush. Moses saw the bush ablaze with fire, but it was not consumed. [3]So Moses thought, "I must go over and see this marvelous sight. Why is the bush not burning up?"

[4]When the LORD saw that he had gone over to look, God called out to him from within the bush, "Moses, Moses!"

"Here I am," he answered.

[5]"Do not come any closer," God said. "Take off your sandals, for the place where you are standing is holy ground."

1 Samuel 22:1-2

Bold, Bodacious and Beautiful

¹So David left Gath and took refuge in the cave of Adullam. When his brothers and the rest of his father's household heard about it, they went down to him there. ²And all who were distressed or indebted or discontented rallied around him, and he became their leader. About four hundred men were with him.

Colossians 3:12-13
¹²Put on then, as God's chosen ones, holy and beloved, compassionate hearts, kindness, humility, meekness, and patience, ¹³bearing with one another and, if one has a complaint against another, forgiving each other; as the Lord has forgiven you, so you also must forgive.

Psalm 119:105
Your word is a lamp to my feet and a light to my path.

Chapter 5: Season of Season of Acceleration (Winter 2020)

Jeremiah 1:5
"Before I formed you in the womb I knew you, and before you were born I consecrated you; I appointed you a prophet to the nations."

Matthew 13:45-46
"⁴⁵Again, the kingdom of heaven is like a merchant in search of fine pearls, ⁴⁶who, on finding one pearl of

Bold, Bodacious and Beautiful

great value, went and sold all that he had and bought it."

Philemon 1:9, 10
9Yet for love's sake I prefer to appeal to you—I, Paul, an old man and now a prisoner also for Christ Jesus — 10I appeal to you for my child, Onesimus, whose father I became in my imprisonment.

2 Timothy 4:16-18
16At my first defense no one came to stand by me, but all deserted me. May it not be charged against them! 17But the Lord stood by me and strengthened me, so that through me the message might be fully proclaimed and all the Gentiles might hear it. So I was rescued from the lion's mouth. 18The Lord will rescue me from every evil deed and bring me safely into his heavenly kingdom. To him be the glory forever and ever. Amen.

Psalm 55:22
Cast your burden on the LORD, and he will sustain you; he will never permit the righteous to be moved.

Chapter 6: Season of Solitude (Spring 2020)

Luke 2:19
But Mary treasured up all these things, pondering them in her heart.

Bold, Bodacious and Beautiful

Ephesians 6:10-18 (See Season of Wondering)

2 Kings 19:35
And that night the angel of the LORD went out and struck down 185,000 in the camp of the Assyrians. And when people arose early in the morning, behold, these were all dead bodies.

1 Thessalonians 5:18

Be thankful in all circumstances, for this is God's will for you who belong to Christ Jesus.

Chapter 7: Season of Lingering (Spring 2020)

Isaiah 35:6
…then shall the lame man leap like a deer, and the tongue of the mute sing for joy. For waters break forth in the wilderness, and streams in the desert;…

Five scriptures that mention dreams:
Genesis 41:1-45

1After two whole years, Pharaoh dreamed that he was standing by the Nile, 2and behold, there came up out of the Nile seven cows, attractive and plump, and they fed in the reed grass. 3And behold, seven other cows, ugly and thin, came up out of the Nile after them, and stood by the other cows on the bank of

Bold, Bodacious and Beautiful

the Nile. 4And the ugly, thin cows ate up the seven attractive, plump cows. And Pharaoh awoke. 5And he fell asleep and dreamed a second time. And behold, seven ears of grain, plump and good, were growing on one stalk. 6And behold, after them sprouted seven ears, thin and blighted by the east wind. 7And the thin ears swallowed up the seven plump, full ears. And Pharaoh awoke, and behold, it was a dream. 8So in the morning his spirit was troubled, and he sent and called for all the magicians of Egypt and all its wise men. Pharaoh told them his dreams, but there was none who could interpret them to Pharaoh.

9Then the chief cupbearer said to Pharaoh, "I remember my offenses today. 10When Pharaoh was angry with his servants and put me and the chief baker in custody in the house of the captain of the guard, 11we dreamed on the same night, he and I, each having a dream with its own interpretation. 12A young Hebrew was there with us, a servant of the captain of the guard. When we told him, he interpreted our dreams to us, giving an interpretation to each man according to his dream. 13And as he interpreted to us, so it came about. I was restored to my office, and the baker was hanged."

14Then Pharaoh sent and called Joseph, and they quickly brought him out of the pit. And when he had shaved himself and changed his clothes, he came in before Pharaoh. 15And Pharaoh said to Joseph, "I have had a dream, and there is no one who can interpret it. I have heard it said of you that when you

Bold, Bodacious and Beautiful

hear a dream you can interpret it." 16Joseph answered Pharaoh, "It is not in me; God will give Pharaoh a favorable answer." 17Then Pharaoh said to Joseph, "Behold, in my dream I was standing on the banks of the Nile. 18Seven cows, plump and attractive, came up out of the Nile and fed in the reed grass. 19Seven other cows came up after them, poor and very ugly and thin, such as I had never seen in all the land of Egypt. 20And the thin, ugly cows ate up the first seven plump cows, 21but when they had eaten them no one would have known that they had eaten them, for they were still as ugly as at the beginning. Then I awoke. 22I also saw in my dream seven ears growing on one stalk, full and good. 23Seven ears, withered, thin, and blighted by the east wind, sprouted after them, 24and the thin ears swallowed up the seven good ears. And I told it to the magicians, but there was no one who could explain it to me."

25Then Joseph said to Pharaoh, "The dreams of Pharaoh are one; God has revealed to Pharaoh what he is about to do. 26The seven good cows are seven years, and the seven good ears are seven years; the dreams are one. 27The seven lean and ugly cows that came up after them are seven years, and the seven empty ears blighted by the east wind are also seven years of famine. 28It is as I told Pharaoh; God has shown to Pharaoh what he is about to do. 29There will come seven years of great plenty throughout all the land of Egypt, 30but after them there will arise seven years of famine, and all the plenty will be forgotten in

Bold, Bodacious and Beautiful

the land of Egypt. The famine will consume the land, 31and the plenty will be unknown in the land by reason of the famine that will follow, for it will be very severe. 32And the doubling of Pharaoh's dream means that the thing is fixed by God, and God will shortly bring it about. 33Now therefore let Pharaoh select a discerning and wise man, and set him over the land of Egypt. 34Let Pharaoh proceed to appoint overseers over the land and take one-fifth of the produce of the land of Egypt during the seven plentiful years. 35And let them gather all the food of these good years that are coming and store up grain under the authority of Pharaoh for food in the cities, and let them keep it. 36That food shall be a reserve for the land against the seven years of famine that are to occur in the land of Egypt, so that the land may not perish through the famine."

37This proposal pleased Pharaoh and all his servants. 38And Pharaoh said to his servants, "Can we find a man like this, in whom is the Spirit of God?" 39Then Pharaoh said to Joseph, "Since God has shown you all this, there is none so discerning and wise as you are. 40You shall be over my house, and all my people shall order themselves as you command. Only as regards the throne will I be greater than you." 41And Pharaoh said to Joseph, "See, I have set you over all the land of Egypt." 42Then Pharaoh took his signet ring from his hand and put it on Joseph's hand, and clothed him in garments of fine linen and put a gold chain about his neck. 43And he made him ride in

Bold, Bodacious and Beautiful

his second chariot. And they called out before him, "Bow the knee!" Thus he set him over all the land of Egypt. 44Moreover, Pharaoh said to Joseph, "I am Pharaoh, and without your consent no one shall lift up hand or foot in all the land of Egypt." 45And Pharaoh called Joseph's name Zaphenath-paneah. And he gave him in marriage Asenath, the daughter of Potiphera priest of On. So Joseph went out over the land of Egypt.

Daniel 2

1In the second year of the reign of Nebuchadnezzar, Nebuchadnezzar had dreams; his spirit was troubled, and his sleep left him. 2Then the king commanded that the magicians, the enchanters, the sorcerers, and the Chaldeans be summoned to tell the king his dreams. So they came in and stood before the king. 3And the king said to them, "I had a dream, and my spirit is troubled to know the dream." 4Then the Chaldeans said to the king in Aramaic, "O king, live forever! Tell your servants the dream, and we will show the interpretation." 5The king answered and said to the Chaldeans, "The word from me is firm: if you do not make known to me the dream and its interpretation, you shall be torn limb from limb, and your houses shall be laid in ruins. 6But if you show the dream and its interpretation, you shall receive from me gifts and rewards and great honor. Therefore show me the dream and its interpretation." 7They answered a second time and said, "Let the king tell his

Bold, Bodacious and Beautiful

servants the dream, and we will show its interpretation." 8The king answered and said, "I know with certainty that you are trying to gain time, because you see that the word from me is firm— 9if you do not make the dream known to me, there is but one sentence for you. You have agreed to speak lying and corrupt words before me till the times change. Therefore tell me the dream, and I shall know that you can show me its interpretation." 10The Chaldeans answered the king and said, "There is not a man on earth who can meet the king's demand, for no great and powerful king has asked such a thing of any magician or enchanter or Chaldean. 11The thing that the king asks is difficult, and no one can show it to the king except the gods, whose dwelling is not with flesh."

12Because of this the king was angry and very furious, and commanded that all the wise men of Babylon be destroyed. 13So the decree went out, and the wise men were about to be killed; and they sought Daniel and his companions, to kill them. 14Then Daniel replied with prudence and discretion to Arioch, the captain of the king's guard, who had gone out to kill the wise men of Babylon. 15He declared to Arioch, the king's captain, "Why is the decree of the king so urgent?" Then Arioch made the matter known to Daniel. 16And Daniel went in and requested the king to appoint him a time, that he might show the interpretation to the king.

Bold, Bodacious and Beautiful

17Then Daniel went to his house and made the matter known to Hananiah, Mishael, and Azariah, his companions, 18and told them to seek mercy from the God of heaven concerning this mystery, so that Daniel and his companions might not be destroyed with the rest of the wise men of Babylon. 19Then the mystery was revealed to Daniel in a vision of the night. Then Daniel blessed the God of heaven. 20Daniel answered and said:

"Blessed be the name of God forever and ever,

to whom belong wisdom and might.

21He changes times and seasons;

he removes kings and sets up kings;

he gives wisdom to the wise

and knowledge to those who have understanding;

22he reveals deep and hidden things;

he knows what is in the darkness,

and the light dwells with him.

23To you, O God of my fathers,

I give thanks and praise,

Bold, Bodacious and Beautiful

for you have given me wisdom and might,

and have now made known to me what we
asked of you,

for you have made known to us the king's
matter."

24Therefore Daniel went in to Arioch, whom the
king had appointed to destroy the wise men of
Babylon. He went and said thus to him: "Do not
destroy the wise men of Babylon; bring me in before
the king, and I will show the king the interpretation."

25Then Arioch brought in Daniel before the king
in haste and said thus to him: "I have found among
the exiles from Judah a man who will make known to
the king the interpretation." 26The king declared to
Daniel, whose name was Belteshazzar, "Are you able
to make known to me the dream that I have seen and
its interpretation?" 27Daniel answered the king and
said, "No wise men, enchanters, magicians, or
astrologers can show to the king the mystery that the
king has asked, 28but there is a God in heaven who
reveals mysteries, and he has made known to King
Nebuchadnezzar what will be in the latter days. Your
dream and the visions of your head as you lay in bed
are these: 29To you, O king, as you lay in bed came
thoughts of what would be after this, and he who
reveals mysteries made known to you what is to be.
30But as for me, this mystery has been revealed to me,
not because of any wisdom that I have more than all

Bold, Bodacious and Beautiful

the living, but in order that the interpretation may be made known to the king, and that you may know the thoughts of your mind.

31"You saw, O king, and behold, a great image. This image, mighty and of exceeding brightness, stood before you, and its appearance was frightening. 32The head of this image was of fine gold, its chest and arms of silver, its middle and thighs of bronze, 33its legs of iron, its feet partly of iron and partly of clay. 34As you looked, a stone was cut out by no human hand, and it struck the image on its feet of iron and clay, and broke them in pieces. 35Then the iron, the clay, the bronze, the silver, and the gold, all together were broken in pieces, and became like the chaff of the summer threshing floors; and the wind carried them away, so that not a trace of them could be found. But the stone that struck the image became a great mountain and filled the whole earth.

36"This was the dream. Now we will tell the king its interpretation. 37You, O king, the king of kings, to whom the God of heaven has given the kingdom, the power, and the might, and the glory, 38and into whose hand he has given, wherever they dwell, the children of man, the beasts of the field, and the birds of the heavens, making you rule over them all—you are the head of gold. 39Another kingdom inferior to you shall arise after you, and yet a third kingdom of bronze, which shall rule over all the earth. 40And there shall be a fourth kingdom, strong as iron, because iron breaks to pieces and shatters all things. And like iron

Bold, Bodacious and Beautiful

that crushes, it shall break and crush all these. 41And as you saw the feet and toes, partly of potter's clay and partly of iron, it shall be a divided kingdom, but some of the firmness of iron shall be in it, just as you saw iron mixed with the soft clay. 42And as the toes of the feet were partly iron and partly clay, so the kingdom shall be partly strong and partly brittle. 43As you saw the iron mixed with soft clay, so they will mix with one another in marriage, but they will not hold together, just as iron does not mix with clay. 44And in the days of those kings the God of heaven will set up a kingdom that shall never be destroyed, nor shall the kingdom be left to another people. It shall break in pieces all these kingdoms and bring them to an end, and it shall stand forever, 45just as you saw that a stone was cut from a mountain by no human hand, and that it broke in pieces the iron, the bronze, the clay, the silver, and the gold. A great God has made known to the king what shall be after this. The dream is certain, and its interpretation sure."

46Then King Nebuchadnezzar fell upon his face and paid homage to Daniel, and commanded that an offering and incense be offered up to him. 47The king answered and said to Daniel, "Truly, your God is God of gods and Lord of kings, and a revealer of mysteries, for you have been able to reveal this mystery." 48Then the king gave Daniel high honors and many great gifts, and made him ruler over the whole province of Babylon and chief prefect over all the wise men of Babylon. 49Daniel made a request of

Bold, Bodacious and Beautiful

the king, and he appointed Shadrach, Meshach, and
Abednego over the affairs of the province of
Babylon. But Daniel remained at the king's court.

Numbers 12:6
And he said, "Hear my words: If there is a prophet
among you, I the LORD make myself known to him
in a vision; I speak with him in a dream."

Acts 2:17
"'And in the last days it shall be, God declares,
that I will pour out my Spirit on all flesh,
and your sons and your daughters shall prophesy,
and your young men shall see visions,
and your old men shall dream dreams;...'"

Job 33:14, 15
14For God speaks in one way,
and in two, though man does not perceive it.
15In a dream, in a vision of the night,
when deep sleep falls on men,
while they slumber on their beds

(End of dream scriptures)

Psalm 46:10
"Be still, and know that I am God.
I will be exalted among the nations,
I will be exalted in the earth!"

Bold, Bodacious and Beautiful

Mark 4:26-32

26And he said, "The kingdom of God is as if a man should scatter seed on the ground. 27He sleeps and rises night and day, and the seed sprouts and grows; he knows not how. 28The earth produces by itself, first the blade, then the ear, then the full grain in the ear. 29But when the grain is ripe, at once he puts in the sickle, because the harvest has come."

30And he said, "With what can we compare the kingdom of God, or what parable shall we use for it? 31It is like a grain of mustard seed, which, when sown on the ground, is the smallest of all the seeds on earth, 32yet when it is sown it grows up and becomes larger than all the garden plants and puts out large branches, so that the birds of the air can make nests in its shade."

ABOUT THE AUTHOR

Gini Noble called New York City her home for thirty-six years. She now lives in Phoenix, Arizona.

Made in the USA
Las Vegas, NV
26 December 2023